A LEGAL HISTORY OF THE ENGLISH LANDSCAPE

A LEGAL HISTORY OF THE ENGLISH LANDSCAPE

Christopher Jessel

WS
&H

Wildy, Simmonds & Hill Publishing

Copyright © 2011 Christopher Jessel

A Legal History of the English Landscape

British Library Cataloguing in Publication Data
A catalogue record for this book is available from the British Library

ISBN 978-0854900879

Typeset in Times New Roman by Cornubia Press Ltd
Printed and bound in the United Kingdom by Antony Rowe, Chippenham,
Wiltshire

The right of Christopher Jessel to be identified as the Author of this Work has
been asserted by him in accordance with Copyright, Designs and Patents Act
1988, sections 77 and 78.

First published in 2011 by
Wildy, Simmonds & Hill Publishing
58 Carey Street
London WC2A 2JF
England

FSC
www.fsc.org
MIX
Paper from
responsible sources
FSC® C013604

Contents

List of illustrations

Foreword

The landscape we see today is the product of thousands of years of evolution, as land has been shaped, reworked and managed by successive generations. For WG Hoskins the landscape was 'the richest historical record we possess'. He likened it to a palimpsest (an ancient manuscript with successive layers of writing), or to a symphony featuring a variety of movements and musical motifs.

To the trained eye the landscape can reveal much about the past, or at least prompt us to ask the right questions of other historical sources. What do those bumps in the ground mean? Why does the road make a sudden ninety-degree turn? Who put that avenue there, and why?

Sometimes the influences on landscape are purely physical. The course of a river or the fold of a hill are determined largely by geological processes that have been underway for millennia. We have little control over such things, although on our coasts we are starting to see the impacts of changes that humankind has wrought over the last 300 years. The weather, the seasons and sudden unexpected catastrophes, such as droughts and floods, can all affect landscapes in unpredictable ways.

But for the most part the landscape is a human construction. The way a society organises itself is expressed visibly through landscape, whether in the form of the great landed estates with their parks, fields and wooded belts, or in the endless rows of terraced housing to be found in nineteenth-century industrial towns. The very word 'landscape', borrowed from the Dutch vernacular, was first applied to cultural depictions of places in paintings and sketches, rather than to the physical places themselves.

The National Trust now looks after more than one in every hundred hectares of England, Wales and Northern Ireland. Our founding statute, the National Trust Act 1907, gave us the power to hold land inalienably, meaning that the will of Parliament is required in order for us to divest ourselves of such land. This gives us a long-term perspective, since any declaration of inalienability obliges us to take into account the interests of future generations. A subsequent Act of Parliament gave us the power to hold covenants over land, and not just land immediately adjacent to our own property.

Such legal developments have had a significant impact on today's landscape. The Hambleden Valley would look very different today were it not for the restrictive covenants that we hold over it. England's coast and countryside would have suffered much more sprawl and development were it not for the National Trust, as well as other legislative protections such as National Park status and the powers in the planning acts to protect green belt.

The law is a melody that runs throughout the symphony of the English landscape. This book reminds us of the important role that the law has played, and continues to play, in shaping our surroundings.

Dame Fiona Reynolds, DBE
Director General, National Trust

Preface

The visible landscape of town and country which we see about us is the result of hundreds of years of change. Since the publication of *The Making of the English Landscape* by WG Hoskins in 1955, landscape history has become an important and popular study. Underlying many of the changes are the legal rules which made them possible and in this book I have sought to outline what those rules were and how they themselves altered over the years.

The history is important but this is not only of historical interest. A lawyer may be asked to advise (as I have been) on who now owns the ground under a modern highway on the course of a Roman road or on a boundary dispute whose origins go back to the terms of an Anglo-Saxon charter. In recent years, courts have had to consider issues going back for centuries, such as a farmer claiming a right of common exercisable one year in three on a former common field,[1] the rights of a borough corporation to property granted under a sixteenth-century charter,[2] the obligation under an eighteenth-century Inclosure Act to maintain a hedge,[3] and the people entitled to a closed village school under a nineteenth-century settlement.[4]

It follows that while my account is in general chronological, I have not kept strictly to time. The law of the land has grown gradually, almost invisibly, with only a few major changes as in 1066, 1660 and 1925. Therefore, a chapter can include a comment on the way some apparently ancient law survived until a time outside its evident dates, often to our own century. Ways of thinking and values, particularly about social status, have changed a great deal over the years, but the way modern lawyers reason and reach a conclusion has much in common with that of their predecessors and many of the rules and institutions which earlier generations developed are still in use today.

---

[1] *Hall v Moore* [2009] EWCA Civ 201.

[2] *Ipswich Borough Council v Moore* [2001] EWCA Civ 1273.

[3] *Marlton v Turner* [1998] 3 EGLR 185.

[4] *Bath and Wells Diocesan Board of Finance v Jenkinson* [2002] EWHC 218 (Ch), [2003] Ch 89.

Glossary

Adscriptus glebae	inscribed to the clods; applied to *coloni* then to bondsmen
Beneficial ownership	right to enjoy land as distinct from formal title
Beneficiary	(*cestui que* use or *cestui que* trust) person having right to enjoy land
Bondsman	free man bound to service of a lord
Bookland	Anglo-Saxon landholding under grant by the king
Borough	town administered by a corporation
Burgh	Anglo-Saxon strongpoint, often nucleus of later borough
Case	lawsuit often a reported decision.
Castle guard	form of tenure by garrisoning a castle
Charter	documentary grant usually by the king
Civil law	law derived from Roman sources
Civitas	political community, also citizenship, also territory
Claimant	litigant who starts legal proceedings
Close	enclosed agricultural land
Common	area of waste or rough grazing subject to rights of common of persons other than owner
Common, rights of	rights of grazing, to take turf, wood, etc; exercisable over waste or over land of another person
Common field	open field subject to rights of common enforceable at common law
Common law	English law; law administered by common law courts as distinct from equity; judge-made law as distinct from equity; law of all England as distinct from custom; law derived from English rules as distinct from civil law
Commonable field	open field subject to informal practices or to customary rights similar to rights of common
Commons, House of	part of Parliament representing people of England
Company	modern form of corporation usually engaged in commerce

Consols   consolidated stock; permanent interest-bearing
                                government securities
Contingent remainder   right to land which might arise in future
Conveyance   document transferring title to land
Copyhold   land held by copy of court roll within a manor
Corporation   group of people having a single legal personality
Court   legal authority such as judge, formal local assembly,
                                king and advisers; mostly refers to forum for
                                resolution of disputes
Custom   ancient practices recognised as legally binding
Customary freehold   form of copyhold
Defendant   litigant against whom legal proceedings have been
                                instituted
Doom   law made by an Anglo-Saxon king
Enclosure   creation of closes out of open fields or waste
Entail   arrangement for land to descend within a family
Equity   laws developed by the Chancellor to ameliorate the
                                strictness of the common law
Farm   originally leasehold, later any agricultural unit
Fee simple   form of tenure amounting to absolute legal title
Fee tail   right to land held under an entail
Fiction   legal pretence to enable procedure designed for one
                                purpose to be used for another
Folkland   ancient form of Anglo-Saxon landholding
Frankalmoign   form of ecclesiastical tenure
Freehold   the nearest English law recognises to ownership of
                                land
Guardianship   government protection and maintenance of ancient
                                monument
Heir   person who succeeds to land, usually on death of a
                                former owner
Herepath   Saxon military road
Hide   Anglo-Saxon measure of land able to support a
                                substantial household containing about 120 acres
                                plus further rough grazing
Highway   public road or path
Hundred   unit of local administration comprising 100 hides
Impeachment for waste   right of a person with a future right to land to prevent
                                a current owner committing waste
Imperium   Roman suzerainty
Inclosure   conversion of common land to severalty
Knight service   form of tenure by military service
Landed estate   large area of land administered as a single unit

Landlord	owner of superior interest to holder of a lease
Law report	account of a case which might be quoted as a precedent
Lease	right to hold land for a limited period of time
Legal estate	formal title to land recognised by common law
Loanland	Anglo-Saxon predecessor of lease
Local Act	Act affecting a locality
Lord	holder of land with superior rights
Lords, House of	part of Parliament representing powerful landholders
Manor	customary jurisdictional rights over various tenants and lands
Mortgage	arrangement that if a borrower of money defaults the lender can sell his land to repay himself
Novel disseisin	form of speedy procedure introduced under Henry II
Nuisance	infringement of legal rights by neighbour
Open field	arable land arranged in strips without physical boundaries
Park	originally land set aside to contain deer; later an open grassy space for recreation either private or public
Parliament	assembly comprising king, Lords and Commons with power to make law
Perpetuity	future time beyond which legal rights may not be created
Possession	occupation of land
Precedent	law created by decision of a court
Private Act	Act affecting a family or a locality
Province	Roman unit of administration comprising several *civitates*
Public Act	Act altering the general law
Rent	payment for the use of land
Rentcharge	annual sum payable by freeholder
Reversioner	person with a right to inherit land after the death of a current owner
Seisin	right to possession capable of basing a claim to land
Settlement	arrangement for keeping land in a family
Severalty	private land free of common rights
Shire	unit of local administration centred on a town designed for defence against Vikings
Slave	human being owned as property
Socage	form of tenure, usually agricultural
Sovereign	person or organisation with no earthly superior
State	organisation of a sovereign country having international status

Statute	law made by Parliament or under its authority
Tenant	holder of land
Tenure	holding of land; also legal rules governing that holding
Term	fixed period of time for duration of lease
Title	evidence of right to hold land
Toll	payment for use of facility such as road or port
Traditio	Roman law informal conveyance
Turnpike	eighteenth-century system for improvement of roads paid for by tolls
Use	holding of land for benefit of another person
Villein	substantial bondsman
Waste (activity)	change in land, eg by demolishing or erecting a building, working minerals or felling timber
Waste (land)	unoccupied and uncultivated land
Works Act	Act authorising construction of works, such as canal or reservoir
Writ	summons to court to determine a dispute

Chapter 1

Introduction

LAW AND LANDSCAPE

This book explores how the law has influenced the way the landscape of England has changed over the centuries.

Men and women have made the landscape of England. Until modern times and the invention of machines, they did it by manual labour with help from oxen and horses. Starting from an environment of hills and rivers, rocks and soils, trees, grasses and reeds, they cleared the woods, drained the marshes, dug mines and built houses and towns, roads and canals, forts and tombs. Sometimes they did this work for their own purposes as individuals or families. Sometimes they did it as members of a larger group, acting under the direction of an overseer. In either case, they were guided by needs and ideas. The needs were those of farmers who grew crops or kept animals, of soldiers defending or controlling territory, of priests serving in holy places, of travellers passing across the country and by everyone needing a roof over their heads. The ideas were what we would call technical or architectural, social, political, military, economic or religious.

Law is one of those ideas. Law and legal rules are tools for making human societies work. Although law itself came to England with the Romans, long before that, men and women had to solve the problems which we deal with under the law. For us, the law regulates our relationships and it sets out the ways in which limited assets are divided among people who would like to have them. In the development of the landscape, the land is the most important asset. As the old saying goes, they are not making any more land, so what we have must be shared out. The law sets out the rules for sharing.

People change the landscape by using these ideas to create or change or replace fields and woods, settlements and roads, watercourses, castles and shopping centres. They do it by having control over the land. This book describes how that control comes about, how some people exercise it and how others in turn control that exercise. We will come across ideas, such as rights, ownership and agreements, which may at first sight seem obvious, but the way earlier generations understood them was often different from us. As we trace the means of control down the centuries, a number of themes recur. They are security, inheritance, disputes and transfer.

In the rest of this introduction I will explore those ideas and consider how people use the law and how it works. That may be found helpful in understanding how and why the law has developed. Those readers who wish to get on with the story of the landscape and its law may prefer to move immediately to Chapter 2 and come back to the discussion later.

SECURITY

Security concerns the right of someone to remain in control of a piece of land. It applies to a householder who wants to be sure she can bring up her children in a safe home or a trader who needs to know he can always sell from the same shop. Until modern times, the greatest part of the story concerns the countryside and so it will be simplest to refer to a farmer. Although farmers and others involved with land can be men or women, and they may gather in families or groups or be organised as a company, historically most were men and so I will refer to he as including she, they or it, bearing in mind, as we will see, that many arrangements were possible.

A farmer will not grow crops or graze cattle or sheep on the land unless he can be sure of his return. His work in sowing and cultivation must be rewarded by peacefully taking the harvest. He must know that he will be able to keep the milk or wool, hides or meat that his beasts produce. He needs to know that no one will throw him out and take the products he has spent time and energy in producing. Therefore, in some sense he must have control over them and the land on which they grow, and other people who belong to the same social group in which he lives must respect that. We will see the variety of ways in which this control can be worked out but the simplest and most obvious is to set apart a specific area which the farmer either owns or holds as tenant. That area will be defined in some way and many such areas together make up the landscape.

At first thought, ownership seems a simple idea. So it is for a thing, such as a spade, or even a cow. Ownership of land is not so simple. Land has existed for millions of years. It includes not just the occupation of the soil, but the right to share in the value created by working it. It includes minerals deep below the surface and the ability to take or kill the birds that fly over it. Every handful of soil contains countless bacteria, worms and other small creatures. The benefits from land can be shared in many ways and different parts of the ownership can belong to different people. It involves not just the terrain and its produce but at certain times in the past has included humans who live and work on it, slaves, serfs, tenants and farm labourers. It also involves people who live nearby and have concerns about how it is used – a field may grow weeds which can spread, a wood may be a fire risk or a building may overshadow a neighbour's house. We will see how the ideas of ownership and property and the right to treat land as a personal belonging only took their modern form in the seventeenth century.

Ownership can be divided. The most important division which plays a major part in the story arises under a tenancy. Although the word 'tenant' is nowadays used for a person with a short-term right to occupy land, in law it simply means holder and can refer either to an owner or an occupier. Usually, the tenant has (or once had) a duty to a lord or landlord to pay rent or perform other services such as fighting in a war.

Some types of holding, such as where the owner had (in law: was tenant in) the fee simple, lasted forever and they became freeholds. Others were copyholds, some of which were also perpetual. Other arrangements known as leases are either for a given time or term, or made under an agreement which either party, the lord or landlord and the lessee or termor or tenant, can bring to an end. If the tenancy is a short one, for a season or a year, we may not think of the tenant as the owner although we will see that in the sixteenth century the law came to give him ownership rights for the time he had the land. If his rights under his lease last for many years or even centuries, he may have a greater claim to be seen as the owner than the freeholder, who may just get a modest rent.

I will have much to say about tenancies and leases. First, the way people see the relationship between the parties can change over the centuries. Sometimes, as in the eleventh century, people who once would have been regarded as owners come to be seen as having a more precarious situation. At other times, as in the sixteenth and the twentieth centuries, people whose predecessors began as tenants may themselves become owners. Secondly, lawyers have used leases for all sorts of purposes – as mortgages, as procedural devices on the sale of land or in disputes about ownership and in family arrangements. So a historian coming across a person called a tenant or a document called a lease cannot assume any specific relationship to the occupation of land. Leases have been found to be flexible devices to modify the strict letter of the law, and to call a person a tenant may not by itself define his rights.

Ownership may also be divided among several people at the same time, such as brother and sister, husband and wife, a group of farmers who all graze their cattle on a piece of land, or it may be regarded as belonging to successive generations of a family. Ownership of minerals or of the right to kill birds and game may be separated from ownership of the land. All of these affect the way in which someone who appears to be the owner can control the use of the land or the extent to which his power to make changes is restricted. I shall sometimes refer to men or women or institutions as holding or occupying land as well as owning it but twenty-first century ideas will not always describe how people understood their situation in the past. Security may therefore rely on ownership but that can take different forms.

INHERITANCE

Inheritance expands the idea of security from an individual to his family after his death. If a man has worked a farm all his life and raised a family, he will want his widow to be secure in the family home, for any young children to be brought up safely and for older children to take the land on in his place. If he has several children, there is a question of who will take what when he dies.

The geology and form of the landscape of northern France is similar to that of southern England but, until a few years ago, if you had travelled through the two countries you would have seen a difference. In parts of Normandy were broad areas with few hedges but within them were many differently cultivated strips of land alongside one another. In Kent there have long been fields, more or less square in shape, surrounded by old hedges.

There are several reasons for this but one of the main ones is the difference in the rules of succession on death. In France it is common, and used to be invariable, for a family's land to be divided up in pieces among the children and grandchildren. In England the land is regarded as a thing on its own. The right to share in the value of the land may be divided but the land itself will be kept together. It will go to one child, often the oldest, but sometimes the youngest, son. He may buy out the interests of his brothers and sisters or he may pay them a rent but it is unusual for the land itself to be split up.

As control of land brought wealth and political power, it became important for those who had these things to ensure that their land would pass complete to their heirs so that any influence a landowner had in his community would belong to his descendants. Some scholars consider that historically family rights preceded individual ones. We shall see how family property was important in England in times such as the thirteenth and eighteenth centuries when it was entailed or in settlement. In such a case the present head could use it or let it during his lifetime but he could not sell it, so it was kept intact. Family ownership of land tended to inhibit change in the landscape because what one person handed on to the next generation had to be what he had received from his own ancestors.

DISPUTES AND TRANSFER

The third theme occurs because there may be arguments leading to formal legal disputes. Different people may claim ownership or occupation of land. Members of a family may disagree about who gets what when an ancestor dies. There can be problems about straying cattle eating a farmer's crops, the spread of disease, a cockerel making too much noise, blocked drains, the use of trackways or the obstruction of a view. Above all, there are boundary problems, one of the most fertile sources of work for lawyers and, it must be said, one of the most tedious. The laws of Babylon and ancient Israel were concerned with this as were the earliest Anglo-Saxon laws and it continues to take up much of the time of judges today. As rights to security and inheritance depend on what the law will allow to be enforced in courts or in other ways of resolving disputes, it is the key to those rights. In reference to lawsuits I will use modern expressions (different ones have been used in the past), so that a person who has suffered a wrong and brings the suit is called the claimant and the person who resists the claim is the defendant.

The final theme is transfer. If a person has established secure rights which he can defend in a dispute, then he has something he can pass on to another person in return for a benefit. In historical times and within societies which have a settled market in property, that has most often been by sale for money or sometimes by exchange for other land. This involves the procedure of transfer of title, and the records of such deals are second only to those of disputes in telling us about how people used and occupied land over the centuries. A society which allows easy transfer of land will be one in which the landscape will change rapidly as new occupiers with new ideas buy in to the countryside. For that reason, many static societies have inhibited sales and we shall see how the effect of the strict settlement system of the eighteenth century was to entrench a small group of hereditary landowners in power and wealth and how, despite that, people found ways to build mills, canals and railways and expand the towns.

Title is important. It gives security. It can be inherited by the next generation. If you have title you will win an argument. You will control the land and can either make those changes you want or prevent others doing what you do not want. Therefore, much of this book is concerned with title to land, which confers the power to cut down trees, dig minerals, build a house, or erect a tomb, a church or a factory. But the idea of title took time to emerge and so did the corresponding idea of owning land.

THE USE OF LAW

Law achieves its purpose – to help people live together in society – in two ways. One is where a problem has arisen. This may involve what we call the criminal law, an assault, a killing or a theft. In practice, that is a small part of the work of lawyers although it is a part that many who are not lawyers think of first. More important are civil disputes between parties where one has a claim against the other. There may be an existing conflict over land or the occupation of it. Perhaps a man has pulled down a fence along the boundary or built on land claimed by his neighbour. In such cases, the lawyers are asked to advise the parties to the dispute, if possible to negotiate a solution, and, if not, to argue the case before an impartial third party, now called a judge or arbitrator.

The second, and more important, way the law comes into play is long before any conflict has occurred or even seems likely. Its function is, by using the experience of many cases, to prevent a dispute arising in the future. This is the reason for the long intricate documents known as deeds and contracts which go on for pages in technical language, dealing with all sorts of remote possibilities. That is conveyancing. It is also the reason for the survival of many ancient laws, some of which we will examine in this book. By using the experience of past disputes, lawyers have developed rules which can be effective in preventing the same problems arising again.

In most of this book I will refer to England and the laws of England. That is because the other parts of the British Isles and Continental Europe have their own laws. The laws of England have never governed Scotland. At times in the past they have applied in Ireland and Wales but Northern Ireland and Wales now have their own law-making assemblies and in the future their laws will become (as in the past they were) different from those of England. However at times, such as during the Roman Empire, after the Norman Conquest and since the United Kingdom joined what is now the European Union, Continental law has affected what is done here and in the future there will be more influence from overseas. Correspondingly, the common law which developed in England in the thirteenth century has spread to other parts of the world and the ideas which I will discuss have influenced the laws in many countries.

There are several relationships which recur in different societies and which the members of those societies reflect in their laws. One is between owners and occupiers of land. Another is the way in which one person wishes to control the way his descendants benefit from land while, in their turn, those generations want to make their own decisions. Another is the balance between the need that leaders and groups of people have (nowadays through the planning system) to regulate and organise the landscape as a whole as against the wish of the individual occupier to do what he wants with his own property. Another is between the government, or what in modern times has come to be seen as the state, especially in its need for revenue, and the landowner who wishes to retain what the land produces. All of these have affected the development of the landscape and have been worked out through the law.

In what follows I have selected a few problems which recur down the ages to tell the story of how law has affected the landscape. Traditional legal histories contain a mass of details of interest to lawyers. Here I have tried to give a broader account to those who have little or no previous knowledge of land law or its ways. I need to say, however, that the way lawyers reason and develop their ideas can often seem strange to those not familiar with the law.

In part, that is because of a never-ending conflict between certainty and flexibility. The law has to be certain so that people know what their rights and duties are. That is especially important for property law which controls the landscape and which affects the livelihood of many people over a long time. That means it alters slowly and with difficulty. That, in turn, means it often gets out of date with changes in society and technology. Those affected need to deal with their affairs to meet new conditions, and their lawyers have to find ways to do it. There are a number of methods. One is to use legal fictions, making a new approach look as if it was an old one. Another is to find an argument that the old laws do not quite cover the new situation and therefore it is possible to squeeze the new solution to a problem through gaps in the old law. It will be evident that this can lead to complications and we will see several examples. Over the centuries, legal arrangements have become ever more convoluted as each generation tries to get round rules and restrictions imposed earlier. So the law becomes almost too complex to understand. But the client who is hiring the lawyer is a practical person, and wants to get to a specific outcome as simply (and cheaply) as possible.

Furthermore, the law does not enforce itself. In recent centuries there have been a variety of public officials, such as inspectors and police and planning officers, who are paid to see that certain public laws are observed. In former times, monarchs had little money or inclination to do that. In any case most issues were regarded as private matters between his subjects and not for interference from on high. So laws would only be enforced or court action taken if it suited someone to pay for it. That person would only do so if there was money at stake, either to promote a new project which would make a profit or prevent someone doing something which would cause him loss. Similarly, where a change in the law was required, an individual or a group of investors often needed to promote a new Act of Parliament. Most of the developments in the law we will consider were, therefore, initiated by private people in order to achieve a particular benefit for themselves. They might not have been too concerned with the wider effect on society but others learnt from their efforts and used them to gain different ends. The law tended, therefore, to change bit by bit without any logical plan.

The law of the land has responded to the needs and desires of those who live or work or take pleasure on or from the land. It has reflected changes in society and technology, in the amount or distribution of wealth and in the possession or exercise of political influence. The story that follows is about the way that law has been used in determining the shape of fields, the layout of roads, the building of castles, churches and houses and the way that these products of human labour are spread across the landscape.

Chapter 2

Prehistoric to AD 43

Before the Romans came there was nothing we would recognise as law. There was no writing, therefore no title deeds, no Acts of Parliament, no textbooks, no reports of the decisions of judges. There were only accepted ways of doing things that varied among the numerous societies which occupied different parts of England over more than 4,000 years. So how did people resolve the problems that could arise from competition over the resources of the countryside – the issues that we deal with by invoking the law?

FIRST FARMERS

Imagine a scene soon after the earliest farmers began to cultivate the land. The very first may have been immigrants from France, Germany or Spain, or they may have been people born in England who learnt new techniques and imported crops or animals from overseas. Although they did not know it, the crops and animals came from ancestors which people had, thousands of years before, learnt to domesticate in the Middle East. Over the centuries, farmers spread the new ways across Europe. Some time before 4000 BC, one of those early pioneers settled somewhere in England, perhaps near the sea and made a field for his crops or his beasts. When he died, his family made a great tomb for him on the hillside. It was designed to be large enough so that in time it could take the bodies of several generations of his descendants. In the autumn, when the mourning was over, his children went out to one of the clearings he had used. Where he had made a rough enclosure, they began to replace the bank or hedge with a proper fence, made of stakes cut from the surrounding woods.

A group of men and women appeared from those woods. They and their ancestors since the beginning of time had been accustomed to hunt and to gather fruits and roots from this land. They had seen the new farms with some curiosity and growing concern. If things continued, this would interfere with the running of the deer and the growth of the wild plants. If the farmers were strangers from across the water they were damaging the land. Even if they were the children of local people, the new ways would disturb the traditional ways and means of livelihood.

The encounter was peaceful. There was a discussion. The farmers explained that this land was cleared and cultivated by their father who was now dead and had become an ancestor who desired his descendants to have forever the land he had given them. The hunters pointed out that the farmers were damaging the lands on which their own ancestors had run. Eventually, one of the farmers gave one of the hunters a woollen cloak to keep him warm; the hunters accepted that the farmers could stay and they departed.

This little scene is imaginary and probably it was never like that but it illustrates some of the themes we will encounter in the story of the way the law makes the landscape. Something not too unlike this did happen three or four hundred years ago when colonists from Europe went to North America and Australia, as Peter Minuit bought Manhattan Island in 1626 for a few tools and some cloth. We can, therefore, look at these ideas as they existed before the complications that modern society has brought and we can also consider how it was possible in a country before law.

SOLVING LEGAL PROBLEMS BEFORE WE HAD LAW

Farming takes time and trouble. The first man (or, less likely because of the physical labour, woman) to farm a piece of England had to create a field. He cleared stones and trees or bushes from his arable land used for crops or he made pasture for his beasts by burning the land so it would grow a grassy sward. Where he intended to grow a crop, he turned the sod to provide a bed to take the seed which he then sowed. He had to protect the growing crops from competition from weeds and to water it in case of drought. He needed to be sure that if he did all that, he could then reap the harvest in peace to have the grain that he needed for food and for next year's sowing. He might not use the same plot of land every year. As successive crops were grown, so the fertility of the land fell, and unless the farmer restored it by fertilising (the use of manure was a later discovery) he had to move to another piece of land, but he had to be sure he could do so. He needed to know that no one would interfere with his cultivation. If he grazed cattle or sheep, he needed to protect them from wandering off and to provide sheltered places against the heat of summer or the cold of winter.

The ways in which farmers obtained this security varied over the prehistoric centuries and between the differing terrains that make up the geography of England. Most often they relied on their neighbours to support them in a dispute. If a man was born into a society, grew up knowing the people farming adjoining lands, one family marrying into another, then there was pressure to conform. Someone who violated established ways would be an outcast, for in a fragile society at risk from disease and famine, a threat to one farmer's security was a threat to all. Neighbours would stick by each other, respect one another's land and band together to resist outsiders. Also, if the farmer died, his family would be protected in their inheritance by those who lived nearby, many of them his own kin, for they knew that if they did not then their own widows and children would also be at risk.

Disputes likewise would most often be settled by neighbours. No doubt in many times and places rivals might fight out their differences – perhaps two brothers might have a duel to see who would inherit their father's land. But in any settled society such private fights had to be kept under control or they would threaten the whole community as each combatant called on friends and relatives until all were fighting. Such a society would quickly fall prey to organised outsiders.

Sometimes if there were powerful or respected leaders they might decide who was right or who could occupy land. That became more common as time passed and aristocrats and kings developed their fortunes and gathered dependant followers. For much of prehistoric times, society was not sufficiently organised to have such rulers to give formal decisions. Sometimes judgment in a dispute might be left to the spirits. The rivals could consult them by observing the flight of birds or the shapes of clouds. But even such things had to be interpreted and the wisest elder would be asked to do that. So in practice it is likely that arguments came to be resolved according to the opinion of neighbours and they would tend to reach similar conclusions in similar circumstances.

Finally, a difficult matter can be resolved by a deal. In our story the hunters, realising the greater force of the farmers who could, if thwarted, get their friends to help, agreed to give way and let the farmers stay in return for a cloak. In our society that would be a sale, signified by transfer of title to the land. Over the centuries, there were many different arrangements for neighbours to allow a young man to take on land formerly occupied by a senior, or for a shepherd to move his flocks from one region to another in peace. Such changes were made possible by gifts, by invoking the will of the spirits, by threat of force or withthe consent of elders.

DIVIDING THE LANDSCAPE

No record has survived of the thoughts and ideas of the people who lived here in the periods called the New Stone Age or Neolithic Age and the Bronze Age but, as there were no documents of title and no recognisable system of law, we can say that they did not own the land in our terms. They occupied it, they grazed their sheep and cattle, they made stock enclosures to confine them for the autumn culling and they had areas in which they grew crops. Archaeologists have found traces of enclosed fields as far back as the early Neolithic Age.

We are used to fields being surrounded by a hedge, fence or wall, perhaps with a ditch, but these are not essential. Often, animals can graze in open country over common land but sometimes a farmer needs an enclosure to confine them and stop them straying. He also needs a barrier to deter wild animals such as deer which may eat the growing shoots or in prehistoric times wolves which might take lambs. If there is mixed farming, he wants to prevent the cow getting into the corn. And in any human society there may be thieves who will steal the livestock or casual wanderers who may damage the crops but who may be deterred by a hedge or fence. Once such a barrier exists it takes on a life of its own. It becomes not just a physical thing but a mental idea, distinguishing mine or ours from what lies beyond.

We can see this from the great landscape features sometimes called reaves. Andrew Fleming, an archaeologist working around Dartmoor, studied these long features, running for many miles across the country.[1] They consisted of a set of main banks, with lesser banks branching off them, thereby creating a system of fields. He found they dated to the Bronze Age and must have been laid out by a central authority, or perhaps several, each of whom controlled large tracts of land and could organise the labour to build the system. Plate 1 shows a map of part of the system. Since then, other archaeologists have discovered field systems of a similar date in many other parts of England. The most likely explanation is that they were for stock rearing, but the best guess is that they had to be installed at a time when there was growing competition for land and some rule was needed to decide who could use one area rather than another. In short, they had what we would regard as a legal setting, to divide the resources used by one group from those of another and to set boundaries.

The landscape may not just have been divided into economic zones. Indeed, we cannot expect the people of those times to have thought in the same way as we do or to have made the same distinctions. We, for instance, distinguish private property, such as houses, fields and shops, from public land, such as government buildings, places of worship, recreation grounds and common land. Some archaeologists believe that in early prehistoric times people made a different division, into the lands of the living and those of the dead. Some places, such as burial mounds, certain stone circles and perhaps special springs and groves, were regarded as the place of the spirits or the ancestors. Others, such as arable fields, grazing lands, houses, fishing streams and perhaps some of

---

[1]   Fleming, Andrew, *The Dartmoor Reaves* (Batsford, 1988).

the hill tops known as causewayed camps where people might gather for meetings and feasts, were for the living. Both had their special places, sometimes linked by long parallel lines of ditches known as cursuses running across miles of country.

There must have been rules to divide and protect these distinctions. Most people of course would have respected the places, both those of the spirits and those used by others for making a living, but there were always dissenters, criminals and those who did not conform. Suppose a farmer thought that a particular area set aside for the ancestors looked like productive farming land? Suppose when a man died, his kin wanted to bury him in a mound on land where their neighbours grazed their sheep? We do not know, for example, if Stonehenge was readily accessible to anyone or whether access was restricted to a few privileged people. If the latter, how was this enforced? Would the community impose a penalty such as exile or was it left to the spirits?

In our society, such matters are decided by the pressure of economic need, by national policy determined by politicians, by the special sanctions that religion places on sacred sites and by the general views of people in society, and they are then worked out though legal rules. In early times, people did not make such distinctions. So a sanction could be what we would call religious, by believing that an offender had displeased the spirits, or political by exiling him from the assemblies where his neighbours gathered, or economic by cutting him off from any dealings with his fellows. We can get a hint of this from the observations of anthropologists in the simpler societies which survived until the nineteenth and twentieth centuries, although they existed in very different parts of the world and we must not assume that Prehistoric England resembled them.

We cannot expect that any one explanation will work throughout this period. In the 4,000 or so years between the first farmers in England and the Roman conquest, there were many different societies which came into being and disappeared. There were also people living in different parts of England, among the mountains of the north, the wetlands of East Anglia, the flat country of the Midlands or the river valleys of the South – different societies developed with different ways of sharing their resources. Even so, we can say that for most of the people politics, religion, economics and society were the same thing, part of the same life. There were few specialists. Some were rulers although their power depended on those who worked on the land. There may have been religious experts we might call priests. There must have been smiths who worked the metals. There are indications of trade, in stone axes, in gold objects, in bowls and jars and clothing and no doubt many other products which have perished, and some people would have spent part of their time in commerce. But most worked the fields or herded the beasts. Their concerns were to protect their ability to bring in the following year's harvest and to keep their herds safe from predators, both human and animal. They had dwellings but they were not substantial.

Some writers suggest that at this time land was owned in common. I think that is a mistake. First, as we will see, the idea of ownership developed later. Even the Romans did not see it quite as we do and the full implications did not emerge until the seventeenth century. People who lived in a locality might indeed have taken the view that any land in the area could only be exploited by members of their community and outsiders were not welcome. They might then have come to accept some sort of communal responsibility for the land. However, only an individual or a family would cultivate a particular piece of land for crops or occupy a specific home. Secondly, the idea of any common thing is a sophisticated one and unlikely to have been held by a simple society. When we speak of land being owned in common, we mean that a few individuals or families share its resources and divide the value between them. In modern times, we may be referring to ownership by a company, by government or under a trust, but, as we will see, the concept of a corporation, a state or a local authority capable of owning land is a recent one. In the past, we may mean that the land is regarded in some way as belonging to a higher power, such as a god who protects the community.

We know from texts excavated in Iraq that in the valleys of the Tigris and Euphrates from the third millennium BC people understood that the land belonged to the gods and humans simply managed it for them. Those societies had what we would recognise as law. One of the most famous collections was an engraved stone bearing the laws issued by Hammurabi who ruled Babylon from around 1792 to 1750 BC, which corresponds to the middle Bronze Age in England. The laws are said to have been issued on the instructions of the gods. They included provisions about the exchange of fields, neglected buildings, pasture and, as irrigation was especially important, agricultural drainage. Likewise, in Egypt at the same time there were what we would understand as legal procedures although, as the king was himself a god, they could hardly be distinguished from religious petitions and commands. It is unlikely that anyone in those countries had ever heard of this island; perhaps a rumour of distant cities might have reached people here. However, even though the idea of law as such was already in the world it would not have affected people in England. They lived in small societies without writing or elaborate institutions. They had no need of it and did not know it. They subsisted by ancient practices tempered by fighting.

IRON AGE

From around the eighth century BC until the Romans came, hill forts dominated the landscape in many parts of England. Their remains survive to our times. They are enclosures on the summits of strategic hills, set around with ditches and ramparts and designed to be defended against attack. Some archaeologists think they were built for display, to declare the importance of the leader who organised their construction or of the people who occupied them, but they look as if intended for war and they stood out like the castles which later generations sometimes put in the same place.

Although some scholars believe that hill forts were communal enterprises, it is more likely that they were planned by individuals who also controlled the surrounding countryside. This introduces a form of organisation which will be one of our main topics and which dominated the landscape until around 1900. That is power concentrated in the hands of an individual, a member of a small group of aristocrats or gentry who, by the use of an institution later known as the landed estate, could direct the lives of people in rural areas. Much of the story told in this book involves estates, how they were consolidated, passed down the generations and dissolved. It is a key element in the way the powerful arranged the countryside.

Any agricultural society will be governed in that way. This is because while agriculture produces an economic surplus, it is only a small one. Before agriculture, when people hunted and gathered from the wild, they neither could nor wanted to make or keep a surplus. Since the Industrial Revolution, industry has produced enough wealth to be spread around and the result has been democracy. But in between, when nearly everyone worked on the land and raised crops and stock, a farmer could get just a little more than enough to live on. He would find in the autumn that he had sufficient grain to make bread for his family for a year, to provide seed corn for the following year's crops and enough over to sell in order to buy an iron plough-share or other equipment he could not make himself. Or he could produce leather from skins to clothe his family, meat and milk to feed them with a little over. Beyond this was a surplus, a little more than he needed to survive. That could, in principle, be handled in two ways.

Imagine two neighbouring societies. In one, a small group of fighters have power over everyone else. They leave enough to the farmer for bare subsistence and seize the surplus, in the form of rent or taxes or under any one of a number of names, to make their own lives easy. They are the warriors and rulers. In the other, the farmers live at peace, each keeping the whole of his small surplus and trading it for little luxuries. They can make pleasant homes and life is good.

In time, the aristocrats will want to expand their power. The free farmers are not fighters. The warriors spend their time training and using their wealth to make weapons. If they attack, they will incorporate the farmers into their country and dominate them. So the farmers have to defend themselves and the only way is to ask some of their number to become professional soldiers, paid for by their fellows so they have the time to train. As they cannot spend time farming, they will have to be allocated lands to produce an income to keep them and that will have to be provided by the farmers out of their surplus. These soldiers will come to have more in common with the aristocrats next door than with their own fellows. They will develop a code of honour needed for military discipline, and come to expect the contribution as their right. In time, the former free farmers will come to be subordinate just like their counterparts across the hills.

In a world where income comes only from land, a few powerful men will control that land and make others subject to them. So it was in early Britain. This may go back to the time before men started to use iron weapons. The authority of the leaders who laid out the reaves may have come from the community or from military power. Most people had to spend their lives producing food, fuel, clothing and other means of subsistence. Even the smiths, potters, shipwrights or minstrels who were able to supplement their living by getting a return for practicing their skills would have had to devote much of their energies to their farm holdings. Few of them would have been free of work on the land.

In the Iron Age, the evidence suggests that society was ordered by a small group of powerful and wealthy men and women, who did not have to guide the plough or milk the cow. They could live in relative luxury and when they died they were buried in style, often with their swords or jewellery or chariots. They made the great hill forts, some of which were no doubt defences for the common good on the boundaries of the little kingdoms of the time, while others were the bases for purely local rulers. Many of these hill forts were densely occupied but they were not towns as we know them with councils, local bylaws and privileges. Other rich men or women lived in large dwellings known as round houses, well built of timber, perhaps controlling a home farm or an estate. Later, just before the Roman invasion, we begin to find settlements with numbers of substantial dwellings at places such as St Albans, Colchester and Silchester, but they seem more to be associated groups of rich men's residences than urban complexes.

These societies had a simple organisation which, while not governed by law, could still use some legal ideas imported from across the Channel. They had money and leaders who the Romans recognised as kings. Julius Caesar came to Britain in 54 BC and wrote to the people of Rome an account of his visit, putting what he found in terms the Italians would understand. He described some of the peoples as a *civitas*.[2] That word has been translated as city-state, canton and tribe, but it has no exact English equivalent and it is better to use the contemporary term. The Romans applied it to most of the small independent peoples who became incorporated in their empire around the Mediterranean and also to those they encountered north of the Alps. It really means political unit (the nearest Greek equivalent is *polis*) or legal community. It applies first to the free men and sometimes women who counted, who could make their own decisions, owned property and had, in a related meaning of *civitas*, citizenship of their own country. It also came to mean the territory of land occupied by the community. The *civitas* might or might not have been governed by a king but would in practice have been run by a group of nobles. In Greece or Italy it had its own laws, it had a system of land proprietorship and of rules which governed the relations between the powerful aristocrats, the farmers and the unfree, who ploughed the fields and herded the cattle. A British *civitas* would not have had all these features, particularly laws, but it was close enough to be called one.

Even the ordinary folk may have had some claim to their land. Caesar, when describing Gaul across the Channel, says that the common people had nothing[3] but that may not have applied in Britain or everywhere. Across England are many so called celtic fields, the size of paddocks, roughly square in shape. We can still recognise some on hillsides where centuries of ploughing have caused the soil to roll down hills to the boundary, so making a series of terraces which survive in downland. In Cornwall, there are some ancient massive stone-walled enclosures which go back to Iron Age times. At Dicklesburgh in Norfolk, landscape historians have recognised a large area of cultivated fields laid out in a grid pattern. A Roman road cuts across the field pattern at an angle. If it had been there first the fields would have been laid out parallel to it, so they must be earlier.[4]

Some of these small enclosures did in a sense belong to their cultivators. The fields show signs of permanent use over many generations, and were most likely inherited from grandfather to son to grandson. The family had some lawful right to make them, since the making involved building walls and banks and digging ditches. That is something that might have been ordered by a landowner but mostly it was the work of men who expected that they and their families would continue to benefit from the investment of time and money.

However, neither the nobles nor the cultivators owned the land in our sense. They could not sell it – there was in any case no land market. There were iron

---

[2]   Eg Caesar, Julius Gaius, *de Bello Gallico*, 5.20.

[3]   Ibid, 6.13.1.

[4]   Williamson, T, 'Early co-axial field systems on the East Anglian boulder clays', (1987) 53 *Proceedings of the Prehistoric Society* 419–31.

currency bars, and later gold coins, in circulation, minted under the authority of the kings, but it is not clear what they were used for. Even in Iron Age Britain, a few coins or a mass of iron would not have amounted to the value of a farm let alone an estate. All, rich and poor alike, were as much bound to the land as they were entitled to it, as son followed father.

If a noble prospered and attracted followers, or if his people increased after a time of peace, they might have begun to make new fields or pasture their flock further away from his dwelling. That might have led to an argument with a neighbour over these resources. Caesar says that in Gaul the leading men submitted such boundary disputes to the decision of the druids.[5] They are often thought of as priests, sacrificing to the gods and collecting sacred mistletoe, but we can also see them as judges, perhaps among the few who could read and write (in Latin for there was no British literature) and therefore as advisers to kings. There were some shrines and other sacred places, such as groves and springs, as well as holy places inherited from earlier centuries, such as Stonehenge. The decision-making power of the druids would extend also to other boundaries between *civitates*.

Apart from the hill forts and temples there were few permanent structures. Even substantial round houses could be built or pulled down in a few hours, although if kept in repair they might last for 100 years. If a powerful warrior decided he wanted to make a house in a new place, or a king gathered his nobles around him in the loose collection of separated households which was the nearest they had to a town, no one could stop them. The fields by contrast were permanent. Once men had laid out good land and banked it round with a hedge planted on the bank, it was a sound investment and would remain. It was vital to the economy.

Political organisation was subject to constant change. England was, to outward appearances, split among a dozen or more *civitates* but, unlike the stable communities around the Mediterranean, these were ephemeral, dependent on the military skill and reputation of a chieftain. On his death or defeat, they could be reconfigured or incorporated in another unit and his sons might have had only a slender chance of succeeding. It is therefore unlikely that they had any tradition of long-standing rules to regulate them. We know less about the noble estates but these too would have been transitory, although where a former leader had a competent son he might hope to take on his father's power. Among the cultivators of the land we should expect stability to be more important. Knowledge of every field and wood was important to get the best out of it and that could only be learnt by growing up on it. Generations could have followed, tilling the same soil, leading flocks and herds to the same pasture.

---

5   Caesar, Julius Gaius, *de Bello Gallico*, 6.13.

There was little in the way of rights. The local community would have recognised that a widow or child could take on the land of a former cultivator. Among the powerful, there would be a small governing group, often gathered around a king, although it seems that some *civitates* were run by aristocrats without a single ruler. It was with such small groups that the Romans dealt when they arrived, and by ruling through them they were able to incorporate Britain into their empire.

Chapter 3

Roman – AD **43 to 450**

IMPERIUM ROMANUM

In AD 43, the Roman emperor Claudius ordered his legions to incorporate Britain into the empire. Since Caesar's time, the Romans had claimed a form of superior governance called *imperium* over the *civitates* of southern Britain. Now they asserted it with their army and established Britain as a province. When they came, they made roads through the countryside, stationed forts in strategic places, founded towns and built comfortable country houses across the land. Some came to settle here but more significantly they persuaded local rulers to adopt Roman ways of living. Most important of all, they brought the law.

Soldiers impressed the first signs of conquest on the landscape and military need did not respect any legal rules. There was indeed a legal basis for the occupation. It was the respect for the *imperium* which British rulers had acknowledged since Caesar's time. Claudius was also asked to intervene by Verica, a claimant to the kingship of the *civitas* of the Atrebates. But the reality was force of arms. So when the generals built forts and made roads to communicate between them, they did not take time to respect any rights of the local people.

However, soldiers cannot control by force forever and as the legions moved north into unconquered territory, leaving the settled lands of the south, there had to be a civilian regime. This varied between *civitates* and therefore the rules governing changes also varied. The Romans had to deal with each *civitas* through its rulers – king or council of nobles – on the basis of law, otherwise there could be no stability. They had long experience of this. In early times when the Roman Republic was expanding through Italy there was a system of unequal treaties.[1] Under this the Senate and People of Rome made a treaty

---

[1]   Sherwin-White, AN, *The Roman Citizenship* (Oxford University Press, 1973), p 121.

(*foedus iniquum*) with the territory to be incorporated in the Roman *imperium* which governed matters such as trade (*commercium*), marriage between citizens of Rome (and of its other allied *civitates* already in the empire) and those of the newly incorporated *civitas* (*connubium*), and freedom of movement (*migratio*). By the time of the conquest of Britain, the Romans no longer used these treaties as such but they had to make similar arrangements. This is sometimes called a *lex provinciae* but that term may not be contemporary.

The emperor (or his governor) had to define the rules to integrate the newly incorporated peoples into the empire. Most humble farmers will have hardly noticed the conquest. They went on cultivating their fields or herding their sheep as their ancestors had. For the aristocrats there were indeed differences. They had to adapt to the ways of the new rulers. The most important features were that the *civitas* had to pay tax, and the Roman authorities had a monopoly of force, that is capital punishment and making war so that the British leaders had to put away their swords. But apart from a few defined matters, the *civitas* remained as it always had been. It might now have been a 'friend and ally of the Senate and People of Rome' but in other respects it retained its laws and its rulers kept their positions. In law, the empire expanded not by annexing a *civitas* into the territory of Rome itself but by the Senate and people (acting through the emperor) establishing *imperium* over its rulers and incorporating it into a province. The Roman empire was not a state in the sense that modern countries are or nineteenth-century empires were. As well as *civitas* and *imperium* the Romans had several related expressions, such as *patria* (fatherland) or *respublica* (public state of affairs). *Roma* referred either to the city or to a goddess who guided the destiny of the nations associated with her in the *Orbis Romanus*, the Roman World under the protection of the emperor who, while not himself a god, exercised divine power. But the empire was seen as consisting of and being run by individuals and not as some abstract collective entity.

The emperor appointed a governor, in the case of Britain based in London, and the territories were subject to his jurisdiction. In theory, *provincia* described his sphere of responsibilities; in practice it referred to the area he controlled. Most of the surviving histories say relatively little about *civitates* and more about provinces because they were written by men who were or had been officials based in Rome and they saw things from the point of view of the imperial authorities. But for ordinary people the *civitas* was more important. We can tell this from surviving accounts relating to the Mediterranean, but the same would have applied in Britain. For instance, the Acts of the Apostles (written before 100) tells how wandering Christian preachers mainly had to deal with the *civitates* although occasionally they came across Roman provincial governors. Likewise, the letters of Pliny the Younger (written around 112) who was a senator and, at the end of his life, the emperor's special envoy to and governor of Bithynia and Pontus in Asia Minor, show that his duties involved dealing with issues affecting the *civitates*.

So in Britain there were two overlapping systems of law. One was Roman law itself which in turn had two aspects. The first was imperial control representing what we would call public law of crime, taxes and the military which governed the making of forts, roads and public buildings. The second aspect was private law between the Roman citizens who came here to live or trade and which dealt with rights affecting their houses, shops and villas.

The other system was the local law of each *civitas*, which could vary from one to another and which governed the dealings between native folk and their own farms and fields. As we have seen, unlike the peoples of Athens or Judea or the other communities of the Mediterranean, the peoples of Kent or Cornwall or the Midlands had no law as such before the Romans came. They would, however, have had some practices for instance about sacred places, such as springs, groves and temples, which would be recognised by the authorities. They had other rules, perhaps concerning boundaries or inheritance, which varied from one locality to another. These became the basis of what can now be recognised as domestic law. In addition, once Britain was part of the empire there were a host of other matters, such as sale of land, loans and commercial contracts, for which the local folk had to adopt rules from Roman law and these became incorporated in the law of the *civitas*. In this remote province, therefore, people came to take on the laws of Rome more than did those with a longer history of their own culture.

THE OLDEST KNOWN LAWSUIT

These two systems acted on one another. An instance is the case of *Bellicus v Silvinus*[2] the earliest known law suit in England. It concerned the sale by Titus Valerius Silvinus to Lucius Julius Bellicus in the year 118 of a five-acre wood called Verlucionium in the territory of the Cantiaci, who lived in modern Kent and adjoining lands. We do not know why Bellicus wanted to buy it. Perhaps he intended to fell the timber and then sell it for fuel or use it himself; perhaps he wanted the land to build a house. Perhaps he just liked to own a wood. Bellicus and Silvinus were both Roman citizens, so when Bellicus agreed to buy the land the contract was governed by Roman not Cantiacan law. Citizens took their law with them wherever they were in the world. This even applied where the contract related to land within a local jurisdiction. However, local factors had an influence. The modern commentator, Dr Roger Tomlin, suggests that the name

---

[2]   Tomlin, RSO, 'A five acre wood in Roman Kent', in *Interpreting Roman London*, Oxbow Monograph 58 (Oxbow Books, 1996), pp 209–16.

of the wood meant 'shining' in the British language and it may have been a sacred grove. If so, it presents a curious legal problem.

If the wood had been in Italy, the contract of sale would have been ineffective. Holy sites were consecrated to the gods and could not be bought and sold. Any attempt to do so did not work. If Bellicus had paid a deposit, he would have been able to ask a judge to order Silvinus to repay it. But this was not Italy; it was the *civitas* of the Cantiaci. Under Roman law, land in provinces could not be owned by a private individual. The law regarded it as belonging to the Roman people or, in the case of an Imperial province such as Britain, to the emperor. In practice, of course, individuals could buy and sell ordinary land but according to Roman law they would transfer a right to possession or occupation, not full ownership. The law would recognise such a transfer of rights.

The issue, therefore, was whether the Roman rules about sacred sites applied to land in Kent or whether, because it was outside Italy, the parties were free to sell and buy possession in much the same way as if they did have rights to the land. Gaius, a famous lawyer, who gave a series of lectures on Roman law some 40 years later, said that a similar rule to that applying in Italy would extend to provincial land.[3] If so, the judge would have recognised the sacred nature of the wood and nullified the sale. It is even possible that the statement of Gaius is based on some actual case.

The idea that someone can have legal rights over land and thereby control it became the most important means of changing the landscape from that time to ours. It gives someone the legitimate power to alter the use, to put up or pull down buildings, to plant and dig. The concept did not immediately penetrate all of society. The Romans recognised the aristocrats as, in a sense, owning the land they controlled, although, since land in Britain was provincial land (except, possibly, land in the *coloniae* mentioned below), we should qualify this as the law gave an ultimate power to the emperor. It is unlikely that the authorities would, at least in the early years of Roman rule, have regarded the humbler people in Britain as owning the land they farmed.

The road at Dicklesburgh mentioned in Chapter 2 is an instance. It leads to Caistor by Norwich, the Roman town of Venta Icenorum, whose name means the Market *Civitas* of the Iceni. The Romans probably built Venta after they defeated the rebellion by Queen Boudicca in AD 60. The rebellion was put down with force and the lands of Boudicca and her followers would have been forfeit. It has been suggested that the lands of this part of East Anglia then became part of the property of the emperor, known as the *fiscus*, which was used to raise money for government, either by being directly farmed with the profits going to

---

3   Gaius, *Institutes*, 2.7.

the government or by being let to tenants at a rent. By contrast, in another *civitas*, that of the Dobunni in the West Midlands, it appears that in AD 43 the Romans were welcomed as deliverers from domination by their neighbours. The nobles co-operated with imperial authorities and in consequence got their reward. In later Roman times, this became a prosperous area with villas amid private estates belonging to established landowners.

As I explained earlier, the road at Dicklesburgh cuts across the pre-existing fields. We should not expect that the cultivators of the fields were compensated. Possibly the noble with ultimate control might have been, if he had not been involved in the rebellion, but no one would have been concerned about the common folk.

TOWNS

Although the Romans drained marshes, dug mines and built military works such as Hadrian's Wall, the most significant change they made to the landscape of Britain was to found towns. These were small by our standards, covering a few acres but they had a big impact on the surrounding countryside. They were the centre of a network of roads. Some were great imperial public ways (*viae*) built by the legions, running between the towns. As they served the defences of Britain, they were well maintained. There were also local routes known as vicinal ways. Some of those were ancient tracks; others were made by local farmers coming to the town to buy luxuries and pay their taxes. These were rarely paved and users got by as best they could. The wood in the *Bellicus* case is described as lying on a vicinal or local road.

Towns could have one of three types of legal status. The most important were the colonies (*coloniae*). This institution started when Roman citizens went to live in nearby territories, often to garrison them, and under the empire they were treated as legally part of Italy, however far away. Some of them had special rights called *ius italicum*. Although the colonies were situated within the area of a *civitas*, they, with their own territory around them, were in law separate. Their free inhabitants were Roman citizens and the law they used was Roman law. The colonies, such as Colchester, Gloucester and Lincoln, had all the attributes of a Mediterranean town with a market place (*forum*), temples, perhaps an amphitheatre and race track. Their first occupants were veterans retired from the army who were supposed to compensate the natives (that is the aristocrats) for the land they took, but the historian Tacitus says that at Colchester they did not do so[4] and that was one cause of the rebellion. Tacitus was the son-in-law of the

---

[4]   Tacitus, Cornelius, *Annals*, XIV.31.

governor Agricola who encouraged the building of temples, forums and houses[5] and who may have ensured that compensation was paid if other settlements were established. After a couple of generations the residents would have been born in Britain and never visited Rome, but they were nevertheless Roman citizens. Within the towns were of course houses, some grand dwellings for the wealthy, others more humble. There were shops and workshops. Most were held on lease (*locatio conductio*) but some may have been owned by their occupiers and, if so, the tradesmen could sell them.

Within the colonies there was a good market in land. A tablet found in a well at Chew Stoke near Bristol in 1954 is an extract from a sale deed, probably a *traditio* or transfer.[6] The document itself is written on a piece of wood. Once it had the names of parties on it but they have been crossed out, possibly because it was then used by a lawyer as a precedent, a standard form on which to base particular transactions. The surviving text forms part of what lawyers today would call a title guarantee. These were originally used in Italy because the formal method of transferring land there was by an ancient and solemn procedure called *mancipatio*. In practice, it was so cumbersome that people ceased to use it and instead simply handed land over (*traditio*) supported by a less formal document. This initially involved a risk that, since the formalities had not been complied with, the formal ownership or *dominium* remained with the original owner and even though he had been paid, he (or if he died his heir) could claim still to have the land. In response to this, Roman law developed a principle of equity under which the nominal owner was compelled to recognise the rights of the buyer. Although, therefore, the law came to protect this informal method of selling land, it was not quite as good as the formal procedure, so the seller also agreed to guarantee the title of the buyer. English law has parallels to these, one in the use, which will be considered in Chapter 10, and an other in the title guarantee, which is still an important part of contemporary conveyancing.[7]

Strictly, the approach used in relation to what was called Italic land was not relevant to provincial land in Britain, where in Roman law land could not be owned, but such guarantees had become usual and helped to overcome any technical defects in title to rights of possession. For instance, there might have been rights attaching to the land under the law of the *civitas*. The function of the guarantee was to say that if the buyer was evicted by someone claiming rights, then the seller would make good his loss. The commentator on the Chew Stoke tablet considers it to have come from a colony for that reason, perhaps on the

---

[5]   Tacitus, Cornelius, *Agricola*, 21.

[6]   Eg Turner, EG, 'A Roman writing tablet from Somerset', (1965) xlvi *Journal of Roman Studies* 115.

[7]   The Law of Property (Miscellaneous Provisions) Act 1994.

grounds that if the colony had *ius italicum* then *mancipatio* would have applied and so a title guarantee would be necessary. That seems unlikely but it was still a useful device. It indicates the activity of the land market, and possibility for changes by new owners.

A second type of town was the municipality (*municipium*). The only known instance in Britain is Verulamium, St Albans. Plate 2 shows a reconstruction of part of the town. The inhabitants had joint citizenship, both of their *civitas* (in this case the Catuvellauni) as well as being Roman citizens, but the *municipium* was not regarded as a part of Italy. The third type was what is known as a *civitas* capital, the principal town of a *civitas*. These were most like the Mediterranean concept of a *polis*, namely a built-up area surrounded by countryside, where all the free inhabitants, or in Britain the better off, had a say in communal matters. They had many of the civic amenities such as a market place but their status was purely local. While some of their residents would have been immigrants, most of the people would have been of local origin.

The towns and the *civitates* were self-governing in the sense that they ran many of their own affairs, but we should not think of them as local authorities in the modern sense. The Romans had only a limited idea of a corporation. They had a few institutions, such as partnership (*societas*), and some idea of municipal ownership of facilities, such as a market building or a theatre, but it was not full ownership. The municipality, which operated through a council of decurions, could not sell or let the town buildings, which were not regarded as property but as a public facility. Debts owed by or to a town council were separate from those of its members.[8] Likewise, temples had land but, as we saw in the *Bellicus* case, sacred land could not be sold so it cannot be regarded as owned. However, unlike medieval corporations, these were not seen as legal persons.

The emperors encouraged the decurions as local leaders to provide costly facilities, such as aqueducts or theatres, out of their own money. This was known as *munera*. At first it was voluntary, and provided a means for the leading citizens to demonstrate their wealth and civic virtue. As time went on it came to be seen as a burden and became compulsory. Under the late empire, taxes had to be directed to the support of the army, the imperial court and the defences of the empire against barbarians, and there was less public money so that much of the infrastructure of a province had to be met from local sources. Taxes would go some way but the demands of a new fort, of the repair of Hadrian's Wall and of the roads came first.

Hadrian's Wall had originally been built and repaired by the legions, but in the mid-fourth century there is evidence in inscriptions of repair work being done

---

[8] Digest of Justinian, 3.4.7 (Ulpian).

by the *civitates*.[9] They also repaired the roads.[10] This work was organised by the decurions as members of the council of the *civitas*. Since they were personally responsible for taxes (although the rescript of Constantine, mentioned below, modified the rule), this may have been an occupation to be avoided. But in Britain it was still important. The inscriptions may mean the decurions paid for the repairs as *munera* and they arranged for the work to be done by their tenants and slaves who, in an economy moving further away from the use of money, owed labour services instead of rent.

COUNTRYSIDE

In Britain, towns were not a source of wealth but, as administrative centres, consumers of it. Although there were markets for farm produce and craft centres for specialist work, such as mosaics, they relied on officials and rich landowners for their revenues. Towns were imposed on the landscape, to encourage a feeling of belonging to the culture of the empire. The real wealth of Britain lay in the countryside. Some products are well known. British woollen cloaks, which came from the sheep that grazed on the downs, were famous. There was gold to be mined in the Welsh hills and tin in Cornwall. There were renowned hunting dogs, again raised on farms. Britain was a source of slaves, perhaps raided from the peoples of remote regions of Wales and Scotland, perhaps raised in the country districts and herded down the trade routes to the markets of Rome. The soil and climate were good for corn and wheat and oats. It was expensive to use land transport for distribution, but most parts of England are close to the sea or a river and the produce, once loaded on a barge or ship, could be taken to feed the garrisons of Germany. So the countryside had to be exploited and, particularly in the fourth century, at a time when much of the empire was in economic difficulties, while the towns declined, the countryside of Britain prospered.

The land was farmed under several different systems. First were the imperial estates, the *fiscus*. These were managed by two different methods. One was for the emperor's slaves to cultivate some of the land and alongside them might have worked a few hired hands. Both slave and nominally free lived in shacks, built to the minimum standard. The fields were as large as the geography of the landscape and the methods of proper farming could take. It was a matter of exploiting the land and people for the benefit of the treasury and the needs of a distant government. The other method was land let to tenant farmers, *coloni*, as mentioned below.

---

[9]   Collingwood RG and Wright RP, *Roman Inscriptions of Britain* (Oxford University Press, 1965), Nos 1843, 1844, 1962.

[10] Ibid, No 2250.

Then there were the great private estates called *fundus*. Some certainly were owned by absentee landlords who never came near Britain. In the late empire, there is a reference to a wealthy lady, Melania, who had inherited from her father estates all across the empire including Britain.[11] She herself lived in Rome although she fled to North Africa to escape the uncertainties of the invasion of Italy in 410. Before that happened she became an enthusiastic Christian, adopted the life of a nun, sold her estates and gave the proceeds to the poor and to the Church. She is said to have freed 8,000 slaves and possibly some of them were British. Her generosity and the scale of her wealth are untypical but there must have been other investors in land. As it happens, Britain had been in revolt since 406 and been cut off from Italy, so the estates here cannot have had much value to someone living in Rome.

Rural estates might vary from 100 acres with a handful of dependant farmers to a large *fundus* running for miles. If the owner was not resident, he would have a bailiff to look after the estate and collect the rent, see to the repairs and generally supervise activities. Other estate owners lived in Britain in comfortable stone-built villas on which they spent large sums on mosaic floors and fine wall paintings. In order to do so, they must have had full rights to their estates and had confidence that their heirs would be able to inherit them. There is some indication that rich men in the fourth century may have bought land here to find a refuge from troubles on the Continent.

A villa was the centre of an estate that produced an income. It may have been let under *locatio conductio* to tenants paying rent in cash but it is more likely that many of them were share croppers paying in kind. Pliny, writing around 100 describes how, even in Italy, his tenants were having difficulty in finding the cash to pay their rent and how he had to commute the rent for payment in kind.[12] His concern was that that would impose a burden on his bailiffs who would have to supervise the crop and arrange for its sale. Britain had a far less developed economy than second-century Italy and payments in kind were universal.

There is a formal letter of the emperor Constantine dated 20 November 319.[13] It may have been a rescript, specific to Britain, or it may have been provided for the whole empire, but only the British version has survived. The emperor sent it to Pacatianus, the *vicarius* or senior governor of Britain, by then divided into four small provinces. It refers to taxpayers (*tributarii*). A *tributarius* was a free landholder with a small holding who was normally liable to pay his taxes direct to the imperial tax collectors. The emperors made laws that even free farmers

---

[11]   Gerontius, *Sanctae Melaniae junioris Acta.*

[12]   Pliny, *Epistolae*, 9.37.

[13]   *Codex Theodosianus*, 11.7.2.

were not permitted to leave the land but they and their sons were bound to stay as farmers.[14] Many of them, burdened by taxes, felt it better to sell up to the local estate owner and accept the holding back on a sale and leaseback as a tied tenant, *colonus*, but some did not do this and were able to retain their rights to their land.

The rescript also mentions *coloni*. The word means cultivators but in this context refers to a special type of *locatio conductio* under which the cultivator was bound to the land by the terms of his tenancy and by status (*adscriptus glebae*: 'inscribed to the clods') rather than (or as well as) by legislation. This word for a tenant farmer is distantly related to *colonia* as a type of town, but the way it was used was quite different. In Italy, it reflected a decline from the status of a free tenant but in Britain some at least may never have been fully free. In many ways, *coloni* were hardly to be distinguished from the better-off slaves. While some slaves operated at all times under orders, others carried on their own farming business under an arrangement called *peculium* by which they were, although themselves property, allowed to have their own possessions including their own slaves and their own land.

The rescript concerned decurions as the proprietors of landed estates. Since they were obliged to be members of the governing council of the *civitas*, they were personally responsible for the taxes due from it. Constantine said that they were only to be liable for the tax in respect of their own *coloni* and *tributarii* and not for the tax on behalf of those on other estates. This indicates that the *tributarii* were also regarded as dependent on the greater landowners. They were modest proprietors who paid their taxes and lived as dependant clients of the powerful and if they did not pay, their own decurion would have to pay on their behalf.

Ploughs and other means of cultivation were simple and so most fields were small. If they changed hands they might do so as individual lots or as parts of small farms. Many celtic fields remained in the same form throughout the Roman period. Others were reorganised, probably as part of an estate, by being planned as rectangular fields. This is often called 'centuriation' by reference to a practice used in Mediterranean lands, but we do not know if the same rules applied in Britain. Such fields would be laid out under the supervision of a trained surveyor employed by a landlord.

In much of the north and west of England, fields were isolated patches amid rough land – wood or pasture. In the better agricultural lands of southern Britain, farms were packed as densely as possible and a traveller would rarely have been out of sight of farmsteads. It would not have been easy to tell, just by

---

[14] Digest of Justinian, 15.1.7.4; Codex, 11.48.

looking at the farmers, whether they were slaves, *coloni*, hired labourers or *tributarii*. Farming methods were the same for all and all alike were tied to their ancestral farms, as much by economics as by law.

LATE ROMAN BRITAIN

After the conversion of Constantine to Christianity, the Church became a major landowner in the empire. We do not know if the bishops had much land in Britain. It is possible that the clergy were poorer here than elsewhere. Some of them needed subsidies to attend imperial conferences and they seem to have supported popular religion. There were church buildings and one has been excavated in Lincoln. At Lullingstone in Kent there was a private chapel in the villa. However, such structures were modest and would not have stood out or dominated the landscape as Saxon or medieval churches did.

The four centuries that Britain was in the empire saw as many changes as any other similar period. In 212, the Emperor Caracalla, shortly after he returned from Britain to Rome, issued the *Consitutio Antoniniana* under which Roman citizenship was granted to all free residents within the *Orbis Romanus*, the Roman World, which probably means all lands within the Roman provinces. This may have affected a greater proportion of the people in Britain than elsewhere as citizenship had already been granted widely over much of the empire but probably less so here. It is unlikely to have had much effect on their daily lives but it would have meant that they could use the rules of Roman law instead of any separate laws which might have applied under the law of their *civitas*. It would affect commercial transactions and possibly landholding but it has been suggested that it did not change inheritance laws.[15]

In much of the empire, wealth became more concentrated in fewer hands, although that might not have made much difference in Britain where most farmers had probably never had much freedom. Taxes became ever heavier and the power of the emperors grew with reorganisation of the administration of government and the imposition of more civil servants to operate it. Local initiative tended to be suppressed in case it led to rebellion. Emperors could and did legislate about anything from the occupation of land to the use of resources for building.

From the third century, there were frequent raids by Saxons, by Picts from Scotland and by Scots from Ireland. The towns needed their own walls to defend themselves. They were authorised, perhaps commanded and financed, by

---

[15] Stevens, CE, 'A possible conflict of laws in Roman Britain', (1947) 37 *Journal of Roman Studies* 132–4.

the government. This might have been the local governor of one of the four provinces into which Britain was divided or his superior, the Vicar of the Britains, or even by the emperor.

In 410, the last legions were evacuated from Britain and it appears that the civil administration departed at about the same time. The emperor Honorius then issued a rescript to the *civitates* of Britain authorising them to defend themselves. This was a formal termination of the Provinces of Britain since the whole basis of being within the *Orbis Romanus* was that Rome would defend the *civitates* and had a monopoly of the power to make war. As there were no provincial governments, Britain became free of imperial control and imperial taxes but deprived of imperial protection.

The *civitates*, which had existed before the Romans came, still existed when they left and the rules of law, including those of private property, continued as before. After the departure of imperial officials, their successors were the decurions and other aristocrats. These men who came to rule Britain regarded themselves as fellow citizens, *cives*, in contrast to the now foreign Romans. For a while, public order continued but it had to change as Britain passed under the control of the Saxons.

In around 500, a monk called Gildas wrote a book denouncing the sins of the rulers of his time. He indicates that there were still courts and legal processes, but in a famous passage he says 'Britain has kings but they are tyrants; she has judges but they are impious'.[16] Although he uses 'impious' as a general term of abuse, it may carry a particular implication here. The word 'pious' usually refers to a man who respects the ways of his ancestors. A king might well be denounced for being tyrannical but a more common criticism of judges is that they are corrupt or slow. Gildas said, amongst other things, that the kings and judges prosecuted thieves across the country but allowed robbers to sit at table with them. This suggests that the general law was being enforced, but he may be indicating that the king had expropriated land that had belonged for generations to families who did not support him and given it to his household warriors for their loyalty, and the judges had upheld the confiscation. Such redistribution of assets often occurs as power shifts and may have been needed to pay for defence, but Gildas, as a defender of the old order, would not have approved.

What effect can we say the Roman period had on the development of the law and landscape of England? First, there were the roads, forts, towns and monuments. The early Saxons made little use of these but knew that they were there. When the time came to make such things themselves they would need

---

[16]   Gildas, *De Excidio Britanniae*, 27.

similar ways of organising the work. Secondly, there was the structure of society, a society which among the Romans operated by status.

Thirdly, and most importantly, was the idea of law. Law affected principally the more prosperous and educated citizens. Humbler farmers still lived according to local practices as their ancestors had done before AD 43. But as the Saxons took over the former lands of the British provinces they also took over a people whose leaders had become used to legal rights and obligations. The earliest Saxon rulers and their followers were illiterate and pagan but they were not isolated. They were aware of ways of doing things which had not been necessary in the lands across the North Sea from which they came. They were, in any case, a minority, so that even as conquerors they had to pick up the local techniques of running society. Once law has come into a country it cannot easily be extinguished.

Chapter 4

Early Saxon – 450 to 867

MANY SMALL KINGDOMS

During the fifth century, Britain ceased to be part of the Roman world and split up into many independent communities. Some were successors to the *civitates* and in them rights and laws continued, though adapted to new conditions. Others were founded by immigrants from across the North Sea, who were pagan in religion and spoke a language similar to that of the people of Frisia and Denmark. The new rulers had their own ways and practices but most of their subjects were descendants of the cultivators of Roman times and their lives may not have altered much.

The imperial administration and army had gone but nothing changed the truth that wealth and power came from the land. Small groups of warriors controlled small territories. After Roman times the population decreased and people could occupy good land without crowding. The evidence suggests that while farmland continued to be occupied and produced the same crops and animals, there were also new techniques which allowed farmers to colonise former woodland. Some of the names which they gave their settlements reflect the clearance of spaces in the woods or by marshes. The old English word *leah* has given us countless place names ending in -ley or -leigh such as Barnsley, Cowley, Wheatley which indicate ancient clearings and which may represent legal or administrative units.

But whether the land was anciently occupied or newly taken in to cultivation, we should not imagine pioneers making new farms in a no man's land. Someone had authority, if not actual control, over every piece of land, as had been the case since the late Stone Age. The occupiers, whether independent farmers or servants or slaves of a lord, needed approval from that authority to cultivate the land and that came by word of mouth or by recognising an existing state of affairs without any need for title deeds or ceremonies. The ability to cultivate the land depended on the leaders who themselves had to take account of law. Both in the kingdoms of the west – which remained British, later Welsh, for centuries – and among the Anglo-Saxons, there was law, at least for the rulers. They claimed legitimacy and sought to impose legal standards. Norms introduced by the Romans had become accepted across western Europe and the retreat of the empire did not change that. Legal documents, although less sophisticated than those of Roman lawyers, are among the earliest records of the new communities in Britain.

The conditions of life were, by the standards of Roman times, miserable. There was no building in stone and little enough in wood. In the east of England, a few towns, such as Verulamium, may have continued as remnants for a while but most were abandoned as the Saxon rulers had no need for urban centres. There is some evidence that they retained some administrative structures – for instance in 628 a man named Blecca was a prefect (Latin *praefectus*) or reeve responsible for local government in Lincoln.[1] In the west, some walled Roman towns survived as the forts of kings. If Continental parallels are any guide, the man who controlled a town retained some legal jurisdiction over the surrounding countryside as the seat of the count or bishop. In England, unless a petty king adopted a Roman settlement as his headquarters it fell into ruin. In time all were abandoned, either because of defeat in battle or because they did not serve the needs of the powerful. But farmers had still to cultivate their fields in order to live and to do that they needed settled security. In a country divided into small independent units, that could only be provided by armed rulers.

Where the fighters needed to protect a stretch of territory, they got their people to make dykes – defensive banks. We find them across the land. They are at the Devil's Dyke at Newmarket in Cambridgeshire, at the Grimsditch at Stanmore to the north of London and at the Wansdyke outside Bath. The greatest of all was Offa's Dyke along the Welsh frontier. Plate 3 shows part of it. These were defensive lines, put in strategic places. Some ceased to be important as war changed boundaries but others remained significant for long enough to create property boundaries. We saw that in the later empire the *civitates* were responsible for repair work to Hadrian's Wall. Their successors organised these local defences in a similar way, as the war leaders drafted people in to make the defences.

Slowly by conquest, by marriage between ruling families and by treaty, the tiny independent communities of England began to collect into larger kingdoms. As the former petty kings joined, either willingly or in deference to superior force, they brought their own followers in. Thus a former king (*rex*) became a sub-king (*regulus*), or ealdorman (*dux* or *princeps*). His followers had a position in the greater kingdom subordinate to his. So each kingdom came to comprise a legally graded hierarchy. This is borne out by the penalties for death or injury

---

[1]   Bede, *Historia Ecclesiastica Gentis Anglorum*, Bk 2, c 16.

which varied according to status. The most powerful kingdoms in the beginning were Kent, based on the *civitas* of the Cantiaci, East Anglia and the two kingdoms of Deira and Bernicia on the north east coast, which combined to form Northumbria. Others were those of the East Saxons (Essex) and the South Saxons (Sussex). The later great powers of the Mercians (in the Midlands) and the West Saxons (in the South West) also formed in a similar way. The kings and great lords controlled, and took revenues from, large areas. Their followers had smaller ones.

LOCAL LAWS

These kingdoms needed laws and their kings needed status and authority, with men of lesser status and authority under them. Since power came from the land, these degrees reflected different landholdings. The more powerful, the nobles, were sometimes called earls and the lesser freemen, churls (*ceorls*). A community comprised earls and churls, who together were freemen, in contrast to slaves and *laets* who may have been the predecessors of *geburs* or serfs. Each of these ranks in turn included distinct grades and each had its own rights and duties.

The rules and practices under which people occupied land and enjoyed security and inheritance rights varied from one settlement or valley to the next. It was a world of isolated farmsteads and hamlets. These settlements did not remain in a fixed place but were rebuilt on a different site every few years as fields became exhausted and the farmers needed new land. Each little community had its own ways and as they gathered into larger units, these ways remained in force, so that how children inherited a farm or a landholder owed duties to his lord (from *hlafod*, which meant loaf-giver) varied over every few miles. The jurisdiction of the lord over the lands occupied under such varying practices of the folk became known as folkland, land held under folk custom.

Custom is a type of law distinct from statute (the laws passed by, or under the authority of, parliaments and other assemblies) and judicial precedent (the law developed by the decisions of judges). It was the main source of rules which governed society in the Saxon realms. It is less relevant now but it still forms part of our law.[2] It was and is most important in relation to land. Custom is not made on a particular day, like the other forms of law. It is a practice which has developed, perhaps imperceptibly, over many years or generations. Some practices remain just that and do not become law. They are simply the way men and women tend to behave, and if behaviour changes then people follow the

---

[2]   *Hammerton v Honey* (1876) 24 WR 603.

new ways. But if people come to regard what they do as binding, then the law will assume that the ancient practice has a lawful origin and will enforce it. We shall see the difference between practices and rights in the context of enclosure of commonable as distinct from common fields. Instances of recognised customs in modern law include the right of local people to play or dance on an ancient village green, the right of fishermen to dry their nets on a beach or the right of inhabitants of a village to take water from a stream. In former times customs, both of towns and villages, could regulate many matters now governed by statutes and bylaws, including inheritance rights and duties to serve the community. The whole system of medieval manors depended on custom but even by then the system was in decline. The great days of custom were before 1066, although new secular legal customs could arise until 1189.

The Saxon kings made statute laws called dooms (*domas*). They were issued on rare occasions, usually after consulting with the great men of the realm, and several have survived. The earliest are those of Ethelbert King of the Kentishmen issued some time around 600. Others are by Ine King of the West Saxons and by Wihtred King of the Kentishmen, both around 690. Much of the content, particularly of these early laws, deals with the attempt to regulate common practices, such as a blood feud, by providing that a money payment, sometimes called wergild, could be made instead of seeking revenge for death, injury or rape. Other laws, especially of the later kings, deal with aspects of family law or trade and highways. They are not, except incidentally, about property law or the rules which affected the development of the landscape. There are two reasons for this.

The first is one which is relevant for property law at all times. Land law involves rights which are long lasting. Also, because of its nature, many people may have different rights in a single piece of land. Such laws need to be well known and certain and to change slowly to avoid upsetting too many people. Therefore, they were not thought suitable for immediate changes of the sort which could be brought in by a new royal law. The second reason reflects back on the local nature of custom. Distinct ways of holding land had grown up in each place and differed from one settlement to the next. They were a slow growth and if the king made changes which might be sensible in one part of his realm it could present problems in another.

A king seeking to assert his power sought to achieve two main aims. One was defence against external enemies. The Anglo-Saxon kingdoms were constantly at war with each other and with their Welsh and Scottish neighbours. War involved small bands of warriors who often campaigned far from home. They had to move fast, and needed roads, just as the Romans had. Some of their roads, which they called streets (from the Latin *strata* referring to the method of construction by building up layers), were those of the Romans, such as Watling Street or Ermine Street, parts of which still continue in use as the A2–A5 and the A1. But other Saxon military roads were no more than routes through the countryside, often winding as they went from one lord's hall to the next or to a ford. These were called army roads, *herepaths*, and many of them form the basis (much diverted and widened) of our main roads today.

The other aim was internal power and here the kings had a problem. To begin with they were little more important than their leading subjects. In many cases it may have been a matter of the chance of battle whether between two leaders of warriors one became a king, and his sons after him, and the other's family declined to the status of landholding nobleman. So the early kings had to assert their authority. In part, they did this by making laws. A king who could do that was in a special position. He was doing what the Roman emperors had done. In this the kings were encouraged by the Church.

THE CHURCH

The Church was ready, indeed eager, to help build up royal power. Some relics of the Church of Roman times remained. The British kingdoms of the west and north remained Christian. Even in the Anglo-Saxon south and east some of the common people may have continued to follow the Christian faith, but initially the lords were pagan. In 597, Augustine was sent by Pope Gregory to convert the English. He landed in Kent and in due course converted Ethelbert, the leading English ruler of his time. Ethelbert may have appreciated that his power might be ephemeral (as happened – Kent was to succumb when greater kingdoms such as those of the Mercians and West Saxons came to dominate the south). He sought the aid and support of the international institution which Augustine represented. The Church likewise needed the protection of a strong ruler in a dangerous land, easily liable to return to paganism, as occured in several places. It needed to establish cathedrals, monasteries and local churches to convert the country.

So the kings encouraged the Church and the Church in turn upheld the position of the kings. The Church could offer legitimacy, by the ceremony of anointing and coronation by which a new king, at the vulnerable time of his succession, came under the special protection of God. In response, the king protected and supported the missionaries by establishing bishops with cathedrals and abbots with monasteries. These needed money (or at least income in kind) to support their work and to allow the monks to preach and pray free from the need to grow corn to make their bread.

The simplest way to do this was to grant land to the Church as an endowment and that had another advantage. The churchmen would be able to control large tracts of the country but as they did not marry and have children there was no need to be concerned about their inheritance becoming a base from which to challenge royal power, unlike the lay nobles who might assert their own independence. The king could control the selection of an abbot or bishop. This partnership led to the organisation of the countryside for production, it allowed the building of abbeys and the large district churches called minsters which could be seen from far across the land. In legal terms it came about by the joint institutions of bookland and the multiple estate.

BOOKLAND

One form of local law-making was by a royal grant of bookland. The clergy encouraged the kings to make laws, just as the old Roman emperors had done; law-making was a royal prerogative and no noble could do that. Bookland involved changing the legal status of an area of countryside. As such it was a form of legislation and it led, through changed legal relationships on the land, to changes in the landscape.

Our historical records contain many books, *boks* or charters. Some originals have survived from Anglo-Saxon times. Many others are later copies or even forgeries but they often include genuine material taken from charters now lost. Most of the surviving charters are Church documents since they kept their records safe. Such evidence became important in disputes over land, especially after 1066. The abbots and bishops, who in the seventh century asked for the first charters, based their request on continental experience where rulers had for long been able to grant lands and their revenues to the Church.

The English adapted the process to their own conditions. The king had the right to take the products of the lands in his control. Not all lands were – many were under lay nobles – but as a result of conquest and the extensive domains inherited ultimately from the Roman fisc, the early English kings had wide lands to support their expenses. From those lands they took benefits. In the Laws of Ine King of the West Saxons is a passage, perhaps added after the first version but still of an early date, which says:

> From every 10 hides shall be paid as food rent 10 vats of honey, 300 loaves, 12 buckets of Welsh ale, 30 buckets of clear ale, 2 full-grown cows or 10 wethers, 10 geese, 20 hens, 10 cheeses, a full bucket of butter, 5 salmon, 20 pounds of fodder and 100 eels.[3]

---

[3]   Laws of Ine King of the West Saxons, c 70, 1.

A hide was the amount of land for the support of one substantial family with its retainers – perhaps about 120 acres of arable land and as much again of rough pasture and woodland. Sometimes the Latin word *tributarius* is used, suggesting a link with the Roman holding of a free taxpayer. The king, at the request of an abbot, granted to his monastery the returns from hides amounting to a few hundred or a few thousand acres, so that the monks were entitled to receive the food rents or 'farms' (*feorms*) instead of the king. They might have to provide services in return – we shall see that in late Saxon times these became known as the *trinoda necessitas* – but they still took a benefit.

The form of a *bok* or charter became standardised and in some ways resembles later conveyances of land. It began with a formal grant written in Latin drawn up by a scribe who was experienced in legal terminology. The charter then included a description of the boundaries of the land, usually in English. These bounds were drawn up by surveyors who were not monks and did not know the learned tongue. They contained detailed descriptions of the landscape saying how the boundary should be drawn along a stream, then in a straight line to a hill, from there to a wood and then passing by a prehistoric burial mound to a standing stone, and so on until the circuit of the land was complete. Finally, the charter was witnessed by a number of prominent courtiers such as bishops and earls.

Although it related to a defined area, the charter was not a grant of land as such. It was a grant of revenues from the occupiers, free or bond, who farmed it and a grant of jurisdiction over their disputes. This jurisdiction was called *soc* and the name Soke remained in use for centuries; indeed the Soke of Peterborough only ceased to be a unit of local government in 1965. But even though we cannot call the holder of bookland an owner in our sense, *soc* carried rights. If the farmer, a socman because he was under the soke, did not pay his *feorm*, the abbot could evict him, and if an occupier of land died without any immediate family to inherit the holding, the abbot could decide what to do with his land, in particular to appoint someone else to cultivate it.

If the Church initiated the law of bookland, laymen were not far behind in adopting it. Sometimes they were men who had done service for the king, and he rewarded them with a grant from the royal estates. Sometimes a family which had controlled their own folkland, and had been accustomed to receive their own *feorms* from the farmers perhaps for generations, decided they wanted a new recognition. This could be important on a disputed inheritance to confirm the claim of the new landholder. This suited the king since if he made a grant of bookland to the family they would recognise that they held it by royal authority. One way in particular, used when a father provided land for a child getting married, was to have the land booked to a family so that it would be inherited by the descendants of the individual or couple to whom the donor first booked it. A law of King Alfred[4] deals with an abuse where bookland was intended to be retained in a family but an owner tried to sell it. This may be relevant to the *Fonthill* case discussed in Chapter 5. Later charters came to be granted by noblemen but they could only do so as being under royal authority.

Jurisdiction and the right to a share in what the land produces, initially in kind but later often in money, are not ownership but they are elements of it. In a country with more land available than people to cultivate it, ownership was less important than jurisdiction over the farmers. Nevertheless, great men had sufficient control to bring about changes in the landscape.

THE MULTIPLE ESTATE

On a large scale this control was exercised through the multiple estate. The idea is better documented across the Channel in the land then called Francia where the great monasteries administered vast domains called (by a term adapted from Roman times) villas, but in England their counterparts did much the same. We know this mainly from place names. When we find names such as Norton (the northern farm or settlement) and Sutton or Much Hadham and Little Hadham, it suggests that a large area of land was under a single administration but different parts were operated in distinct ways. Some farms within the estate concentrated on arable production, others on pastoral. Some produced leather, others milk. Another clue comes from the shape of some parishes, many of which derive from estates. In some places such as Kent or Somerset parishes had (until nineteenth-century reforms) outliers, with the main settlement in one place but summer grazing or access to marshland belonging to the same people many miles away. So a powerful lord could control the use of land across stretches of country.

The proceeds went of course to support the lords (lay and clerical) in their daily lifestyle. Laymen hunted – so areas of land were kept for that purpose even if not on the scale of their Norman successors. Much went to food, clothing and luxuries. But both clergy and laymen also constructed buildings, such as monasteries with surrounding houses, and minster churches, all paid for out of the revenues from legal control of land.

The folk who lived in the estates were dependent on it in a variety of ways. There were free churls and there were serfs, *geburs* bound to the soil like the Roman *coloni*. There were also slaves which were property belonging to the

---

[4] Laws of Alfred King of the West Saxons, c 41.

cultivators or to the monks and lords. Within a bookland, all owed some sort of duty to the holder of the charter but many farmers were independent free men, better seen as taxpayers like their *tributarii* Roman predecessors than as tenants. There was some oppression, of course, and much misery but a free farmer, a socman, could live in his little house by the woods or among his fields. He complained at the rapacity of the great men, as farmers have always complained, but however wretched we might think his bare walls of wattle and daub, the draughts under the roof and the earthen floor, he was, in his own terms, as prosperous as his descendants holding in socage in the fifteenth century.

TRADE AND COMMUNICATIONS

Although most folk lived and died in their own locality, a few great men, kings and abbots travelled not only across England, but even to the Continent. King Ine died in Rome. There was also a flourishing trade in humans, with children from Yorkshire being sold in the slave markets of Rome, although various laws from King Ine onwards prohibited the export of freemen or bondsmen as slaves.[5] There were also merchants who made the first towns. These did not dominate the landscape as later ones did. To our eyes they were modest affairs. Some were coastal ports, such as Ipswich, or Hamwic the predecessor of Southampton. Some were on rivers such as Lundenwic, at the place we call Covent Garden on the Thames. Some were industrial, like Middlewich which produced salt traded throughout England. These towns were the size of a modern village. They did not have self-government but they did need some organisation to settle disputes, decide where someone could make a house, a shop or a warehouse and they had their own rules. They existed by royal permission and therefore enjoyed a degree of protection. The kings could make rules to protect merchants and regulate trade since any source of wealth was a matter for them.

Royal protection extended to the communications between settlements. Apart from the rivers and coast there were land routes. These were narrow, muddy and dangerous but they were necessary. Not only merchants but monks and royal officials collecting the king's revenues (in cash or kind) used them. Apart from the *herepaths* designed for military use, but available to anyone, were ways, *wegs*, such as salt-ways. There were customary ways, leading local people to their minster. These had to run across land in the *soc* of a lord such as an earl or abbot.

---

[5]   Bede, *Historia Ecclesiastica Gentis Anglorum*, Bk 2, c1; Laws of Ine King of the West Saxons, c 11.

Such ways influenced the position of settlements and churches and of facilities for travellers such as the predecessors of inns. Later, villages and towns grew up along them. Like the trading towns they were under the special legal protection of the king and said to be in his peace. The king's peace extended to a few other places, such as his residence, and he also protected ports and churches. Often, the local lord welcomed the money from trade and the benefits of communication, and could offer some protection but, if not, or if the way was threatened by robbers, then travellers needed greater support than the lord could or would give. They could band together to do this but if there was a fight, who could decide who was in the right? In the end, only the king could protect communications.

The Laws of Ine and Wihtred are largely different, even though concerning similar subjects, but there is one which is the same in both and it concerns highways.[6] It provides that if a stranger to the locality goes off the way and neither shouts nor blows his horn, he can be assumed to be a thief and it is lawful to kill him. This law implies that long distance travel was protected provided the traveller kept to the road. The identity between the laws of the two kingdoms suggests either that the kings wanted to have a general code for such routes or that a general international law already existed and they were confirming it.

Such general laws were the exception and few extended beyond the immediate locality. The customs which developed among the early Saxon farmers were suited to their little communities. Most of such rules as existed applied to a fraction of a kingdom, a little patchwork landscape a man could walk across in a few hours. A few applied throughout the little kingdoms into which England was divided. But all that had to change when, from across the North Sea, the Vikings struck.

---

[6]   Laws of Ine King of the West Saxons, c 20; Laws of Wihtred King of the Men of Kent, c 28.

Chapter 5

The Making of the Open Fields – 867 to 1066

Between around 800 and 1100, people rearranged the landscape of the middle of England. The changes were on a greater scale than the creation of the field systems of the Bronze Age. They can be compared to the Enclosure Movement of the eighteenth century which reversed the work discussed in this chapter. In a few generations, vast areas of the Midland countryside were organised in a wholly new system of farming and settlement. The causes were the Viking invasions and the introduction of the eight ox plough. The means were the growth of legal lordship and the local court.

THE VIKINGS

The Vikings, pirates from Scandinavia, struck without warning at Wareham in Dorset in 787 and again at the monastery of Lindisfarne in 793. Over the following years they raided much of England, venturing far from the coast. In 867, a Viking army came to conquer and settle. They destroyed all the kingdoms of England except for that of the West Saxons and even there, after the death in battle of two kings, their brother Alfred was forced into retreat. But he was able to fight back and over the next few years he, his son Edward the Elder and his grandson Athelstan achieved suzerainty over all the land we now call England and created the kingdom of the English.

In order to do so, they had to change the way warriors fought and to do that they had to reorganise the basis of the economy that supported the fighters. In this they were not alone. All Europe was struggling with such attacks. In addition to the Vikings from the north, the Magyars from the east and the Saracens from the south raided and pillaged across the continent and everyone had to deal with the threat. The solution was defence in depth. The rulers of the time lacked resources to defend long frontiers as the Romans had, so instead every valley and every river crossing had its local lord, entrusted with local protection. On the Continent this was known as domainal lordship, from the Latin *dominus* for lord. It led to local independence where fighting men in their castles could operate free from any central control. They developed their own jurisdictions and came to rule their little lands where they could do as they wished.

In England, Alfred's successors were able to keep control of the whole realm. This is partly because of geography: in the low lying country of England with few barriers to travel it is difficult to create defensible frontiers between petty local lordships. There is no equivalent of the Rhineland valleys with towering rocks on which soldiers could build castles. It is also possible that the traditions of the land encouraged this. On the Continent, many landholders regarded themselves as owning their family property known as allodial land. In this country, there was more of a tradition that even the oldest monasteries and the greatest lay lords derived their rights from the king through a grant of bookland. This should not be over-emphasised. After 800, arrangements, sometimes known as feudalism, developed in Italy, France and Germany and they involved an actual or fictional royal grant which came to include the right to administer justice. In England, landholders regarded themselves as having full heritable rights but, as the *Fonthill* case mentioned below illustrates, there was always a last resort to royal justice and protection.

The English kings were able to found strong places, *burhs* or boroughs, such as Stafford, Hertford and Warwick. They were originally forts but several became walled towns. They were central points, where a militia could be assembled, and had walls to resist attack. They were, and remained until after 1066, royal dependencies, deriving their legal status from the king's authority. In the beginning they were creatures of and therefore allies of royal power. Long afterwards some of their successors enlarged their privileges by obtaining further royal charters which gave them a measure of control over their affairs, but the early boroughs were not self-governing corporations in the medieval sense.

They were also supported by a legal obligation, binding on the holders of bookland, to pay towards the repair of *burh* defences. This was one of the *trinoda necessitas* – the 'threefold necessary things'. The other two were *bricg-bot*,[1] the repair of bridges, needed for armies to move across the land, and service in the *fyrd*, the king's army. These duties bound every substantial landholder. Any man rich enough to hold five hides became regarded as a king's thegn, liable to serve in the army or, if he was old or ill, to pay for a substitute.[2]

It was not practicable to set up defences in the same way in the countryside but people still needed to do something about the marauders. The answer was the

---

[1]   Cnut, Statute of Winchester 1020/21, c 66.

[2]   Domesday Book 1086, Berkshire, 56V.

nuclear village, where the local folk could be protected by a hedge. They could choose some of their number as watchmen for raiders, and organise themselves to see off small bands of robbers. They assembled in groups of ten or twelve substantial households, known as the tithing comprising ten hides. That idea fitted well with other developments in agriculture and the local courts.

FARMING METHODS

The agricultural change came because farmers adopted the new technology of the wheeled mould board plough. This had been invented before the end of the Roman Empire but to begin with its use did not spread far or fast. Such a plough was more efficient than the methods in use before. The ploughman could turn over the sod in the autumn so that in winter it weathered to a tilth. But the plough needed skill to make, it used an iron ploughshare and it was expensive. Where there were few people and they were content to continue to cultivate in a traditional way, farmers felt no incentive to adopt a new sort of device. As the population grew and the Viking wars led to a need for the more efficient use of resources, many communities came to adopt the new technology.

At this time horses were too expensive for most humble farmers. A horse drawing a plough needs a special collar and harness which, even if it had been invented (which is not certain) was not in widespread use. So the plough had to be drawn by oxen. The most efficient way of doing that was to harness them in a plough team and because the plough was heavy it needed up to eight of them, particularly in the clay lands which were being opened up to cultivation. Such a team was unwieldy – it was difficult to start and once it had got going it was hard to stop its momentum. So, in some parts of the country, the best design of a field was a long narrow strip, where the team could go steadily up, be turned on a balk at the end and then taken down the strip again. Unlike the traditional small square celtic fields, these had to be laid out across a large expanse of ground, and the strips were so narrow there was no room for fences or hedges. The best layout was a great open field of several hundred acres in which each farmer had his own strips distributed through the field.

Such a system needed co-operation. Few except the rich lords or an occasional prosperous farmer could afford their own plough and team. Instead, each farmer owned one or two beasts which they could share with their neighbours in much the same way as modern farmers share expensive equipment through a machinery ring. The long, narrow, unfenced strips were virtually all boundary with plenty of potential for encroachment and boundary disputes, so it was essential to have a simple means of dispute resolution. Because the strips needed to be ploughed, seeded and harvested at the same time, there had to be some authority who would say when to plough or harvest, and when, once the harvest was taken, the oxen could be let into the stubble to graze.

There were no sheds for the oxen to live under cover. The oxen were hardy beasts which got their sustenance partly from grazing the cultivated land after harvest when it was under stubble and partly from the rough grass growing on the open lands surrounding the fields. Later this uncultivated land was to become common waste and the law came to regard it as belonging to the lord of the manor, but at this time it was better not to regard it as owned in any particular sense – it did not belong to the community. The local lord had jurisdiction over it but in a country with few people and many open spaces, that had few practical implications. Rather, much as in our own time, the open seas belong to no country and any nation can freely take the fish or exploit the minerals on the ocean bed, so at that time any local villager could make use of the products of the unoccupied uncultivated expanses of the land. It was only as numbers of people grew and resources became scarce that property rights developed over the waste.

The strips in the common fields belonged (in a sense) to the farmer who worked them but arrangements differed a good deal. The lord was entitled to some strips. Although a petty thegn might farm his own lands, the great lords and abbots, did not themselves lead the plough or herd the beasts. They had others, particularly slaves, to do it for them. Their own strips were called 'inland' and were on the best land. There were also the predecessors of serfs, *geburs*, who were tied the land. Their status was between that of slaves and free men and they had to do services to the lord or pay rent. There were also some free men who cultivated strips known as warland or outland. They were the successors of the former churls. They paid taxes, *geld*, and had a legal right to depart – perhaps even in some sense to sell up and go elsewhere.

In practice, most people were born, lived and died in the same place, never leaving their ancestral fields. Inland and outland were not physical descriptions of where strips were located but referred to their legal status. None of these different ways of holding or benefiting from land was obvious to an observer. If you walked across a field you could not tell simply from looking which strip belonged to which sort of farmer, although these social differences were important to them. No doubt the free peasants were better clothed and fed, but the life of a slave could be better than that of a *gebur* if he had a good master. The Church encouraged slave-owners to free their slaves, if not in their own lifetimes then on their death by will. As in Roman times, slaves might have been able to accumulate modest wealth.

GROWTH OF LORDSHIP AND THE LOCAL COURT

Across Europe the military emergency of the invaders and then the wars among local lords led to a concentration of power in the hands of great men. That affected their ability to control the layout of land but the existence of powerful men on its own was not enough to create the open fields. The landscapes had been settled for centuries, perhaps millennia. The Romans had reorganised some areas but the changes made in some parts of England at this time were greater. The pattern of small fields was suddenly disrupted. Unlike enclosure, which can occur by gradual encroachments over the years, an open field cannot be established by degrees, although once it is there it may later be extended. At least a substantial part must be laid out at one time. Perhaps a powerful lord whose ancestral lands were cultivated only by his servile dependants could order a new layout but that was not the general position. The power of lords was matched by the influence of communities. The independent small farmers saw the need for both safety and a more efficient system of cultivation. They helped to make it possible through a new concept, the local court.

In England, the oldest type of court of which we know is the Hundred. There was an equivalent in the north called Wapentake (weapon-take) which suggests it was a military assembly, but in the south the Hundred meant 100 hides, about 12,000 cultivable acres with as much again of waste – say 40 square miles or an area 6 miles across, although the size varied in different parts of England. The 100 or so free landholders could gather for meetings and return home within a day. The West Saxons grouped Hundreds into shires and as their kings spread their authority across England they made new shires in the Midlands around what became county towns. Shires had their own assemblies. Likewise, as villages took shape the leading men – perhaps ten or a dozen – formed a tithing.[3]

These assemblies met to sort out matters of local importance. They resolved disputes (for example, over boundaries) and so became in our sense courts of law. In an age without policemen and when royal authority was distant, they also saw to the keeping of the peace and punished criminals. But they did more than that. If they needed rules – to decide who paid for the repair of roads or, in a village, to determine the innumerable issues of cleaning out ditches, looking after the herds, organising gatherings – then they made them. Such rules were not democratic in our sense, since men were deferential to their betters or more powerful members, but in a world where everyone knew everyone else, they were a way of reaching agreement or deciding what to do if agreement was not possible.

---

[3] Eg 6 Athelstan, c 3.

The tithing had a part in the making of the open fields and the village. Sometimes the initiative came from a lord who saw a way to increase his power and control over people by gathering them together but, where geography and geology permitted, farmers appreciated the advantages of the new more efficient style of farming. They could propose it even if the lord was reluctant – for lords could be as conventional minded and slow to change as anyone else.

The circumstances of each settlement were different. As part of the new agriculture it was convenient for people, instead of living in isolated farms, to gather into nucleated villages where they could more easily share resources such as oxen and ploughs, perhaps clustered around a church and a village green. With marauders ravaging the countryside a village could be defended by a group of men more easily than an isolated dwelling. Some localities were converted early, where the farmers saw the need or a powerful lord saw the advantages. Some were converted later, when refugees from the Vikings returned to an abandoned village after the war and could rearrange the landscape. All villages had lords, and in some places there were more than one so that different inhabitants of the village were under different jurisdictions. All villages, however many lords they recognised, had the local tithing meeting, the court leet as it came to be called. This not only provided a means of resolving disputes but also administered matters such as the date for ploughing or when, after harvest, the oxen could be permitted to graze the open fields.

The new system of farming came to predominate in the Midland plain and some other areas but much of the country was not suited to it. The north, the west and most of the south, did not adopt it. The land might be too hilly for open fields or the farmers might concentrate on pastoral farming and not need the layout of arable strips. This was so in those parts of the country called woodland not just because they had many woods but because hedges with trees growing in them divided one field from another, and this gave the countryside a different look from the champion areas of the Midlands where open fields stretched far across the landscape. Much depended on the quality of the soil and therefore the geology. Some decisions depended on the accidents of history. A traditionally minded abbey or a group of free farmers who would not agree to give up the fields their grandfathers had tilled might keep to the old ways so their community never developed open fields. In those parishes the fields were more like what we would recognise as organised farmland, areas of crop or pasture surrounded by enclosures such as banks, hedges or walls which later became known as closes from the Latin *clausum*. This contrast between the so-called champion country of the open field and the woodland areas of the close is found across England.

Where it was decided to form open fields it needed a good deal of organisation to convert a number of more or less isolated farms with their separate plots of land into a coordinated system. Where the lord had a strong control and the farmers were bondsmen or dependants, this could be done by his agents giving orders. In others, especially where there were free socmen or much outland, it needed the co-operation of the landholders. Someone had to lay out the new fields in strips, grouped in furlongs, with the headlands and any trackways for the oxen to reach the fields. There might have needed to be drainage, and the relics of ridge and furrow still visible in some places were as much to guide the flow of water as to mark a boundary.

The system went on developing even after 1066 and the introduction of the manor. I consider that in Chapter 6, but something like a manor was emerging even before the Norman Conquest. A text called the *Rectitudines singularum personarum*, 'the right things for different groups of people', possibly written or edited by Archbishop Wulfstan of York, sets out the description of what is said to be a typical village community around the year 1000. It describes all the groups of men, free tenants, serfs or labourers. These types of status came not from any particular political or legal system but from the nature of the society and economics of the time.

As in earlier centuries, society was still organised by degrees and the rules about land reflected this. The later evidence of the Domesday Book reveals much about the management powers of those who held land before 1066. Some free men and women (for women could hold land) could sell their rights to occupy or take rent from land, others could not. Although all landholders and all free folk had to have a lord, some had the right to change their lord,[4] as the Domesday Book says 'to go with their land to whoever they wished'. That meant that the landholder could chose whose lord had *soc* over him, who could decide disputes between him and his neighbour and who would protect him in case of a challenge to his rights. An effective lord could attract many followers and corresponding influence and wealth. It also followed that if a landholder was not entitled to sell his rights to the land he farmed, then (unless it reverted to his lord on his death) his heirs were bound to inherit it.

THE *FONTHILL* CASE

Some of the changes in attitudes to landholding can be seen in the case of *Aethelm Higa v Helmstan* (c 898) (the *Fonthill* case), described in a letter written from an unknown aristocrat (possibly Ealdorman Ordlaf Wormald) to

---

[4] 4 Athelstan, c 6.

King Edward the Elder, son of King Alfred. It concerned a claim by Aethelm to some land at Fonthill in Wiltshire belonging to Helmstan. The land had once belonged to the lady Aetheldryth. She in turn had received it on her marriage and the case turned on the nature of that gift. There were two types of marriage arrangement. One was for the gift to be outright, so that the recipient could do what she wanted with her land. The other was conditional, so that the land was intended to endow a family and to be kept for the children and in that case, if there were no children, the land might pass back to the family of the person who had originally given it. Aetheldryth claimed this was an outright gift and some time later she sold it to Osulf for a fair price. Evidently, there was a risk of a claim by the relatives of the donor that if it did not pass on to Aetheldryth's children it ought to come back to the donor's family. Aethelm may have been a member of that family. So Osulf (or his advisers) ensured that the sale document was approved by King Alfred and by a number of leading officials to make sure it could not be challenged. Osulf did not keep the land. He may have resold it or given it away and it came to Helmstan. Helmstan was unreliable about property and when he was in trouble, accused of stealing a valuable belt, Aethelm saw his chance and claimed the land on the basis that Aetheldryth ought never to have sold it.

The case came to King Alfred as judge. He directed an inquiry into the facts and Helmstan produced the charter of sale approved by the king. But Aethelm did not accept this and insisted on a further step which involved Helmstan making a solemn oath supported by reputable sureties that the land was indeed his. Helmstan asked the writer of the letter (who had been his sponsor at his confirmation) to help. The writer agreed on the terms that Helmstan gave the land to him but so that Helmstan could occupy it for the rest of his life. He may have known of Helmstan's unreliability so that the arrangement may have been done in this way in part to protect Helmstan from his own folly in case he again did something which might lose his possessions. The writer may also have used this method in order to be ready to answer any claim by Aethelm. Helmstan accepted the terms and transferred the land. Then he swore his oath and won the case.

However, Helmstan could not keep his hands off other people's property and about two years later he stole some oxen and then he was ruined. He was arrested and he fled. His property was forfeit and King Edward (who had succeeded Alfred) declared him an outlaw. He obtained the king's mercy and was allowed to live in England. The writer of the letter took on the land at Fonthill but he did not want to keep it and, in another charter witnessed by the new king, he exchanged it with the Bishop of Winchester for some land at Lydiard. The letter may have been written in the context of a new claim by

Aethelm against the bishop. If so the bishop won, for the Domesday Book over a century later records the Diocese as holding land at Fonthill.

The case illustrates a number of factors affecting landholding. The Anglo-Saxons had well-developed laws of inheritance and dealing in land. There was an active market so it was evident what was a fair price, and a system of showing title by the use of formal documents and, to ensure that it all worked, a procedure to settle disputes. The nobility could take their disputes to the king – lesser men would fight it out in the local court. This shows that land could change hands and the buyer could be secure, so encouraging changes in the use or arrangement of the land.

As indicated, the parties would not themselves have guided the plough. What they bought and sold was the right to the rents and services of the cultivators. At this time there was a major reorganisation of the great landholdings. The writer of the letter does not say why, having just acquired Helmstan's land, he quickly exchanged it with the bishop. A possible reason was that the parties wanted to consolidate their estates. If a lord had much land in one place and a smaller holding in another it could be sensible to dispose of the lesser area for the chance of greater control of the principal estate and sometimes it suited the parties to do this by exchange. In localities where lords were reorganising the fields such a pattern of control (even taking into account that the fields themselves were farmed by slaves, serfs or tenants or freeholders) would make the changes easier to put through.

ORGANISING LANDHOLDINGS

In the earlier Saxon period kings held (and retained) their own great estates in large units of many hides, and when they granted bookland it was also in large continuous stretches. With the new ways of running the countryside a different pattern emerged. First, in order to reward their followers the kings granted small estates – the Old English word is *land* – comprising perhaps 5 or 10 hides out of the royal domains to their followers, who were called king's thegns. These were not great lords but royal servants. They held their land in return for the *trinoda necessitas*; similar patterns were becoming common across Europe. But at the same time, especially after around 1015 when England became part of a Danish empire under King Cnut and the power of great Danish warlords became important, leading aristocrats, jarls or earls began to accumulate collections of such lands. While lesser lords tended to have all their land in one shire, a great man diversified his estates by having them distributed across England. Some of them were administered together, so that if a lord developed a new technique of land management in one place he could have it applied elsewhere. His neighbours would come to know about it, and so the new methods would spread.

England had the most efficient system of taxation in Europe, known as *geld*. This was charged on the hide, and like all tax systems was vulnerable to avoidance schemes, but it worked well enough for kings to be able to support an army, and build churches out of their revenues. At a time when in France and Germany domainal lords were building castles and monks were making fortified abbeys, England enjoyed a degree of settled government. Life was indeed hard for the poor and hardly comfortable in our terms for the rich, but it was, compared with the Continent, a land at peace.

England had strong central government, with a growing common culture across the country. The powerful earls, rather than seeking their own provincial independence as in France and Germany, jockeyed for central control. There could still be undefended villages in the countryside each with a small church built of wood or sometimes of stone (many of which have survived). Often the local thegn lived on his land and could supervise local arrangements though the court leet to ensure that agriculture was efficient and the open fields were cultivated in peace. His own thatched hall was second only to the church in dominating the village street. There were roads, if not good ones, winding between villages and connecting the larger settlements, particularly the shire towns and at least the major roads were under the King's Peace.

There were also the first signs of something that in later centuries would become of great importance – the lease. As we have seen, the Romans had such an institution. Indeed, ever since the invention of agriculture there have been arrangements for farmers without capital to occupy land by permission of, and in return for a benefit to, a powerful person who controlled land. With the end of the Roman Empire the idea of a lease for rent was lost. In late Saxon times, as a money economy began to emerge again, this revived. In addition, the Church adopted the idea of a grant of land for a limited time, defined either by a number of years or for one or more lifetimes. This was initially a way of enabling Church land to be used in the national defence, something badly needed at a time of emergency. Bishops and abbots were strongly encouraged by the king, usually against their will, to grant Church lands to soldiers for a period under an arrangement called loanland, in effect a lease, and the soldiers would then take the revenues. It was not a satisfactory system and was only justified by need. If the lease was short, the occupier did not regard the land as his own and so might not look after it, while the monastery had no control over it while the lease lasted. If it was a long-standing arrangement, the children of the original occupier might come to see it as their inheritance which could lead to disputes when the period ran out. But the lease was to transform the countryside in later years and its origins go back to this time.

Leases were private arrangements between two institutions or people or families. Customary rules continued to govern other rights, especially those of the communities. As men came to live in villages, they needed a system to set out their relationships and it was not possible to devise a new set of rules for each generation or settlement. So the founders adapted traditional customs into standard legal arrangements. If people made a new village they took over a set of customs from an established one. As the physical circumstances of every valley and neighbourhood are different and as events and individuals in the villages affected changed over the years, it became a feature of custom that it was local, that the customs of one locality (vill or parish or, after 1066, manor) were distinct from every other. But there were common features across large parts of England.

For instance one was a right called botes. This authorised the inhabitants of a village to take fallen branches and underwood for fuel, for the repair of houses, for fencing and making ploughs and for other tasks. In some places the folk could take whatever they could get by hook or by crook but no more – they could not cut down trees. In others they might be able to uproot saplings or cut some types of tree but not others. There were many other customs, governing the work a man might be required to do for his lord, or what duties he did for the village or what he could do on the waste, and so on.

Perhaps more important were inheritance customs, which might provide that on the death of a holder his land passed, in whole or part, either to his widow, or to his eldest son, or youngest, or to all his children equally. These could vary, although some were widespread such as gavelkind in Kent under which all the sons shared in equal shares or borough english in places from Nottingham to Sussex where the youngest son inherited the land. Different rules might apply to different pieces of land in one village or to people of different status.

We should not, however, idealise the late Saxon countryside. Fighting was still the common method of resolving disputes – and the pressures of life in nuclear villages led to many violent and vicious feuds – but compared with much of Europe it was a good place to live. That was because overall a strong government had been able to emerge. It was into this countryside that the Normans came, restructuring, rationalising, reforming and oppressing to make a more efficient system.

Chapter 6

Norman – 1066 to 1154

Until recently, any book on modern English land law started with a brief reference to the Norman Conquest. The author would describe the feudal system, the doctrine of tenure and the fee. He would say that they were introduced by William the Conqueror in order to control the country and he would describe how they continued, with adaptations, until the reforms under the legislation of 1925 and indeed afterwards. Modern ideas have changed. We no longer believe in a feudal system as such, nor that 1066 saw a wholesale change from previous laws. But it remains true that there is continuity from that time to our own and while the way we use these concepts is very different from the Normans, we can trace their evolution over the centuries.

One concept which has changed is the extent to which rights and duties relating to land depended on personal relationships. Of course all law is personal. A judge cannot order a field or a house to do or abstain from something. Any law must be addressed to people. But the land law that developed after the twelfth century related rights to interests in property. Before then it was more important to determine who held land and in particular from whom. This is the idea of tenure which still in theory underlies landholding in England.

TENURE AND ROYAL DEMESNE

Tenure derived from methods of securing defence. We have seen how on the Continent domainal lordship developed to resist the Vikings and led to local independence. The word 'tenure' comes from the Latin *tenire* or the French *tenir*, meaning to hold, and in this context to hold from a superior lord who himself held from a greater one, ultimately from the king, or in Germany and Italy from the Holy Roman Emperor. The lord granted land to a soldier in return for some service, usually military. Tenure was based on the ideas of homage and fealty, personal relationships or contracts that bound an individual soldier to his individual lord, so that on the death of either their successors had to make new bonds.

After the Conquest, William needed to control what he had gained. It is likely that he did not want England for its own sake, any more than the Romans had. His home and his interests were in France, the centre of culture and influence. He needed England partly to prevent anyone else controlling an important territory just across the Channel from Normandy, and partly to exploit its assets to finance his bid for power on the Continent. His descendants certainly tried to dominate France as he probably did, although he kept his aims to himself.

William conquered England by force but needed to legitimise his rule. He justified the conquest by claiming to be the rightful heir of Edward the Confessor but his power depended on the loyalty of his knights, whom he rewarded with the revenues from land occupied by working farmers. While most of the men and women who had been leading landholders in the time of Edward lost their lands and status, those who grew the crops and raised the cattle saw little change in their daily lives. They did, however, have to come to terms with new seigneurs who spoke a different language and had foreign ways of governing.

William's advisers used the doctrine of tenure to provide the king's followers with a lawful basis for control of the land. The theories took time to be worked out but the essence was that in return for the duty to serve in war the king granted to his barons the right to hold rights over various parts of the country collectively known as honours as a fief or fee or *feudum*. From this word writers in the sixteenth century coined the word 'feudal' and in the nineteenth century the 'feudal system' or 'feudalism'. The barons in turn granted parts of their fief to their own followers, and so on. This was done by a ceremony of feoffment in which the follower knelt before his lord and did homage for the land. Sometimes the lord handed over a symbolic clod of earth and later this developed into a means by which the parties did not need to be present in person. Their representatives could pass over a box of soil. Later still this became a formal step done by a document between lawyers. It was known as feoffment with livery of siesin and lasted in theory until 1925. Tenure involved a national hierarchy which, through castles and manor houses, dominated the countryside.

There was no allodial land in England. All land came to be held in tenure from the king, either directly or indirectly. At Salisbury in 1086, William obtained from the leading men an oath, binding on all freeholders of land, that their first duty was to serve the king. This was to have an important consequence in the jurisdiction of the royal courts under his successors and therefore the way land law developed. Because a lord was bound to hold a court for his tenants, if all free men were ultimately tenants of the king, they all had access to the justice administered in the royal court.

The king retained somewhere between a sixth and a quarter of the country in his direct control. This was the royal demesne (from *dominium*) and was the predecessor of the Crown Estate. Much of it comprised ordinary farmland from which the king derived the revenue to meet the costs of normal peacetime government. He administered these lands in the same way as other lords as described below. He also retained rights over other lands. These included several towns which were seen, as they had been under the Saxon kings, as under royal protection. In addition, some lands of smallholders who had no immediate lord were reckoned part of the lands of the king even though he did not take direct revenue from them.

Royal lands included much forest. The word 'forest' derives from *foris*, meaning 'beyond' and initially referred to the great wildwoods of central Europe which were far from settled dwellings and were therefore effectively uncontrolled and beyond the reach of regular laws. In England there were no such places and had not been for thousands of years but the terms came to be applied to those tracts of land which were subject to the jurisdiction of the forest laws. In recent centuries the meaning of the word has changed. 'Forest' did not at first refer to trees although in practice many were wooded – and where trees grew, the right to fell the timber was valuable. Others, like the Forest of Dartmoor, could be without any woodland.

The Norman kings established forests all across the country. Some, such as the New Forest and the Forest of Dean, were in woodland country. Others, such as Sherwood and Charnwood, were in champion country. Later writers presented them as an instance of Norman tyranny, and it is certain that William and his successors did seek to establish forests, partly because of their pleasure in hunting, but partly to establish royal jurisdiction over extensive tracts of marginal land. There may have been predecessors in late Saxon times, when the kings also enjoyed the pursuit of deer. The normal law still applied in forests but the special laws which protected game supplemented it. These forest laws also prohibited new villages within their jurisdiction although existing ones remained. The laws were administered directly by royal officials even where the forest land was within a lord's fief, but most forest manors were part of the royal demesne.

MILITARY TENURES

Lands held by men owing military services comprised most of the country. An earl or baron who held his honour from the king retained some manors and their revenues as his personal demesne. He granted others to his followers, who were coming to be called knights, as their individual fees. It is possible that sometimes a knight might accept a baron as lord in a process called commendation, although evidence for that is more frequent on the Continent. The baron retained some residual rights over the knight's fee, and such an intermediate position was known as a mesne lordship. As the baron in turn owed duties to the king, if the mesne lordship disappeared, for instance if it was forfeited for rebellion, the knight would owe those duties direct to his sovereign.

A knight's fee became a standard unit, sufficient to provide an income to pay for a fully armed soldier with his own small following, horses and equipment and of course livelihood between wars. It is possible that initially, as it was provided in order to finance military needs, he was only granted the land for his lifetime. This was known as a tenancy for life. It became an important way of holding land and it will be further considered in Chapter 10 in the context of the settled estates. However, from an early date, probably the first generation after the Conquest, it became established that fees were heritable and a fee simple, as it came to be called, became a permanent possession which, on the holder's death, passed to his eldest son. With the consent of his own lord, the holder could even sell his rights. Consent was needed because military service was personal and the lord would not want the fee to pass to someone who was incompetent or was a personal enemy. If the knight died leaving only daughters, they (or their husbands) would divide it; and it also became possible to split it up and sell off parts.

England had to be pacified by military occupation and much of this was done by building castles in strategic places but, once again, the arrangements differed from the way it had been done on the Continent. In France and Germany, castles could spring up wherever a lord wished to control his domain. In England, they were tightly controlled. In later centuries anyone wanting to erect fortifications needed a royal licence to castellate. Although the formal expression did not exist at first, the principle was there. All castles were at the disposal of the king, whether directly held by him and occupied by a royal official or belonging to an earl or baron. Unauthorised castles were demolished. Any castles that survived were built to serve the interest of the realm as a whole and were spaced across the countryside accordingly. The keeper of a castle held it by a form of knight service known as castle guard.

An example of an important castle is at Oxford which was an established Saxon shire town, the centre of its own territory and on trade routes. William needed to control it. He sent Robert d'Oilly in 1071 who pulled down many houses in a corner of the town and built a strong point which remains the castle to his day. No doubt influential landholders such as monasteries were compensated for the loss of their houses but ordinary men were not. As with the Roman conquest, military need knows no law. But the castle remained a royal not a private one.

William's knights put up innumerable small castles in their holdings. In a newly conquered land where many of the natives resented their depressed status, this was prudent. Many remain as isolated tree-grown mounds in open country or as neatly mown monuments in small towns. The motte, perhaps 15 feet high and surmounted with a small wooden structure, could serve as an effective if uncomfortable strong point for the knights until they had pacified the country. A knight might be left in control, holding the fort to secure the land. His baron granted him land to provide an income to cover the costs.

The rules of military tenure came to be elaborated into many different types. The most important was knight service of which castle guard was a variety as were some forms of sergeanty. There was also grand sergeanty which involved honourable services owed to the king in person, and those duties still exist. All of these military tenures carried not only the duty to serve in war but also other obligations such as wardship, which we will need to consider later.

THE CHURCH

The final part of England was made up of lands of abbots and bishops. Most of these lands were their existing holdings which had often been given to them in earlier centuries as bookland. Although, therefore, the Church did not derive its rights from the Conquest they still came from a royal grant, albeit long before, and were assimilated to the system of tenure. This was a special type of tenure known as frankalmoign or free alms. It carried only a notional duty to perform religious services and applied as much to the great bishops and abbots who were regarded as barons of the king as to the rectors in their parishes.

The equivalents to castles were the abbeys and cathedrals which began to rise over the landscape. There had of course been such buildings before 1066, but the leading clergy were almost all replaced during William's reign by men of continental origin who were scornful of what they regarded as inferior English buildings and had the money and the will to replace them with grand new structures, many of which still survive.

In the villages the parish priest had an endowment to support him in his work. This was partly in land and partly in a form of religious tax called tithe. This was nominally a tenth of produce and in the beginning was probably just that, but as with all taxes it became ever more complex as the years passed. All holders of productive land were under a duty to contribute and if they did not they could be called before the Church courts which were becoming established or the rector could curse the farmer who failed to pay. Tithe was reformed in 1836 but not finally abolished until 1936 and the last vestiges were removed in 1977.[1]

The lands, known as glebe, had been provided by Saxon lords and were now included in the system of tenure. They were little different to other lands and in many cases the rector had to work them along with his fellow villagers. In champion districts they would comprise a number of strips scattered through the open fields.

The parish church itself was consecrated land. While there are still some surviving Saxon churches, the greater number were built or rebuilt in the year after the Conquest, although of course many were replaced yet again in the later Middle Ages or in Victorian times. Around the church was a churchyard, used not just for burials but also as an open space where people could meet.

MANORS AND THE DOMESDAY BOOK

The way the country was administered, whether the royal demesne or Church lands or knights' fees, was through manors. The manor organised and controlled each village and valley tightly. Most manors comprised rural communities where tenure was applied to the holdings of the ordinary farmers on the land but other places such as harbours and mines were assimilated to the system and so were some towns. A manor was an economic unit and the livelihood of many people depended on it. Many manors were either the Anglo-Saxon estates or *lands* which had existed before 1066 or a combination of several. Occasionally, a single manor might be divided in two, for instance where the lord died leaving two married daughters, but the new parts still each had to make economic sense to the cultivators and the officials such as bailiffs who ran them.

We know a good deal about landholding in William's reign because in 1086 he ordered the compiling of the Domesday Book. Historians argue over its purpose but, at the least, it is an important legal text. The men who composed it were not lawyers as the profession did not yet exist but they thought and wrote in legal

---

[1] The Tithe Act 1836, the Tithe Act 1936 and the Finance Act 1977.

terms. The king's officials designed it to show two main features. One was to reckon the value of what he had conquered and he and his tenants held, so that he knew what resources he had to fight and govern.[2] The other was to set out the system of control. It was arranged by shire, indicating that the important royal official was the sheriff, the king's officer in each county. Within shires it was arranged by honour and manor, indicating the network of dependence and control by the greater and lesser lords. The Domesday Book was not just a record of England. It laid down a legal pattern which later generations accepted as given. It was also a detailed description of the landscape of England in 1086.

The compilers of the Domesday Book took continuity from Anglo-Saxon times for granted and in most places set out the name of the person who, in the time of King Edward, had held the manor now controlled by King William or one of his followers. Church manors in general still belonged to the same abbey or diocese. We can also assume that while the lords had changed, the cultivators had not. They continued in occupation as their fathers had before 1066.

The Domesday Book was first of all a list of manors. With a few exceptions, the whole country was seen as being in one manor or another. Each was described – there were so many farmers (describing their different status) and so much land (distinguishing between the demesne land of the lord cultivated by his slaves and serfs and the land of the free tenants). There were so many ploughs and the Book stated whether its compilers thought there could be more – suggesting that one of its purposes was to see if there was unused productive capacity in the kingdom. The Book listed mills, woods (often saying how large or how many pigs it could support), meadows, as well as special features, such as a salt mine or a fishery.

This was a great achievement. It put into a single system all the variety of English lands, hill and valley, coast and plain, nuclear village and scattered farms. It indicated that all England was under the same general law. Once this became taken for granted it would be possible for the great variety of customs and arrangements which existed across the Anglo-Saxon realms to be assimilated to a single set of rules. We will see how 100 years later the king's judges worked out the implications and developed a common law for the whole country.

The lord, as tenant of his manor, was seen as having his legal rights both within it and beyond. A manor became a piece of property in itself and distinct from the lands and services which comprised it. As such it could be bought from or sold to another knight, inherited by a son, given away to the Church or rented out – the Domesday Book includes many instances of leased manors.

---

[2]   *Anglo-Saxon Chronicle* for 1085.

Correspondingly, in the local setting the lord had control over each piece of his own manorial demesne, which included the manor house, his strips and closes and sometimes other property, such as mills and parks. He could do what he wished with them, build or demolish and lease them individually. In time, he came to be recognised as holding rights over other parts of the manor so long as he did not override the rights of the tenants. He could not on his own enclose the waste but, if there was anything extra left after the needs of his tenants were satisfied, then he could control that surplus. He could rearrange the lands, fell woods, drain bogs and put vacant land to cultivation or authorise others to do so.

Within each manor there was a readjustment of status and in many places such freedom as had existed was under threat. The new lords, who had learnt about estate management on the Continent, had different ideas from their Saxon predecessors about how to control the people who lived on their manors and imposed tighter direction. This was part of a movement right across Europe. The former pattern of nobles, independent free farmers, serfs and slaves was changing. Slavery was becoming uneconomic. Slaves had to be looked after and the Church, although with hesitation and inconsistency, encouraged freeing the slaves. The new system of concentrated local communities gathered in a court had no real place for men who, as slaves, were legally property but who could occupy and farm similar pieces of land in a similar way to their free neighbours.

But while slavery declined and the position of former slaves improved, the status of many free, small farmers declined to serfdom. Throughout Europe, lords were able to impose bad customs, *mauvaises coutumes* or *mals usos*, which involved three things. The first was boon work or week work, the duty to do work for the lord, usually limited in time but often burdensome, say three days a week, perhaps more at harvest. The second was merchet, the power of the lord to control marriages of peasant children. In practice, with time, this consent was given in return for a fixed money payment but in the beginning it was used to control movement of people between villages and to ensure that future children were born on the manor where the lord had rights over them. The third was tallage, the right of the lord to require a payment of money when he demanded. In time this too disappeared or became commuted to a nominal quit rent, but in the early days it was a heavy burden.

All these went with the duty to stay on the land. In Roman times a *colonus* had been *adscriptus glebae*, tied to the land, so he could not leave the estate. The same expression now came to be applied to serfs. They were bondsmen, bound to the soil. There was a variety of different forms of bondage both within a manor and in different parts of England. The most prosperous were called villeins, which came to be the general name for them, but there were also coliberts, cottars and many others. The technical term was 'villeins appendant' and while they had no right to leave the manor, equally they had a right not to be moved and could claim to stay on their holding. There was also a less common version, 'villeins in gross or regardant', who were personally bound to their lord and could be moved about.

Some men were able to resist this trend. In particular there were free socmen on many manors, especially in the east of England, who held their land either from the lord or occasionally outside the manorial structure, who were humble in status but could sell the rights to their holdings. Those within a manor owed services of a different sort from bondsmen, which were certain and defined such as cleaning out a specific ditch or taking a prescribed number of loads of the lord's grain to market after harvest.

All were regarded as holding land by tenure. Socmen held in socage and villeins in villeinage. We will see that in subsequent centuries there came to be an important difference between the status of the holder and that of his land but at this time they went together. Tenure involved relationship, that every landholder had to recognise and deal with others, either his lord or his equals, or his tenants. It invoked a community. The reality of life in the small medieval village was farmers constantly on the edge of starvation. In the managed landscapes of the eleventh and twelfth centuries this relationship governed everything. Everyone was involved with land and tenure bound them together.

COMMERCIAL HOLDINGS

This relationship is shown by the surviving evidence of legal disputes. Inevitably, the records relate to the affairs of the greater landholders, the lords and bishops. Most tenure concerned military, ecclesiastical or agricultural holdings but we can see some occupation of land for what we would regard as commercial purposes or on contractual terms. The Domesday Book records a number of *clamores* or pending lawsuits about control of various parts of the countryside and some relate to such matters.

The case of *Robert of Stafford v Kolsveinn*[3] concerned two mills in the village of Barkston near Grantham in Lincolnshire. Corn mills were an important feature in the corn-growing countryside. They were expensive to build and maintain and the cost was paid for by a form of monopoly. A mill belonged to a particular manor and all the tenants of that manor were bound to bring their corn to that mill to be ground and to pay the miller the going rate. If they owed a duty known as suit of mill they were not allowed to take it to another mill whose

---

[3]   c 1086, noted in the Domesday Book, Lincolnshire, 377V.

miller charged less or even to grind it themselves. The miller of course had to pay his lord and if the mill was profitable the lord got a good income from it.

Robert of Stafford was a great lord with manors across England. Kolsveinn was a monyer who minted coins for the king. Kolsveinn held lands at Barkston but there were several other lords with land and tenants there, the holdings probably being intermixed rather than lying in separate parts of the parish. The Domesday Book records him as holding two mills in Barkston. There were also mills in the adjoining village of Marston which was divided between several manors belonging to different lords including Kolsveinn. Some of these were within the soke or jurisdiction of another manor but some had their own soke.

The dispute was over who was entitled to the revenues of the mills. The wapentake court decided that the mills belonged to Kolsveinn's manor and soke at Marston but they also said that in this case the soke of the mills belonged to nearby Grantham which was a royal manor. On any basis, Robert lost the case but Kolveinn may have had to account to the king's officials for part of the profits.

Other disputes were about leases. We have seen how in the late Saxon time the Roman concept of a lease was revived as loanland. In medieval Latin a grant for a time or sometimes for a number of generations was called a *firma* (usually translated farm) because it had a firm or fixed end date, or one which could be ascertained. This was in contrast both to the interests of the free tenants whose rights were indefinite, either for their own lifetime or to run into the remote future as long as they had heirs, and to those of the villeins who were both bound and entitled to hold the land for life. The *firma* gave rise to numerous disputes. Some of these arose because when after Hastings, William handed out estates he found it simplest to allocate to a particular follower all the lands formerly held by a particular defeated Saxon thegn. The new baron took over the lands of his *antecessor* and if he had held some land on lease before 1066 his successor might claim to take it on whether or not he was entitled to. Sometimes in the confused circumstances of the Conquest, a powerful baron with his own soldiers might take control of a piece of land with no evident lord.

The case of *Abbot of St Guthlac in Crowland v Ogier the Breton*[4] concerned a lease of some land in Rippingale in Lincolnshire. It was occupied by sokemen of Ogier the Breton who was a substantial landholder. The Monks of St Guthlac's Abbey claimed that Abbot Ulfkytel (who was abbot from 1051 to 1085) had granted the land to Hereward at farm at a rent to be agreed every year. Hereward, who was known as the Wake, led an unsuccesful resistance to the Conquest. In its account of the lawsuit, the Domesday Book says he broke

---

[4]   c 1086, noted in the Domesday Book, Lincolnshire, f 377.

his lease agreement and fled the country but it is likely his departure was for political reasons. Presumably, Ogier had got control of the land, probably because he had taken on other lands formerly belonging to Hereweard. The abbot (who by 1086 was Ingulf) claimed it back against Ogier and the case was referred to the judgment of the king.

These two cases illustrate how even in the years immediately after the Conquest there was a system of resolving disputes at the highest level and thereby giving security to those with an interest in regulating the landscape. Disputes between humbler men went either to the honour courts or the manor court of a lord or to the shire, Hundred or leet courts which still survived. They were not always decided by legal rules – there were ways of resolving them by ordeals or oaths or combat but this was within the context of overall control which allowed for certainty and for men to occupy their lands in peace.

Leases were also used as a form of investment in land and as a sort of mortgage, and some of the leases mentioned in the Domesday Book may have been of this sort. Under a modern mortgage (from the Latin for dead pledge *mortuum vadium* or *mort gage*) the borrower pays interest and the lender does not directly take the income from the land unless the borrower defaults. The medieval church opposed interest so one way of overcoming this was for the lender to take a live gage under which he took the rents or produce of the land. Such an arrangement could be done by a lease which would end if the debt was repaid. An alternative was a dead gage under which the borrower remained in occupation. In later centuries, mortgages were to have a profound effect on the development of both countryside and town by providing finance for improvements and enabling new owners with new ideas to buy land. The origins of the mortgage lay in the (by our standards) clumsy experiments of the eleventh century.

In the eleventh century such commercial arrangements were unusual and the personal relationships of tenure governed most rights in land. In the following chapters we will see how secure rights to property developed to replace them.

Chapter 7

Medieval Landholding – 1154 to 1348

THE RULE OF LAW

After 100 years, the descendants of the Norman conquerors settled into the country as if they had been here forever. They appeared to hold and manage their land under the same rules as their ancestors but the needs of an established kingdom were very different from those of an occupying force. The institutions designed for the Conquest had to be reinterpreted for a more sophisticated age.

Life and landholding in the villages and among the hills and woods was still governed by the variety of local practices which went back to the Anglo-Saxon kingdoms. Each region had its distinct ways and each manor was a separate unit with its own special customs, unlike those of the next. There was as yet no single national law. However, we saw how the compilers of the Domesday Book tried to assimilate the innumerable local arrangements to a single set of categories. They did it for the purposes of the survey but the Book gained a prestige and an importance as a legal record and so this approach led to the idea that there could be a set of laws common to the whole of England.

The idea of law itself was well established but, although the royal laws referred to humble people and included provisions relevant to them, they were mainly concerned with the affairs of the powerful. The general law was still a minority pursuit under the Normans. Much of what we now commit to legal process was still determined by local consensus or practice of local courts or by customary arrangements which later came to be recognised as law.

Many disputes, and therefore the rights which depended on them, had formerly been resolved by direct action. This concerned individual arguments as much as communal ones. Some of the Saxon royal dooms set out a scale of compensation for injury or for kinsmen to claim in the event of a killing to prevent feuds getting out of hand and threatening the peace. The Normans introduced a more formal trial by wager of battle both as a part of what we would call criminal law to determine guilt or innocence and also to determine civil disputes. This remained available in theory until *Ashford v Thornton* in 1818[1] and was then abolished by Parliament.[2] In practice, it was discouraged after the late twelfth century and became rare because there were better ways to resolve disputes.

More serious were the conflicts between barons. Between 1135 and 1153, England was disturbed by an intermittent civil war between two grandchildren of the Conqueror, Stephen and Matilda, which overflowed into many private local disturbances. In 1154, Matilda's son succeeded as Henry II. He, like his great grandfather, was more interested in his domains in France but he needed England to be settled and peaceful. With his advisers he determined to provide peace. As ever, the most disturbing disputes were about land, especially as many occupiers had been dispossessed in the civil wars. Henry restored order, and created legal procedures to replace both private warfare and also private combats. While there was still a great deal of violence, it became royal policy to keep it to a minimum.

In order to do so it was necessary for the law, instead of being a voluntary addition to society or a means available only to the great and powerful, to enter into its heart so that all people accepted what we call the rule of law and it came to govern any activities of every free person and of many who were not free. Law has two aspects for this purpose.[3] First are the substantive or primary rules which affect our daily lives – such as laws about occupation of and security in land, about the relations of a lord and his tenants and about the rights of different people in one piece of property. The other aspect, known as secondary rules, governs the interpretation, changing and enforcement of the rules themselves, that is about legal processes such as deciding disputes or making new laws or how one person can transfer land to another. Although the two types of law cannot be wholly separated, this chapter is about the primary rules and I will consider the secondary rules in Chapter 8.

In this period, relative peace in England produced wealth which paid for new buildings such as great abbeys and castles. It paid for barns and for the drainage of marshes. It paid for universities (with their college buildings) and for scholars to work out sophisticated ideas in law, philosophy and theology. The early towns developed into centres of trade and commerce, and their citizens began to make fine buildings, lay out streets and market places and build town halls. The few who had power and wealth competed for more and because wealth came from land, the competition was for that. Followers and tenants expected their

---

[1]   (1818) 1 B & Ald 405, 106 ER 149.

[2]   59 GIII, c 46.

[3]   Hart, HLA, *The Concept of Law* (Oxford University Press, 1961).

lord to defend their rights, just as they had at the time of the personal ties under the Normans, for old ways of thinking remained. The loyalty of his followers was important for a lord's standing but, as Henry II forbade private wars, men had to resolve their conflicts not by force but by the law, and the law had to define those rights.

So the law affected how people managed the landscape. That consisted of waste, woodland and farmland, as well as villages, monasteries and the towns. In legal terms that management was reflected in manors, in the nature of freehold tenure and in the corporations both ecclesiastical and lay.

MANOR AND WASTE

In the Domesday Book, nearly all land was reckoned to be within a manor. Each manor had a lord, who might be an individual, or an institution such as an abbey, or who might be the king. Under the rules of tenure, people did not ask about ownership but about who held the land from whom. If you were the man of a lord, you were entitled to cultivate some of the land over which he had jurisdiction and you owed him services in return. They might be personal ones, in his household, or on his farm, or they might be owed rather through the village community, as a herdsman or by serving as a village official. In some places the community and its court controlled many details of daily life. This was especially the case in the champion districts where most folk lived in a village. In the woodland areas where farms were more scattered there was less control. If there were no open fields to regulate, no communal ditches to clear out, there was less need for an assembly to organise them. In those cases control came through the lord's agents, his bailiff and steward, but it would still be exercised though a court.

Since customary rights, which affected most people, could only be determined in the locality, the royal judges who adjudicated on the laws common to the whole realm were not equipped to determine them. This principle prevented the common law determining the rights relating to villein land and inhibited the recognition of what became copyhold rights until the sixteenth century. However, within the manor free tenants and tenants of villein land came to have rights not just in the lands they occupied but also in the other assets of the manor, such as the common waste or the stream. A lord could not simply override those rights even though they were customary and determined in the court which belonged to him, but he could influence the way they worked through the courts of manor and leet which he controlled.

An important instance of the limits of this communal control is the way in which much uncultivated land converted to arable. As the population grew there was pressure on land. Successive generations of fathers could not forever subdivide their small farms among their children and villeins might not have the right to do so. The young men needed farmland. They found it by taking part of the waste, the rough grazing in the champion districts and the heaths, woods and marshland in the woodland areas. They enclosed it within fences or hedges to make it produce crops. They cut down the trees, ploughed up the rough grass and drained the bogs to make fields to grow the corn to live on.

But as we have seen, the waste was not idle land. For thousands of years people had got reeds, wild herbs, fruits and small animals from them. When the open fields were laid out it was part of the resources of the local economy. It was where the oxen, which drew the ploughs, could graze. It was where the woods grew, which supplied fuel and building materials. So if one person took over some of it, he impoverished his fellows. One small encroachment might not seem much, but over a few years many intakes could change the whole nature and appearance of the landscape and the resources of its people.

If we cannot see arable land as owned by anyone, even less can we so regard the waste, but it all fell within the jurisdiction of a lord and within the bounds of a manor. Therefore the lord and the manor court had control of it. If someone wanted to make a new farm the lord or the court could stop him. He needed permission and that could be given in one of two ways, by approvement or by licensed assarting.

Approvement authorised the lord to take, or authorise the taking, into cultivation of part of the waste land. Tenants of the manor had rights to graze or put out their pigs, to cut wood, and to gather timber or turf as fuel or to repair their homes. Those rights were binding on the lord so, in principle, he could not do anything to reduce them. If he did enclose the waste then the villagers might suffer. Often, there was more of it than they needed but they still had the legal right to prevent any encroachment and freeholders could enforce that right through the royal courts. A system developed to allow the lord to approve the surplus. In a sense it was his land but he was not free to deal with it as he wished. The Statute of Merton 1235 is regarded as one of our earliest statutes, although it was made before the existence of Parliament as we know it by Henry III on the advice of Council of the Barons. Chapter 4 enacted a rule that the lord could approve only if he left sufficient grazing for the tenants.[4] The rule did not apply to any other rights of common such as turbary, to take turf, or pannage, to put out pigs, so it had a limited effect but it did permit some conversion of land from waste to arable on the initiative of the lord. He sometimes occupied the

---

[4]   The Commons Act 1235 (20 H3 c 4).

land through his own serfs or labourers but more often would let it to a cultivator for rent.

More important was assarting. At first this was what we would call a trespass. A farmer went out without permission and simply converted some waste land into arable. This was a breach of law and because it concerned the waste not the open fields it was a matter for the manor court, which could fine him for the offence. Often that was the limit of what the court could do. It did not order him to restore the land to waste. Usually the individual loss to his neighbours was small (although as more people did this they lost a good deal by cumulative assarting) and as the fines stayed the same from year to year they came to be a form of rent, payable at the manor court and so received by the lord as part of his income from the manor. Later the lord might grant a licence to assart to a farmer to reclaim part of the waste in return for a regular payment.

The competition for land led to disputes and the surviving court records of the time illustrate them. A typical case is *Etton v Cornborough* in 1204.[5] The de Etton family held land at Gilling in Yorkshire. William of Cornborough made a hedge to enclose part of the common pasture. Geoffrey de Etton complained that that infringed his rights. The procedure was in the action called Novel Disseisin which I will look at in Chapter 8. Judgment was given for de Etton and he also got an award of 12 pence damages. The families went on having legal dealings for some time. In 1219, there was an agreement between Osbert de Cornborough and William de Etton under which Osbert released certain rights in William's common pasture on the waste. William granted Osbert the services of some of the men of the village and Osbert agreed to make a nominal acknowledgment payment of a pair of white gloves each year. This settled the lawsuit by a compromise. In 1252, there was another case between Osbert and William in which Osbert claimed rights in the common pasture and again Osbert released them but kept for himself the right to graze 35 sheep, 10 cows, 16 oxen and four horses. There was also a provision that if William put any goats in the pasture, then Osbert could put 20 goats there as well.

All of this looks like a long-standing dispute about rights over the common waste. The de Cornboroughs initially tried to claim it as theirs and put up a hedge and when that failed they made various agreements with the de Etton lords of the manor to regulate grazing rights.

---

[5] Roll ed Stenton in (1966) 83 *Selden Society* 127.

FREEHOLDS

Most people nowadays consider ownership of the freehold, the fee simple, as equivalent to ownership of land. It derives from the approach taken by the royal judges who developed the common law. They regarded the lord as holding such rights in land he occupied or managed directly. These rights included his manor house and farm buildings, and other land such as his deer park, an area enclosed with banks so designed that deer could leap in but not get out. As that involved control of otherwise wild animals which would roam freely the lord needed royal permission, known as a franchise, to make a park. His freehold also included the strips in the open field which were his demesne on which the villeins laboured for him, and came to include the common waste of the manor.

The judges also considered that the lord had the fee simple in the land occupied by most villagers. Some free tenants of the lord held their land as common freehold and they came to have the right to defend their title in the royal courts of common law. Other free tenants held rights to customary freeholds. Villeins too had customary rights which could be just as definite in their way. Such customary rights, whether belonging to villeins or freeholders, were not justiciable in the royal courts because only local courts could decide local customs. The common law therefore came to regard the lord as holding the freehold in all customary land. He was in principle bound to respect local rights, and most lords did, but there could be abuses.

In the later eleventh century, in England as across Europe, the law also came to define and regulate personal status. As we have seen, some people were free socmen, others were bondsmen, mostly villeins and, although not exactly free, they were not slaves either. Although tied to the land they could own property and had rights. By the thirteenth century the idea developed that their bondage was only relative to their own lord and as regards others they were free.[6] This had an implication for their land. To begin with the land of a free man was free land, or freehold, and he owed free and defined services. The land of a villein was villein land and he owed undefined services, so that he had to come to the lord's service on whichever days custom required and do whatever tasks needed to be done.

Over the years the land became distinct from the holder. Free men came to hold villein land, perhaps by inheritance or purchase. If they did so they had to do the uncertain service owed by the occupier of the land. If the holder was humble he might do it himself and that could lead to a dispute as to whether he was indeed free, but that did not affect the principle. Similarly a villein could hold freehold

---

6   Bracton, Henry of, *de Legibus et Consuetudinis Anglia* (SE Thorne (ed)), f 196b, vol 3, pp 99–100.

land in socage, for instance if he married a woman who inherited it, and if so he only owed free and defined service for that land even while his person remained tied to the manor of his lord.

The ancient services belonged to ancient lands. As farmers claimed new lands from the waste both they and the lords often found it simpler to avoid the complications of traditional customary services. As a result of certain laws of the Parliament of Edward I, it became established retrospectively that, as a general rule, new customary holdings could not have come into existence after 1189,[7] although exceptionally in some manors, when in later years land was taken in from the waste, it might still be regarded as a customary holding.[8] More often, the occupier might pay a rent to the lord at the manor court and be regarded as having a lease. Sometimes he and his family after him came to be seen as holding the land freely. It could be a matter of chance or local practice whether newly enclosed land came to be villein land or as land held on lease or as the freehold of the person who cultivated it.

The freehold is, today, the foundation of the management of the English landscape but it has taken time to develop. We saw how some landholders had tenancies for life and others had fees simple which their widows and children could inherit. As we shall see in connection with settled estates, there came to be also a fee tail which passed down the family. One of the achievements of the judges of the common law was to clarify different sorts of right in the land.

Land was initially held within the relationship of tenure as part of a bargain. If a man holding in knight service did not serve, then his lord could come onto the land and seize enough of his goods to be sold to pay the cost of a replacement soldier; in the last resort his lands could be forfeit. If the tenant died, his widow could stay provided she paid for a fighter – so-called shield money or scutage. Scutage was due to the king. By the mid-twelfth century, he preferred to collect cash and pay professional soldiers rather than have the service of knights, so scutage became a tax.

In time, the obligation of military service became less important and other financial rights more so. They were an important source of revenues, in particular a form of death duties. If a knight died, his heir owed his lord a due known as primer seisin equal to a year's profits. He might have to pay a relief, which in the beginning was a large sum although as time went on, especially after Magna Carta fixed the relief, it came to be eroded by inflation. If the dead man's heir was a young boy, his lord could run the estate for his own benefit

---

[7]   Statute of Westminster 1275 (3 Edw 1, c 39); *Quo Warranto* 1290 (18 Ed 1). See *Dalton v Angus* (1880–81) LR 6 App Cas 740, at 811.

[8]   *Hughes v Games* (1726) Select Cases Temp King 62, 25 ER 224.

until the boy was of age. This was called wardship and the lord might sell the right to the highest bidder. If he left a daughter, then the lord had the right to choose her husband, and to demand a payment for doing so. The right to arrange the marriage of an heiress was worth a lot of money. There were other payments, for instance when a lord went on crusade or his eldest son was knighted. As society changed, these exactions lost any justification and came to be resented.

The holder of the fee had security in his lands so long as he paid the sums when they were due. He therefore had a right of property. It was not yet ownership as we understand it. He could sell his fee or give it away in his lifetime, but only, as we will see in Chapter 8, with the consent of his lord. He was not free to leave the fee by will. If he died it passed automatically to his heir, usually his eldest son or, if he left no son, to be divided among his daughters.

Some of these rules applied to tenants in socage, but farming tenants of manors both free and villein were subject to numerous other burdens. A tenant in villeinage had to work on the lord's demesne and to pay substantial sums on death, succession or marriage. He could not build a house unless his lord consented. In woodland areas, he could not change the shapes of his closes without the same consent. In the common fields, he could not exchange one strip for another or combine two together unless he obtained authority from the lord and usually the court leet. In a closed village controlled by a single lord, the lord also controlled the leet, but, in a village with several lords, the lord of the leet might be different from the lord of the individual on whose death his family inherited his land according to customary rules he could not change.

A customary freehold tenant of the manor might be able to rearrange his land but he was still subject to the rules of the courts, both manor and leet, and local customs spelt out in detail not only how he cultivated the land, but also whether he could sell. On his death his land might be subject to payments to the lord. Customs which varied from one manor to another also governed the way it passed to his children.

OWNERSHIP AND THE LAW OF THE LAND

There was a land market, although still a limited one. It became possible because of a change in the way that both the powerful and the learned regarded land. As discussed in Chapter 8, the old problem had been to find men to farm available land but, as during the thirteenth-century population increase, the new problem was to find land for men to farm. As lords could find cultivators without difficulty, it became important for them to control the land or the buildings and crops on it.

There was also a shift in political and theological ideas about the nature of property and about the community and the place of law. Until the thirteenth century the prevailing idea was that laws and communities related to men, souls subject to God, not to lands and territories. Just as the Romans saw laws as belonging to a community, with *civitas* meaning both the community and the citizenship which denoted membership of it, and only secondarily the territory it occupied, so later generations thought in terms of people.

This accompanied an idea that land itself could in some sense be owned. In the early Middle Ages some theologians had taught that land was a common inheritance. God had made the earth and allowed humans to live on it and cultivate it but 'the earth is the Lord's'.[9] The early Christians were supposed to have held all things in common. It was soon realised that that was not practical for clothes, animals and tools, but land was seen by many as different. They did recognise that land had to be cultivated and so accepted the idea that it could be held and occupied by individuals. That fitted with the ideas of tenure, under which a soldier held the land in return for military services or a farmer was permitted to cultivate in return for his part in producing food. It may be that open fields were seen in some way as communal assets. Although that could only be in a limited sense, as each strip had to be cultivated separately, farming a scatter of unfenced strips did not carry the same control as a hedged field. Now, however, theologians began to accept that ownership of land was no bad thing. Scholars rediscovered Roman law, and the Romans, at least in relation to land in Italy, had a concept of *dominium* which was much like our idea of owning land, although not exactly the same. So they considered that perhaps God had granted land to be used and improved in the same way as other things.

Likewise, lawyers began to regard the law of the land as the same not just for those who happened to be members of a community as such, but for all those who lived there because they occupied land. A villein or customary freeholder could call on the law of the manor not through his personal tenurial relationship with the lord but because he held land, whether bond or free, which was part of the manor itself. Of course some people had always regarded land as in some sense belonging to them. If monks needed to build an abbey or a knight wished to create a deer park, it was the land not the jurisdiction which mattered. Even jurisdiction related to a defined area which the lord could inspect or ride over. Likewise, a socman saw the closes he farmed as his land. However, it took time for the legal treatment of disputes and transfers fully to reflect this.

---

[9]   Psalm 24.1.

People also began to think in terms of the law of the land in the sense of England. Alfred was not called King of Wessex: his title used in formal documents was King of the West Saxons. His successors, from Athelstan to Edward the Confessor, usually called themselves kings of the English, not of England. William the Conqueror was *Rex Anglorum* King of Englishmen. Only in the reign of King John did the term *Rex Angliae* King of England become usual. By that time men were coming to think more in terms of a king over a land, not just a people. If, therefore, this country was a separate realm with its own laws which applied not just to those men who owed services to the king of the English but to all who lived in the country ruled by the King of England, then the laws of the land would also apply to any land as such, irrespective of who held it (although any landholder had to do fealty for English land[10]).

As it became established that a free man could hold villein land and a villein could hold free land, so lawyers began to regard rights and duties as being attached to the land rather than to the occupier. The law applied to the subject matter not to the individual. As indicated, the way laws work is that a judge makes an order against a person, for instance to let a claimant into occupation. But now the thinking behind those orders is to see the land as a thing in itself rather than as what a person happens to be occupying under a relationship with another person. Rights over land had of course been bought and sold since Saxon times but formerly the rights of the buyer had depended on his relationship with the lord of the land and the occupiers. Now they came to be defined by what the law of the country said about the land itself.

The result of these changes, both in high politics and in the understanding of the way land was held, was that ownership of land as such enabled people to do what they wanted with it, just as they could with their table or cow. Tenure continued to be important until the Civil War (and burgage tenure until 1832 as explained later) but that was mainly for the financial returns to the lord which were increasingly resented. We shall see the outcome in considering two important enactments, *Quia Emptores* and the Statute of Uses, in Chapters 8 and 10.

It remains true that to regard someone as owning land as such is simplistic. Many people have rights in the same piece. A villein might cultivate his plot and have the right, provided the manor court was fairly administered, for his widow or children to succeed on his death, but he still owed services to the lord of the manor who had the freehold and who could evict him if he breached the customs. Which of them owned the land? The lord held the common waste but the tenants had grazing rights and the lord could not approve the land and enclose it if he did not leave them sufficient. Who owned the waste? One man had a strip in the open field but his neighbour used part of the end balk to turn

---

[10]   See *Calvin's Case* (1608) 7 Co Rep 1a, 77 ER 377.

his oxen. In a woodland county, a neighbour has a right of way across a close to reach his own fields. One man might be able to kill birds or game on the land occupied by another. There are many different sorts of right that can exist in the same piece of land. If the accepted idea of ownership is too simple, the owner may be able to block access to others, thus destroying a network of rights of way – there were more local paths and ways in the Middle Ages than in our own time. If he owns land through which a ditch carries water and can block it up, his neighbour's land can be flooded.

So instead of saying that anyone owned land, the lawyers said that what you owned was an estate or interest in land, a right in it. One person owned the fee simple in possession. Another, such as a baron or earl, might own a superior fee, with the rights of lordship and financial benefits attached. Another owned the sporting rights or minerals. Another had grazing rights or a right of way. These rights could be elaborated as far as anyone needed to meet the needs of a growing and densely populated agricultural landscape. They provided a means of fitting together the ways that the farmer who grew oats on one piece of land and crossed another to reach his close, the cottager who collected wood for his hearth and the abbot who collected money for his candles, could all get what they required.

CORPORATE ACTION

It was not just individuals who had needs. The landscape changed through the work of many hands. Sometimes that could be organised by one man giving an order to another but what happened if one fell sick or had to travel – to go on pilgrimage or crusade or foreign war? What happened to a great work which took many years when people died or became too old? A cathedral could take 100 years or more to build. In the growing towns, merchants and shopkeepers wanted fine buildings in which to meet – guildhalls and town halls. In the new universities, colleges needed places to teach and to house the scholars and students. The abbeys became large groups of splendid but expensive structures. All of these needed time, money and organisation, and the solution was the corporation.

This was a new idea of the Middle Ages to create an artificial person, an instance of a legal fiction. The law pretends that a group of individuals acting together are for some purposes treated as if they were a separate invisible intangible person. Such a person can hold land or money, can buy and sell, can sue and be sued. A corporation has perpetual succession so that it does not die when the individuals that comprise it die, because they can appoint successors to carry on the work and so they can plan for long periods of time, over generations. It allows a group of people to combine resources in a way that even the most powerful aristocratic family cannot. It is the basis of the companies which dominate the commerce of the modern world.

As we have seen, the Romans had only a limited idea of a corporation. They knew ownership by an individual or a group of people but once the Christian Church began to acquire land for churches and the care of the sick, there was a need for something better. Sometimes the law regarded the land as belonging to the bishop. That could be a problem if a corrupt bishop wanted to benefit his family or an eccentric one wanted to sell it in order to divide the proceeds among the poor. So some donors gave land to God or to St Peter for a church. That also produced difficulties. If someone damaged the building, or if a relative who had hoped to inherit the land given to the monastery claimed it, then God or St Peter could not appear before the king or a judge to argue the case.

So the practice developed of giving land to the abbot and monks as a body, who collectively had to decide on changes. The dean and chapter held the cathedral, and the master and fellows (most of whom were in holy orders) held the university colleges. This could also apply to secular use. Towns held their markets through the mayor and burgesses, guilds and livery companies held their halls through the master and members. The king controlled this right and any group of people who wished to become a corporation had to pay for the grant of a franchise to do so.[11] In order to distinguish dealings with common property, corporations had a common seal, which they used in the same way that a noble would use his personal seal instead of a signature. Curiously, it took until 1989 for the law to permit corporations to sign instead of sealing documents.[12]

Corporations were therefore able to change the landscape in a way not open to the individuals who made them up. There was, however, one big problem with ownership by a corporation – whether a monastery, borough or college – precisely because it did not live and therefore did not die. The land was said to pass into the dead hand, *mort main*, of the corporation. So the lords lost their revenues due on death of a tenant or on succession by a child. Many lords accepted this but the king insisted on control. If someone wanted to transfer land to a corporation, he needed a royal licence in mortmain to do so and had to pay for it.

The rules about freeholds and corporations which lawyers worked out in the years between the accession of Henry II and the Black Death were important for the way the English landscape developed. We should not think that England was

---

[11] Statute of Quo Warranto 1290 (18 E1).

[12] The Law of Property (Miscellaneous Provisions) Act 1989 and the Companies Act 1989.

alone in this – similar moves were taking place across Europe – but in England there were some special features which allowed the common law as we know it to grow in a way that Continental systems did not. The combination of a strong royal power with rights of private citizens led to a flexible but still certain set of laws which allowed people (still principally but not exclusively the powerful few) to exploit the landscape while having regard to the needs of their neighbours.

These rights existed only so far as they could be enforced, for a theoretical right without a remedy is an illusion. Therefore, there needed to be institutions to secure them, to resolve disputes and where necessary to make changes. To that we turn next.

Chapter 8

Courts, Charters and Statutes – 1154 to 1348

LEGAL PROCEDURE

Security and the freehold did not operate on their own. If someone claimed a right which was disputed, he needed to enforce it and, as combat was discouraged, he could only do so through a legal procedure. It is those processes which have determined the rights and the way our landscape is parcelled out and rearranged. In the early periods we know most about the aristocratic disputes. In Saxon times these could be settled by the king, as we saw in the case of the land at Fonthill. The Domesday Book also indicates that King William heard issues between his greater subjects.

Henry I appointed justices to hear disputes. His grandson Henry II issued commands or writs to the great lords to determine matters between their tenants in their honour courts. Where that was not possible he sent judges round the country to adjudicate, and established royal courts in London. If two rivals claimed a piece of land, the judges had to decide to whom they should award it. The rule that emerged was that the person who could show the oldest peaceful possession, known as seisin, would win. To do that he had to show that he, or his father or grandfather or someone from whom they had bought the land or by whom they had been given it, had lawfully held it before the rival claimant or someone through whom he claimed. This could involve a detailed and solemn enquiry into the history of the land including whether some suggested hand-over was according to law, or it might require an investigation of how a disputed boundary had come into existence. The royal Chancery developed a procedure called the Writ of Right through which a jury could be summoned to hear witnesses and examine documents and a judge could consider legal arguments. If the matter was within the jurisdiction of a lord, the king's writ could order him to do justice. However, we know most about the royal courts.

That procedure could take months (or years if one of the parties was away on crusade or ill) and so Henry also provided some swifter remedies called

Possessory Assizes which determined who had last peaceably held seisin of the land. If a man had been evicted (the legal term is 'disseised') by a rough neighbour, or if he had been away when his father (from whom he inherited) died, and someone else moved in, the king would order him to be put into possession. If the evictor (the disseisor) claimed that in truth that the land belonged to his own family and all he was doing was to reclaim by force what was rightfully his, then he could bring a Writ of Right to claim it. In practice one of the Possessory Assizes, called 'Novel Disseisin' was the most flexible and most used. We saw an instance in *Etton v Cornborough* in Chapter 7. A claimant had to show that unjustly and without judgment he had been dissseised of a free tenement. These two elements, seisin and a free tenement, were strict conditions to ensure that only certain types of claim, principally from substantial freeholders, could be brought before the judges.

Seisin was at first a normal word in everyday use which developed a legal meaning. In the end, the lawyers took it over as a technical term and laymen ceased to use it. Although disseisin was a major cause of disturbance it was not the only way disputes could arise. Another procedure which was to be of importance for the development of the landscape was legal nuisance. This was concerned with interference with rights other than occupation of land. These procedures were distinct and if a man had a dispute he (or increasingly the professional lawyers he employed) had to use the right one. Henry of Bracton, a judge who edited and published a book *On the Laws and Customs of England* in the mid-thirteenth century, gives an example.[1] Suppose the boundary between two manors runs down the middle of a river and one of the neighbours makes a fish weir obstructing the flow thus harming the other. If it was built wholly on the land of the defendant, then it was not a dispossession and the claimant could use an action in nuisance. If it was built wholly on the land of the claimant it was a disseisin and he could use Novel Disseisin. If it was built across the river, then it will be both and Bracton discusses which procedure can be used – for the law did not permit a person to make two claims for a single injury. In this case Bracton concludes that the claim ought to be in nuisance. Nuisance was to have a long history in the law of the landscape and it is still important in environmental law. Nuisance still governs the relations between occupiers of land. If a fire spreads from one person's land to the next holding, if he pollutes a stream or diverts it, his injured neighbour will claim in nuisance.

In principle, these procedures were available to the holder of any fee but they were of course expensive. In practice, a socman would use the local courts where similar procedures developed, although local justice could sometimes be rough and ready. Sometimes, therefore, a persistent small freeholder would seek

---

[1]   Bracton, Henry of, *de Legibus et Consuetudinis Anglia* (SE Thorne (ed)), f 234b, vol 3, p 196.

to assert his rights in the royal courts of common law. This was, as I will explain, in contrast to the position of villeins and of the growing number of leaseholders who had no legal right to claim their land in the royal courts.

There was a great variety of courts; the problem was often to locate the right one. The manor court handled disputes between tenants both free and bond, including grazing over the manorial waste. It decided the rights of the manorial socman according to common law but those of other free tenants of the manor and of villeins according to local custom. If there was a dispute affecting two manors held from the same baron it went to his honour court. The shire, Hundred and leet courts were, in a sense, royal courts and administered common law although modified to suit local conditions. In settlements with one dominant lord, known as closed manors, the leet and Hundred tended to become his private courts and to be assimilated to the manor court. Elsewhere, in open villages often with several lords, the leet retained a jurisdiction over the open fields. The shire or county court originally had a general jurisdiction but over time it was whittled away in favour of the royal courts.

There were also separate Church courts which decided issues such as legitimacy or the inheritance of goods. These were wholly independent of the king and issues over their jurisdiction led to the quarrel with and death of Archbishop Thomas à Becket. Cases in them were subject to appeal to the Pope and were decided according to the civil system derived from Roman law. The growing towns developed their own municipal or market courts to resolve differences between their citizens about trade or building disputes or the clearance of rubbish. Tribunals called courts of pie powder decided disputes in the market; borough courts dealt with property disputes. This maze of jurisdictions could be confusing but its very existence shows the penetration of the rule of law.

STATUTES AND THE KING'S CHARTERS

Although the law can develop through the decisions of judges, there is a more direct means. Acts of Parliament or statutes were to become the most important way the law changed the landscape. There will be many instances in this book and nowadays statutory powers are universal, so we need to have an idea of why and how they worked. Acts start by saying that they are enacted 'by the Queen's most Excellent Majesty' but they go on to say it is 'by and with the advice and consent of the Lords Spiritual and Temporal, and Commons, in this present Parliament assembled, and by the authority of the same'.

The Saxon kings issued their dooms and sometimes said they did so on the advice of the *Witan*, their council of wise men. William I and his successors simply made law, just as they decided disputes. While they were strong that is how the government effected the few changes that they needed. A century and a half later King John faced a rebellion by his barons and he was compelled to make a formal agreement to consult them. The idea of such consultation was by then becoming widespread all across Europe. Kings and great lords began to listen to their leading followers in formal assemblies which came to be called Parliaments from the French *parler* meaning to speak or talk. The Barons who, at Runnymede in 1215, made the king sign the Great Charter Magna Carta were not a parliament as such but simply a gathering of those barons who fought him.

A charter is a grant of some right. Any lord could issue one but the most important were royal charters like the Saxon books. The king could grant a charter conferring the right to operate a ferry, to castellate a manor house, hunting rights known as free warren or a franchise of deer park. A charter could authorise a market to help found a new town. Once the people of the town had organised themselves, the king might grant them a charter to enable them to become a corporation. Magna Carta was greater than other charters but it was drawn on the same legal principles of a grant of rights.

John renounced Magna Carta at once but he died soon after and in 1217 the guardians of his infant son Henry issued a second version which is the basis of the later law. The Charter was reissued during the thirteenth century until the final edition in 1297 which was a real statute because it was made by Parliament. The most famous passages in the 1215 Charter are Articles 39 and 40. They were re-enacted as Article 29 of the 1297 version which is still in force and provides:

> No Freeman shall be taken or imprisoned, or be disseised of his Freehold, or Liberties, or free Customs, or be outlawed, or exiled, or any other wise destroyed; nor will We not pass upon him, nor condemn him, but by lawful judgment of his Peers, or by the Law of the Land. We will sell to no man, we will not deny or defer to any man either Justice or Right

Magna Carta had little direct influence on the landscape. An exception is the provision (revised in subsequent versions) that tidal rivers could not be put in 'defence'. Inland fresh waters were held with the land through which they ran, so that if, as we have seen, a river divided two manors, the boundary ran down the middle of the stream. Tidal waters in contrast belonged and are still presumed to belong to the Crown. The early kings had been ready to grant rights over them to individual lords, so that they could enjoy exclusive fishing rights. Magna Carta prevented that and said that for the future the king would not grant private rights over tidal waters. That is still the case, so that if today someone wants to build a quay or make a harbour he will need statutory powers. At present, these are conferred by the Transport and Works Act 1992, but until that was passed any promoter of such works had to get a Bill through Parliament. However, Magna Carta did have a more profound impact on the way the landscape could be changed. For our purposes there are two important points. The first is the reference to a free man being disseised. The other is to the law of the land.

The reference to disseisin as it stands is to land. It meant that no free man could be deprived of his freehold land without the lawful judgment of his equals in status. (Villeins and leasehold land were different.) This meant that he could not be thrown out of the land he occupied without having his case referred to a court and decided by a jury. In principle, that applied to any freeholder, not just the great lords but also the humble socman. That might mean a royal court or it might mean the court of a lesser lord. Article 34 of Magna Carta 1215 specially preserved the right of lords to hold courts but in practice the quality of justice and the standard of legal argument in the royal courts was so much better that, in time, it meant that the private courts lost jurisdiction. However, the cost and complication of litigation was often such that until the development of the action of trespass, as discussed in Chapter 9, it could be difficult for a householder to get justice.

The same principle came to apply to other forms of property. After all, if a free man holding freehold land were to be subject to a heavy debt he would have to sell his land. It therefore extended beyond private debts to the potential debt of taxation. It followed that a free man could not be compelled to pay tax without a decision of his equals. It was not possible to consult everyone in the country every time the king needed to raise revenue so, during the reign of Henry III, the custom developed that representatives of the communities across the realm would attend on the king to give consent. This power over taxation did not extend to ancient revenues from the royal demesne or from seigniorial rights and where possible the kings tried to rely on those sources to avoid having to deal with Parliament.

The council of the barons became the House of Lords, and the representatives, two from each shire and borough, became the House of Commons. Lords were entitled to be present because of their status and birth. In order to carry authority, the Commons needed to be chosen by the people from whom they came. Initially, the chore of going to London (or wherever else the king wished to meet them) was seen as a tiresome burden and the first members of the House of Commons emerged as leading figures who accepted attendance as a public duty. In later times, being an MP became a sought-after privilege and if there were more candidates who wanted to be members than the two available places, there had to be an election.

It became the practice of the Commons not to give the king the tax money he wanted until he remedied some grievance and reformed the law. Every session of Parliament became a haggle between royal ministers and the representatives of the shires and boroughs. In time, the king found it useful not just to grant their requests but to be able to change the law in this way. The rule developed that the law could be altered by, and only by, Parliament by an Act or statute made by the king with the consent of the Lords and Commons. We will see how this power was to become the biggest source of landscape change in future centuries, but in the Middle Ages statutes were modest affairs. Only a few exceptions so changed the law that we can mark their effects on the countryside. Many statutes were more in the nature of grants and hardly to be distinguished from charters.

Statutes were therefore infrequent but as they could change the law, the ability to do so by judicial procedure issued by the Chancery diminished. The common law became settled and in principle it did not change. In practice, the judges had to and could adapt it to new conditions but that took time and depended on the chance that a new case in which a current issue was in dispute came before a court. As land became a commodity, and the common law recognised that rights over land could be owned, and as the rules which governed those rights became fixed and detailed, they provided a certainty which meant that landholders knew (or could find out from their lawyers) just what their rights were. Once they knew that, they had something definite which they could sell for another similar bundle of rights elsewhere. The common law applied to all land throughout the country irrespective of local custom. Magna Carta applied the law to all free men whatever their wealth or status.

Magna Carta 1215, the Great Charter, was so called because there was another charter, the lesser Charter of the Forests of 1217. This did have a direct impact on the landscape. Both nobles and common folk hated the forest laws. The lords resented not being able to exploit them – either for the pleasure of hunting (and for its food) or to incorporate forest land into their estates without royal permission. The common people suffered from the enforcement of the forest laws and their restriction on taking game for the pot, and the barrier to assarting. In the royal forest, any encroachment would be punished by the king's servants. In an age of land hunger, the forests could not be taken into farming. The kings of course needed timber for royal buildings, for castles and houses. Where the forest grew good trees they would donate them to favoured builders, for instance for a cathedral. But most of the resource was preserved for royal use, not least hunting. So at a time when in the shires the knights and lords encouraged, or at least permitted their tenants to reclaim the waste of their own manors, in the vast areas of forest the kings were preventing it. The forest laws by this time extended to about one-third of the area of the south of England. The Charter of the Forests said that no new forests could be created and the king disafforested many lands. This represented the end of Crown attempts to control ever larger areas of land use, although where the forests remained the laws stayed. Over the centuries the controls were relaxed until they were finally repealed by the Wild Creatures and Forest Laws Act 1971.

SEIGNIORIAL REVENUES AND THE POWER OF SALE

Although there was relatively little major legislation there is an important exception in the statute *Quia Emptores*, which is the basis of our present law of freeholds and particularly the freedom to sell and buy them. Under the original rules of tenure, while holders of land could sometimes transfer it they did not have an unrestricted right to do so. First, as we have seen, the idea of owning land as such was only developing slowly. Of course, people had bought and sold for centuries. In Saxon times, as we saw in the *Fonthill* case, some people were noted as having the right to sell land and the Domesday Book specially records that as a noteworthy feature. Nobles had sold and bishops had bought but not quite in our terms.

When there was a small population and plenty of land it was more important to have the services of serfs and other cultivators than the control of vast acreages. So when nobles referred to selling land or bishops to buying it, they were less concerned about the area and more about acquiring the services of those who worked it. It was of course important to have land that was fertile or well drained but, if there was no one to plough it, good land was no use on its own. After 1066 the doctrine of tenure emphasised the services a tenant owned his lord (and the protection the lord owed his tenant). The relationship of homage and fealty were more important than the land itself.

As peace and prosperity led to growth in population, the situation changed. Farmers competed for land so that if one farmer was disobedient or incompetent, the lord could easily get another. The land itself came to be in short supply. Men did what they could to expand it. This was an age of colonising steep hillsides, of efforts to reclaim marshland and, as we have seen, of assarts and approvement. But such areas were only available because they were the second-best land. Previous generations had chosen the better land which remained in cultivation. So control of that land came to be more important than control of the cultivators.

The existing rules led to a problem. In a world where the identity of the holder and his relationship with his lord are important, he, cannot simply sell land to whoever he wishes. We saw this in connection with military service and the knight's fee where the land was provided for the support of a warrior. He might want to sell a manor to someone else who had a lot of money but would the buyer be loyal and able to fight? Equally if a farmer holding in socage owned ploughing services on the lord's demesne and wanted to sell, the lord had to consent because he needed to know that the buyer could at least steer a plough. So the rule developed that a lord had to give permission for an existing tenant to be substituted by a new one who would then owe the dues and services from the land.

But with time this no longer made sense. As fees could be inherited, then on the death of the holder they might pass to a widow, or a young child. These family members had a right to the land (even if the lord controlled them when they were young and arranged their marriages). As society became more sophisticated, men wanted to be able to sell their hereditary land. A holder might have got into debt. He might have wished to go abroad or spend the proceeds of sale on making a fine house elsewhere. Usually the lord would consent to a sale but only in return for a payment – which could be a big share of the sale price.

But by the same token there was nothing to stop the tenant allowing someone else to hold the land under him so long as he remained accountable to his own lord. It might have been a stranger who was prepared to pay money for the land or the tenant might have given it to a monastery or to his son. Here there was another motive. If the holder kept the land until he died his son would have to pay a relief or primer seisin when he took over and if he was a child the lord would have wardship and take (or sell) the profits of the land until the heir was of age. If the holder remained as tenant he did not need his lord's consent because he continued to owe the seigniorial duties. So he granted a freehold sub-tenancy to his son (the arrangement was known as subinfeudation) in return for an annual rent of a rose at midsummer. If he died, the lord was entitled to collect his dues calculated by the value of the holding. He could take the revenues but the right to receive midsummer roses was not worth much. Likewise, the holder could subinfeudate on a sale for an immediate payment of the purchase price and an annual rose. So the lords lost out, and the greatest loser was the king. Edward I wanted to take steps to protect the royal revenues but the landholders were unwilling to give up rights which by then they regarded as established.

These issues were resolved by a compromise in the statute *Quia Emptores* 'Whereas purchasers of land …', one of the earliest Acts of Parliament, passed in 1290. It gave effect to a deal. First, the Act prohibited future subinfeudation or the creation of new mesne lordships in fee simple. (It was still possible to subinfeudate other types of freehold.) Whenever in future a tenant in fee died, his lands would be subject to seigniorial dues which, for the time being, could not be avoided. In return, the statute provided that the landholder was free from the need to obtain the consent of his lord to a sale by substitution. That did not initially apply, at least in theory, to situations where the king was the immediate lord but with time it became the case. So freeholders could freely sell or give away their land. Over the centuries, intermediate or mesne lordships tended to disappear and eventually nearly all land became held directly from the king and dues became a royal tax.

The result of this freedom to sell and buy was significant in the shaping of the landscape. Unlike a tenant of villein land, a lay holder of a freehold (whether knight or cultivator) could, after 1290, sell it in pieces, could divide it between buyers or aggregate it with other land. By this time, manors were fixed and their boundaries could not be altered because they were seen as units of custom, and people could not freely change the boundaries within which customs operated. But any holder of a piece of land held in fee simple, either within or outside a manor, could now sell without restriction. A buyer with access to money could build up fields from strips; he could acquire land for building or merge two farms to make a larger one or sell off an unwanted part of the farm. The process took time but in the long run the idea that freehold land was freely alienable allowed towns to expand and farms to change in shape and size.

The rules were different for the Church which, as we have seen, had lost a lot of land to soldiers in the tenth and eleventh centuries. So the Popes, who in Rome were claiming the power to make laws for the whole Church, enacted that ecclesiastical lands must never be sold.[2] The land was held in mortmain and was always free of the payments due on death and succession. The price for that certainty was inflexibility. The boundaries of an estate, once given to the Church, were fixed. The estates and farms of laymen might be altered but the landscapes of monastic or bishops lands tended to become fossilised.

An outright freehold did not meet all needs, particularly where land belonged to a family rather than an individual. We will look at family settlements in Chapter 11. Here I need only say that there was a variety of arrangements to secure inheritance rights. One was the position of a tenant for life, often employed in that context. Another was that if a man died then his widow could occupy or take the rents from one-third of his land for the rest of her life under the right of dower – whether or not she remarried. (There was an equivalent right for widowers by the 'courtesy of England' called curtsey.) Where someone held land in that way his rights were limited. In particular, he could not do anything

---

[2] A long series of provisions, including Canon 44 of the fourth Lateran council in 1215 and culminating in a papal bull *Ambitiosae* 1468 of Paul II.

that damaged the land or affected the interests of an heir who would become fully entitled to it.

An example is the case of *Mortimer v Thorpe*.[3] William de Mortimer held the manor of Scoulton in Norfolk. He died in 1297 leaving a son, Constantine. His widow, Alice, married John Thorpe, who was a royal judge. Alice (and therefore her husband) had dower in Scoulton. Dower gave the right to enjoy the land but not to do permanent damage. In particular, the life occupant could take botes – underwood and fallen branches – but not fell timber trees. In this case, Constantine complained that his mother and step-father had caused widespread damage to lands, houses, fishponds and inhabitants by ruining a building worth £10, and a stable worth 100 shillings, by felling and selling 400 great oaks worth 10 shillings each and 2,000 smaller oaks, by uprooting 2,000 saplings, felling 400 alder trees, 100 maple trees 400 beeches and 60 apple trees, by digging pits and selling the clay, draining fishponds and taking the fish and expelling two villeins from the manor. These round figures are estimates but they indicate the size of the devastation.

The Thorpes defended the case. They did not dispute the facts. No doubt they were evident to any one who visited Scoulton and indeed the royal writ directed the sheriff to go in his own person to the lands. Instead, they claimed they were simply taking their normal botes and the reasonable profits from the land. The court was not persuaded and they were held liable and in mercy, that is subject to a penalty.

The rules that developed between 1215 and 1348 still form the basis, although much altered, of our own laws of secure occupation of land, of the way it is inherited from one generation to the next, of the way disputes are resolved and the way rights to land can be transferred. Medieval law was not ours. That is not just a question of language – although it took many years for the Latin and old French to be put into English. More important are the differences in the way people thought and their attitude to society. In the following chapters we will see how significant changes came after the Black Death.

---

[3]   (1313) Year Book 6 Ed II ed Vinogradoff and Ehrlich Selden Society (1917) 91, 94.

Chapter 9

Security and Property – 1348 to 1660

APPARENT CONTINUITY, UNDERLYING CHANGE

The Black Death reached England in 1348 and killed somewhere between a third and a half of the people. It brutally solved, for the time being, the population problem and eased the pressure on land. Over the following centuries the population increased until it surpassed the former level, but by then the economy had developed.

To outward appearance much of the countryside hardly altered. In the champion country, many open fields laid out in strips remained until the nineteenth century. In the woodland areas, the ancient banks enclosed arable or pasture where they had been for centuries and sometimes are still today. Where in the thirteenth century coastal marshes had been reclaimed and converted to arable land, it continued to be cultivated but only towards the end of this period was there much new drainage in the Fens or elsewhere. Roads were few and rarely in repair. After the expansion of the thirteenth century, towns stagnated under the hereditary control of a handful of burgesses, London being the major exception.

Yet behind the apparent stability there were deep changes. In towns and villages in the fifteenth and sixteenth centuries, modestly affluent citizens built new houses and others converted medieval halls to comfortable private homes. After the Dissolution of the Monasteries, newly rich men pulled down the emptied abbeys and put up their own mansions. There were new business structures in commerce which needed workshops and offices. There was consolidation of holdings so that where once the lord had shared the open field with twenty tenants, now half a dozen farmers managed the strips.

In the same way, the law of landholding seemed at first sight hardly to change. The Writ of Right and Novel Disseisin were, in principle, the basis of legal claims and remained so in theory until the Real Property Limitation Act 1833. Tenure was in law the abiding principle of holding land so that James I and

Charles I enforced seigniorial dues as a source of royal revenues independent of Parliament. Yet, like the physical landscape, so the intellectual one of law saw hidden changes. The last reported, unsuccessful, case of a claim that a man was a villein was in 1617.[1] Villein land was held by free men, often by investors from a nearby town. It became known as copyhold because the evidence of the holder's title was a copy extract of the court roll of the manor which recorded his purchase or inheritance. Other land was held on lease and the occupier was called a termor because he held it for a fixed term. The development of the writ of trespass transformed the status and security in their land of the yeomen of England. These were the small freeholders, leaseholders and copyholders – people who were neither great nor humble. They obtained security to build houses and lay out their fields. The whole economy changed from one based on a system of self-supporting manors to a more commercial world. Trespass reflected the law of men of business.

There was no need to invent new forms of law for the new conditions. That had been done in the creative period of the high Middle Ages. Instead, lawyers took the old materials and gave them a new substance. Judges (the greatest of whom was Sir Edward Coke) did not so much shape as reshape the law. In so doing, they prepared the way for the triumph after 1660 of private property. Parliament, which included many lawyers among its members, adapted medieval rules and sought to control the power of the king.

England remained an agricultural economy and therefore society, politics and military force were still controlled by a tiny aristocracy. However, in contrast to the time before 1348 when the country was dominated by seigniors and ecclesiastics, and the time after 1660 when the squires managed their own estates without interference, this period gave to ordinary farmers, sometimes called the middling sort of men, a security and certainty they were not to know again until the twentieth century.

One reason was that on the battlefields, from Crecy in 1346 to the New Model Army in the Civil War in 1649, knights bearing swords and charging on horses did not decide the conflict: winning depended on ordinary men, the yeomen, using long bows or muskets. They included small freeholders whose land was worth 40 shillings a year who were entitled to vote in elections to Parliament, as well as termors and copyholders who were not. The logic of society meant that the powerful had to take account of those on whom power and wealth depended. Power itself at this time belonged to the kings. They gained the support of the gentry and the farmers while weakening the aristocracy. Great men who sat in the House of Lords were of course important, but in the Wars of the Roses many noble titles were forfeited and at the Dissolution the abbots were removed.

---

[1] *Pigg v Caley* (1617) Noy R 27, 74 ER 997.

Power came to depend not so much on lordship as on royal favour and the rulers could rely less on great lords and more on the gentry who sat in the House of Commons and on the yeomen who voted for them. The law reflected this and in a time when wealth still depended on farming, the law protected the farmers who fought.

We need to consider two particular developments. Both appear to involve purely legal issues but both had long-term importance for the way great landowners and more humble occupiers alike controlled, worked and built on the land, and for the security they enjoyed and the rights of inheritance they could pass down the generations. One, which I consider in this chapter, was the way the judges adapted the writ of trespass to protect the termor and the copyholder and indeed the freeholder. The other, discussed in Chapter 10, was the development of the use (which later became the trust) both before and after the Statute of Uses to simplify land transactions within families and on sales to strangers. By contrast, the developments we looked at in earlier chapters, the freehold, the corporation and the manor, were less evident. They were still there and still important but once the ideas had been worked out they did not, for the time being, need further refinement.

LEASES

The Black Death killed so many people that there were fewer mouths to feed across the country and therefore less demand for grain but the same amount of arable land to grow it. So prices fell. Many of the assarts which had expanded arable into marginal land were no longer needed and their occupiers abandoned them. As death rates among villeins were so high and as those who survived could escape from their ancestral villages to others where their status was unknown, there were fewer farmers left to cultivate the land. Lords who needed labour to run their own demesnes found there was no one available. They found it uneconomic to farm in hand and they came to prefer that others should take the business risks of the market.

They therefore turned to leasing. They could not attract men to farm the traditional villein holdings on the harsh terms which had applied before 1348 and which, in the competition of an overcrowded island, men had been obliged to accept. The rule that no new customary tenures could be created after 1189 reflected a real difference in the letting of land. Although ancient villein tenements could be granted out again as copyhold on the same terms to a new occupier, any rights to occupy demesne land or land which the lord had bought had to be as freehold or by agreement on lease. Bracton, in the thirteenth century, discusses the difference between villein land and conventional agreements.[2] In practice, most agreements were on standard terms but in theory they were the subject of negotiation and the terms (unlike fixed customary holdings) could change from time to time.

The result was twofold. First, lords were glad to get men to run the smallholdings vacated by dead or departed villeins on whatever terms they could. They would accept any competent farmer with no questions asked. If the man was himself a villein from a distant manor, escaping the law, the new lord (or landlord as he now became) took him for the sake of the rent he would pay. He in turn was prepared to pay rent in cash under a lease from selling his produce in the market, but not to give labour services in week works and boon works labouring on the lord's land (as described in Chapter 6). So what had been tiny subsistence units – and in the early fourteenth century it is common to find holdings of half a virgate, 15 acres – became less common. A commercial farmer, even on a small scale, needed more land and legal security in his occupation of that land. Farms became bigger (although still small by our standards) and began to occupy substantial parts of the countryside, either as collections of strips scattered through the open fields or as adjacent closes, as single units. On copyholds, the lords commuted the services in kind for fixed quit rents which came to be eroded by inflation.

Secondly, as the lords gave up running their own demesnes they put them to farm. This expression, which is the origin of our modern term for food production, meant that the landlord granted out the land for a firm or fixed period. (Another explanation derives the word from the Old English *feorm* or food rent but that is less likely as Latin *firma*, not English, was used for the document which set out the terms.) The Domesday Book mentions manors which had been put to farm[3] so that a lessee ran it in place of the lord but after 1348 there was a new approach. The lord leased the demesnes to an experienced farmer, often the former manor bailiff who had previously run the business for him. The new farmer was interested in the land he could control – the arable and pasture. He did not want the bother of dealing with the manor court, with collecting various payments such as fines and amerciaments, with procedures for assembling the homage and so on, but these still had to be done. The village affairs still centred on the manor court (now divided into court baron for freehold tenants and court customary for the copyholders) and the court leet but the commercial tenant paying a rent wanted something different. The business of the court became run by a steward who, in time, came to be a lawyer practising in a nearby town.

---

2 Bracton, Henry of, *de Legibus et Consuetudinis Anglia* (SE Thorne (ed)), f 168, vol 3, p 33.

3 Eg Pettaugh Suffolk 440 v.

COMMERCIAL FARMING AND INVESTMENT

In many parts of the country, profits from commercial farming were less in crops than livestock. Even before the Black Death, English sheep were profitable and much royal revenue depended on taxing wool.[4] But, in the Hundred Years War with France, Edward III needed to attract wealth and to discourage any support that the wealthy communities of the Netherlands could give to the French. Flemish towns, such as Bruges and Lille, had grown rich on trade, including taking English wool and weaving it into cloth so adding value to a product they could sell at a profit. Edward got his Parliament to pass laws encouraging the production of cloth in England[5] and encouraging foreign merchants to come and work here, thus encouraging industry in the towns and creating more wealth, which then became invested in land.

Wool remained a valuable export. The great monasteries, with their international connections, were in the forefront, and dealt on a large scale with Venetian merchants who found it worthwhile to buy fleeces in vast quantities, which in turn meant wool production on an industrial scale. Instead of the eleventh-century herds of pigs, lords or their tenants now ran sheep. All across the country, wherever the land was suitable, fields were converted to pasture, smallholders put out of their lands and a single shepherd sat where once a whole community had lived and worked.

The matter became a national scandal. A famous denunciation was made by Sir Thomas More in his *Utopia* published in 1516 in which he says:

> your sheep, that were wont to be so meek and tame, and so small eaters, now, as I hear say, be become so great devourers, and so wild, that they eat up and swallow down the very men them selves. They consume, destroy, and devour whole fields, houses, and cities.[6]

Contemporaries saw that numerous beggars were on the roads. Modern historians believe that this was because by the sixteenth century the population was again growing and many young men were unemployed. A farm would only support one son where three had grown up and so the younger ones left for the hope of a better life and job in the town. At the time, people believed that they came from being thrown out of their holdings by rapacious landlords who were trying to enclose ancient farms for sheep walks. In 1517 and 1518, Cardinal Wolsey as Lord Chancellor initiated over 200 prosecutions in the Court of Star Chamber, many of which ended in conviction. There were indeed large scale

---

[4] Eg 11 E3 (1337).

[5] Eg 27 E3 c 4 (1353).

[6] *Utopia*, Book 1, adapted from Robinson's 1551 translation.

changes in many farming areas and in a rough age some were made by force. However, the evidence suggests that even though some whole villages became deserted, many of them had failed economically though changing markets and exhausted soil. Although no doubt some profiteers were deterred, the efforts of the government did not wholly succeed. Members of Parliament were elected from the shires and were ready to tolerate enclosures by their neighbours even if they did not do it themselves. Wolsey needed to get some taxes passed by the Commons and, as part of the deal to do so, abandoned his prosecutions.

Enclosure was not just for sheep: as the horse-drawn plough began to replace oxen a close could be a more efficient method of farming arable land than a strip in the open field. I will look at the general enclosure movement in Chapter 12. Here, I consider the terms under which farmers occupied the enclosed lands, either in the champion country or the lands in the woodland areas which had never been open fields. The initiative was with freehold owners. If they were great landowners, they did not want to carry on the business themselves. Even lesser proprietors might not be able to do so if the land belonged to a widow or young children, so they leased out the land to someone who did want to carry on the business.

At the same time there was another pressure for change. Although, in general, towns did not expand nor were new ones founded, there were still prosperous merchants. A first generation trader made his money in town and kept it there but his sons and grandsons wanted something different. There were no stock exchanges or insurance policies and land was the only safe means of storing wealth or building up status in society. A man who had made his fortune and wanted to be sure that his descendants would be secure and respected had only one way of doing it: he had to put his money into land. The land might be freehold but if that was not available he might take a copyhold or a long leasehold.

Both the investor and the working farmer needed one essential, namely security. The buyer of a lease or copyhold wanted to be sure that his money would be safe and he would not lose his purchase (and with it his rental income) to an overbearing landlord or an evicting lord of the manor. The tenant needed to be sure that he would be able to remain in occupation. Freeholds were safe, although the legal remedies to protect them were the now antique and expensive procedures of Novel Disseisin and the like which, after centuries of legal complications of the sort described in Chapter 1, had lost their speed and efficiency. Neither leases nor copyholds enjoyed proper security. As land became more important to men of modest substance, who had the knowledge and the money to fight cases in the royal courts, they sought a better way.

EJECTMENT

The solution was the development of the action of trespass into the procedure known as ejectment. It worked by protecting the rights of leaseholders as a type of property and was then extended to copyholders and freeholders. This is one of the greatest creative achievements of English law. It has not been fully reflected in the Continental systems based on Roman law where, even now, a lease is regarded primarily as a contract, not as creating a form of ownership of land. This sometimes causes problems in incorporating European Union law into our system.

Copyhold rights depended on local custom and could only be enforced in the manor court. That court was run by or on behalf of the lord of the manor and initially the copyholder could not appeal from any arbitrary decision of the lord's steward to the royal courts however much it was against custom. Traditional lords, such as landed families and monks, tended to respect ancient rights but if the lord was determined to evict a farmer in order to enclose, then the copyholder was left without a remedy. He could not use Novel Disseisin because although he was seised he did not have a free tenement since even though he was personally free, his land was not. After the Dissolution of the Monasteries, when many manors came into the control of new men, many of whom had made their fortunes in a tough world, the position was even less secure.

Leases, by contrast, depended on an agreement which granted possession and not seisin. A leaseholder or termor could not use Novel Disseisin either but in his case it was because however free the tenement itself, he was not seised but only possessed of it. The normal remedy for a broken contract is a payment of damages. Thus if the landlord evicted the tenant, the tenant had a claim for money compensation. That was not adequate where the investor had bargained for the right for himself or a sub-tenant to occupy the land itself. Furthermore, if a stranger (someone who had no existing relationship with the lease) evicted the tenant, he was even worse off. His lord was not at fault and he had no contract with the stranger on which he could sue. It is possible that many unscrupulous lords, who had granted long leases and then found a more profitable use for the land, conspired with a stranger to evict the tenant, but even without such abuses the position of the tenant was weak. Yet leases were becoming more common with rich men investing in them. A prospective landlord, wanting to attract a tenant, needed to be able to assure him that he would be protected in his occupation. Therefore, the law had to change so that the leaseholder became, for the duration of his lease, more the owner than his landlord.

The procedures were worked out by judges and the royal Chancery over the centuries. The technical details are set out in specialist legal histories and here I need only summarise the development in broad outline. By the end of the twelfth century, a termor could bring an action of covenant against a landlord who had broken the contract and evicted him. Around 1230, a new writ, *quare ejectit infra terminum*, 'because he was ejected before the end of his term', allowed a termor to recover the land from someone who had bought the land from his landlord.

Meanwhile, a new remedy was emerging, in the form of the writ of trespass. The word 'trespass' simply meant wrong as in the Lord's Prayer 'forgive us our trespasses as we forgive those who trespass against us'. In legal terms, trespass began as a crime. It was a way that royal officials kept the peace by punishing those who broke the law and the writ alleged the trespass had been done 'by force of arms against the peace of our lord the king'. It could be used in three ways. One was trespass against the person – assault. The second was against goods – mainly theft but also damaging goods or simply detaining them wrongfully. The third was trespass against land. Land disputes were the most serious and most liable to lead to private warfare so the king's officials needed to control it. Anyone who interfered with the peaceable possession of land committed the offence.

At the time, the line between what we would now call criminal and civil procedures was blurred so a litigant could seek to use what started as a criminal procedure to assert his rights. As it originally related to crime, it was a matter for the royal courts. Under the Possessory Assizes such as Novel Disseisin, an artificial meaning had, as a result of hard fought litigation over the centuries, been given to the idea of seisin. By contrast, interference with the right of a leaseholder to farm his land or live in his house, that is to possess his land, was a fact. If someone simply entered on private land, perhaps to damage buildings, the holder of the land (whether leaseholder or freeholder) could take an action called trespass *quare clausum fregit*, 'because he has broken into his close' (although it could be used not only to defend a close but also crops in a strip in an open field), but that was not sufficient to recover possession.

The next step was a form of trespass called *ejectione firmae*, trespass 'by the ejection from his farm', that is his leasehold. This could be brought against anyone who ejected the termor but he could only get money compensation. The rightful occupier did not recover possession of the land. However, during the fifteenth century the judges began to give a remedy to recover the land itself and this was upheld by a case in 1499.[7] As a result leaseholders were able to use this new efficient procedure but freeholders, who were in theory obliged to use the

---

[7] *Anon* 14 H7, noted in Fitzherbert, Anthony, *Natura Brevium*, 220 H.

Writ of Right or Novel Disseisin, could not. As we have seen, if the law laid down one procedure it was not open to a litigant to seek to use another devised for different circumstances. But the lawyers found a way.

They did so through the ingenious device of ejectment. This reached its full development in the eighteenth century but, since its origins were earlier, this is a convenient place to describe it. It worked by the use of a legal fiction. Suppose Henry Brown claimed freehold land of which William Smith was in occupation and did not want to use the old actions. If they had been rival leaseholders, Henry could have used the procedure in trespass which was quicker and more efficient. He was not allowed to do so directly but if he granted a lease and his tenant was ejected from the land, then the tenant could use it. As the procedure developed in its classic form, Henry pretended to grant a lease to an imaginary John Doe. Henry's lawyers then wrote a letter to William describing the lease, how John Doe had entered the land and had been thrown out by an equally imaginary tenant of William's called Richard Roe. Indeed, the letter pretended to come from him and he told William that he did not intend to defend the claim but would leave it to William to do so, the letter ending 'your loving friend, Richard Roe'. The judges allowed the parties to go through this rigmarole so that they could use trespass.[8]

Just as a tenant for years or a freeholder could use trespass, so, in the course of the sixteenth century, the royal judges allowed the copyholder to do so and thereby conferred security. Because villeins, so long as they existed, were supposed to do personal services for their lords, they were forbidden to leave the holding, so they could not let it on lease. That restriction continued to apply to copyhold land. However, during the sixteenth century this came to be seen as unjust. The judges developed the law to presume a general custom that allowed copyholders to lease their land for a year and so fictitiously to do so to an ejected tenant. As the remedy depended on the claimant being a leaseholder it did not matter whether his landlord had a freehold or copyhold. Once copyholders could assert their rights indirectly through a fictitious tenant and the action of ejectment, they could defend their titles to the copyhold in the royal courts instead of the manor court.

CONSEQUENCES OF SECURITY

The result was to confer security on all sorts of landowner – as we can now call them. Anyone, whether a great lord with large estates, a gentleman owning a handful of farms, a small freehold farmer, a tenant either for 30 years or from year

---

[8] See Blackstone, Sir W, *Commentaries on the Laws of England*, 3.203.

to year, or a copyholder, had protection under the same law. If anyone tried to interfere, these landholders could go to court and get a judgment in their favour which they could then get the sheriff to enforce. They had security of title.

This provided a firm legal basis for what used to be called the Great Rebuilding. Castles and churches survive from the earlier Middle Ages, as do a few manor houses and town houses of prosperous merchants and occasional farmhouses, but large numbers of ordinary houses found in towns and villages and on farms across the country begin to date from this period. The process was spread over a long time and, where once historians saw it as concentrated in the sixteenth century, recent research has shown it as more diffuse. Over time, solid structures replaced the simple shacks in which most people had lived until then. Houses of stone, brick and timber were expensive to build and could only be put up once the builder could either accumulate or borrow enough and a lender, as explained in Chapter 11, needed security. Plate 4 shows some cottages built in 1557. No one would go to the cost and trouble of building a house, shop or tavern unless he could be sure that either he, or his family on inheritance, would keep it long enough to recoup their investment or would ultimately be able to transfer and sell it, or preferably both. The ability to sell depends on good title. Unless a buyer (with proposals for a new house or new field layout) can be sure that, if he (or his rent-paying tenant) is evicted from the land he had bought he will be able to go to court and get it back, he will not spend the purchase price in the first place.

There was a parallel development in contract law. Here again there were medieval procedures in the action of Covenant but they were as cumbersome as those to recover land. Instead, the courts developed a new remedy of Trespass on the Case, known as *Assumpsit* on the basis that a party had assumed responsibility for his performance. The result was, for instance, that a building contractor and a landowner could make a contract to erect a house in the knowledge that if the landowner did not pay or the builder did not build, the other had a swift and simple remedy in the courts.

By the nineteenth century, the procedures fashioned with such trouble were looking absurd and political philosophers such as Jeremy Bentham lampooned them ('A fiction of law may be defined a wilful falsehood, having for its object the stealing legislative power, by and for hands which durst not, or could not, openly claim it; and, but for the delusion thus produced, could not exercise it'[9]). By then they were overdue for replacement by something more rational, but in their time they changed the face of England.

---

[9]   Bentham, Jeremy, *Works*, vol 1, p 243.

In particular, ejectment conferred such security that 'an Englishman's home is his castle'. The expression comes from *Semayne's Case* in 1604, where the judges resolved:[10]

> And in this case these points were resolved. 1 That the house of everyone is to him as his castle and fortress, as well for his defence against injury and violence, as for his repose.

Those words in Sir Edward Coke's report lie behind the saying that an Englishman's home is his castle. It is no figure of speech. The court was literally extending to each householder the legal protection once enjoyed by a lord within his moat.

Peter Semayne had a claim for repayment of money he had lent to George Berisford. Berisford's goods were in a house in Blackfriars in London on which he and Richard Gresham had a lease, and when Berisford died it became Gresham's alone. Gresham refused to release the goods to Semayne to sell to repay the debt. Semayne therefore applied to the sheriff to break into the house to seize the goods but he did not get an order from a judge allowing him to do so. At Gresham's request the court forbade it. If the door was open or if the householder invited him in, the sheriff could enter or if the court ordered possession he could break down the door but he could not, without a court order, use force to enter on the property of another.

This rule was coupled with the now ancient law in Magna Carta that a free man need only answer for his land in the courts and the security which all, whether freeholders, copyholders or leaseholders, enjoyed. These together made up the idea of property as a basis for national life. Property could belong to humble men as well as great, to townsmen as well as country dwellers. Within his property an owner was sovereign and could do what he wished with his land. This idea came so to govern our approach to the countryside that it still affects the way, for instance, that we plan buildings or control pollution.

---

[10]   (1604) 5 Co Rep 91a, 77 ER 194.

Chapter 10

Law and the King – 1348 to 1660

DISSOLUTION OF THE MONASTERIES

This period saw the use of Acts of Parliament in a way that had not been contemplated before in order to make a truly revolutionary change in the law. We saw how the power of the Anglo-Saxon kings had been bolstered by the Church, which had built up a jurisdiction parallel to the king's courts. Now that link with the international Church centred in Rome was broken. The Ecclesiastical Appeals Act 1532[1] (often called the Act in Restraint of Appeals) established that in England there was to be one supreme system of law, a situation that lasted until the passing of the European Communities Act 1972.

The details of the Reformation settlement are beyond the scope of this book but one immediate change which affected the development of the land law was the Dissolution of the Monasteries in 1536 and 1537. When Henry VIII broke with Rome he needed, even more than his predecessors, the support of those who counted in the country, not just the nobility but even more the gentlemen. He also wanted money. The Church had, since Saxon times, been extremely wealthy and monasteries held something like a quarter of the land of England, although much of that was uncultivated moor and mountain.

Henry and his councillors used Acts of Parliament to dissolve the monasteries and abbeys and forfeit their lands. Using Parliament in itself was not new: it had frequently intervened in such matters but never before on so great a scale. Vast areas passed from the Church to the Crown. By dissolving the abbeys and taking over their lands, much of which he then sold, the king achieved several things. He obtained their wealth for himself. He removed what many of his subjects had come to see as an anachronism. Above all, by passing over the lands to his more prosperous subjects, he bound them to the new Church order. If there was a conflict between their lands and their faith, the king was clear which would win.

---

[1]   24 H8 c 12.

So it proved when after his death his daughter Mary tried to reverse the Reformation and she had to accept that monastic lands would not be restored.

Some of the lands passed to courtiers and other investors. New landlords replaced institutions which had run their manors and estates for centuries and they had new ideas about land management. The old abbeys fell into ruin, some of which, such as Fountains Abbey and Rielvaux, remain to be visited today. Others, such as Buckland Abbey, were turned into private houses. Many monastic buildings were quarried for stone to build new houses. So with legal structures: some of the Church lands passed as intact units but others were parcelled up or combined so that ancient estate boundaries changed. These arrangements came to form the nucleus of some of the novel types of estate which were to control the countryside until the nineteenth century.

As we have seen, the boundaries of an estate, once given to the Church, were fixed and the land was held in mortmain. As society changed, pressures built up over time. The Church had met these by granting leases of land to farmers or neighbouring gentlemen, who came to hold Church land on lease as part of their own estates. The laws against alienation had not entirely held up the productive reorganisation of land. At the Dissolution the Crown sold much of the land freehold. An existing occupier was often in the best position to buy his land. Other estates came to speculators who intended to resell and lands changed hands again and again until the market settled down.

The purchasers saw themselves as owning the land in a sense which the abbots (who had no children to inherit after them) had not done. For a time the sudden flurry of transactions gave land more the character of a thing that could be bought and sold than of an unchanging inheritance. *Quia Emptores* had in some ways anticipated this attitude by allowing free sale of freeholds, but that applied only to the lands of lay subjects. The effect of the Dissolution was that potentially any land (even though once it had been given to pious causes forever) could come on to the market. Other sales of traditional Crown land, both by Henry and by his daughter Elizabeth, added to the supply. Even though after 1660 land was to resume its character as a long-term inheritance, the way people understood the nature of land had changed.

THE STATUTE OF USES

This linked to another issue which partly derived from the same causes as had led to *Quia Emptores*, namely a device known as a feoffment to uses. It allowed one person (or, more often, a group of people known as feoffees) to hold land 'to the use' of another (the beneficiary or *cestui que use*). The land was apparently in the name of the feoffees and their rights to it would be upheld by the common law courts so that if the beneficiary claimed the land against them, the common law judges would uphold their legal claim. This could work injustice and the Lord Chancellor, who was said to keep the conscience of the king and who had the power to do justice according to equity in his own court of Chancery, would enforce the use and compel the feoffees to deal with the land on the beneficiary's behalf.

The use seems to have existed in Norman times[2] but it was developed to provide land for a new type of building, the friary. In 1208, St Francis of Assisi founded the order of Franciscan Friars. They were committed to poverty and unlike orders of monks which could own their abbeys and estates through a corporation comprising the abbot and chapter, the friars were forbidden to hold property. They became popular preachers and expanded across Europe. They needed buildings, most often in towns (unlike the more rural monasteries) for churches and hospitals. They attracted the charity of wealthy townsmen who wanted to give them land. The solution was to put land into the name of nominees or feoffees to the use of the friars. The feoffees held the land and allowed the friars to occupy it or take the income. Many of the religious buildings which filled medieval towns were held in this way.

Another benefit of the use related to sales. The complexities of title were such that it could take lawyers months or years to sort out the formalities. So the buyer would pay over his money and go into occupation. The seller retained nominal title pending completion of the formalities and held it to the use of the buyer. As we saw in the context of the Chew Stoke title guarantee, the Romans had a similar system and it was subject to the same abuses. The seller might want to repudiate the deal, or he might die and his son might want to get the land back. In order to give the buyer security, the Lord Chancellor, by a development similar to the procedure we saw in Roman times about the *traditio*, and probably influenced by it, granted the buyer the right to enforce the use.

A private landowner could likewise take advantage. If he expected to be out of the country for a long time, he could put the land into the name of feoffees who could manage it for him. If he wanted to give the land to his son while the son was a child, a spendthrift or irresponsible, he could ensure it was properly run. At a time when land could not be left by will, a landowner could create a use to the same effect by giving it to feoffees, who would ensure that instead of the land automatically passing on his death to his legal heir, normally his eldest son but sometimes a disliked or incompetent relative, it went to whoever he decided and he could even control how the land passed in future generations. Such a

---

[2]   The Domesday Book, Bedfordshire 210V Wyboston. See Maitland, FW, 'The Origin of Uses', in *Collected Papers*, vol 2.

settlement employed the use to create a succession of life tenancies. These could include provision for the estate to change hands on a future event which might or might not occur, called a contingent future interest or contingent remainder. An example might be 'I give my manor of Dale to my feoffees to the use of my son John for life but if he shall become a Roman Catholic the land shall be held to the use of my son Edward for life'. The use was said to shift from John to Edward.

However, the use had another function which harmed the king's revenues. *Quia Emptores* had stopped the old device of avoiding seigniorial dues by subinfeudation and, incidentally, led to the disappearance of mesne lordships, so that by the sixteenth century most freehold land had become held directly of the king. Landholders still wanted to avoid dues, especially wardship, and their lawyers developed a new method. A landholder granted his lands to feoffees to hold to his use during his life and then to the use of his son. When the father died, the king had no claim to his dues or to wardship of the son because the legal tenant was a group of feoffees. They had not died so the young heir was not subject to the law of wardship, and he could be brought up by someone his father trusted not someone who had paid the king a lot of money for the right to despoil the lands. The feoffees also decided whom a daughter would marry instead of someone who had bought the right from the Crown.

Henry VIII needed to defeat what he regarded as tax avoidance. In 1535, Parliament passed the Statute of Uses which executed most uses, that is it transferred the fee from the feoffees to the beneficiary who became the legal owner. Accordingly, when the beneficiary died the king was able to claim his wardship and other rights. Judges, who were appointed to do the king's will, kept uses under control so long as seigniorial dues were important for Crown revenue.

A side-effect of the use and the Statute of 1535 was a method of simplifying conveyancing. If there was a contract for sale, and the money was paid, instead of the seller retaining title to the use of the buyer, the buyer automatically took title. This was known as bargain and sale. It was a simpler procedure than feoffment at a time when, following the Dissolution, a lot of land was on the market. Indeed, it was too easy for land to be transferred secretly or even by mistake. In addition, the king needed to know who the landholder was in order to recover his dues. The Statute of Enrolments[3] therefore provided that bargains and sales had to be enrolled in a public registry. Buyers and sellers did not like having their dealings known and the solution was another fictitious lease. If a lessee was already in possession of the land and was acquiring the freehold, publicity and therefore enrolment were not necessary. The seller granted the buyer a lease for a year and the next day released the freehold to the lessee

---

[3]   27 H8 c 16.

without publicity. Bargain and sale with lease and release became the standard means of transferring freeholds. In time, of course, it came to be seen as an outdated procedure, but executing a use was so simple that Parliament only finally abolished the procedure and repealed the statute, as well as the by then long obsolete procedure of feoffment, in 1925.[4]

The Statute of Uses had long-term consequences for retaining family estates. This will be considered later, but one aspect was that when it abolished the device of giving land to feoffees to the uses of the owner's will, the result was that on his death it passed automatically to his legal heir. Landowners had become accustomed to varying such rules by making a will and in 1540 the king responded to pressure from Parliament and assented to the Statute of Wills which allowed a testator to dispose of freehold land. As a result, the will of a wealthy man came to assume an importance which, over the centuries, has been fully exploited by novelists to set up or resolve their plots.

Another aspect for family estates concerned contingent remainders. The law required that there had always to be a landholder in possession or with the right to take the rents. When the Lord Chancellor recognised shifting contingent remainders, that did not affect the rule as the feoffees to use were the legal owners throughout. When the statute executed the use, the common law judges accepted that contingent remainders could still operate so that the freehold itself could now shift from one life tenant to another depending on contingencies.

A third aspect was to lead to trusts which I will also consider in the context of estates. In 1646, after the Civil War, Parliament abolished seigniorial dues.[5] That was one of the few acts of the Interregnum confirmed on the Restoration by the Tenures Abolition Act 1660, which converted virtually all freehold tenures to socage and abolished wardship and other dues. After 1660, therefore, there was no longer any need for the prohibition on the use. The judges could not disregard the Statute of Uses but they came to recognise something which was a use in all but name, that is the trust. The trustees could hold land on behalf of beneficiaries.

---

[4] Law of Property Act 1925, ss 51, 207, Sch 7.

[5] LJ Vii 183, 24 February 1645/46, Ordnance for Removal of the Court of Wards.

PROPERTY, STATE AND SOVEREIGN

As the sixteenth century passed into the seventeenth, a more fundamental issue came to light. The Tudors ruled by the grace of God but their considerable power was exercised under and through the law. For that reason they took care to ask Parliament to change it when necessary. James I, and even more so, Charles I, had a more elevated understanding of their role by virtue of the Divine Right of Kings, embodied in the idea of the sovereign. The king was the summit of society and, more important to some, was anointed and recognised by God as being responsible for the care of his subjects. Although he could not change the law, he could determine how it applied in cases of public need and the judges did his will. If the realm was in danger it was for the king to take measures to defend it and, in the view of Charles I (upheld by the judges in *R v Hampden (the Ship Money Case)*[6]), only the king could decide if there was such a danger. If there was he could call on the resources of the realm without needing to rely on taxes which had to be voted by Parliament. The *Ship Money Case* concerned the right to demand a financial contribution, but where wealth came from land, an attack on men's purses was seen as an attack on their property and therefore on their stake in the country. The representatives of the country in Parliament saw themselves as reflecting property interests and they felt under threat from the king's claims.

Charles I did not, and would not have wanted, to attack property as such. The Crown was the greatest landholder and Charles himself sought to raise revenues by draining the fens, exploiting the forests and increasing rents of Crown farmland. But his subjects were concerned at the extent of his demands. They worried that a powerful king who could collect revenues without reference to Parliament could override their rights in their own lands. Ship money was an instance of that. Landowners also resented the exploitation of seigniorial revenues, such as wardship through the Court of Wards.

This concern to defend property was important among the issues which led many otherwise loyal men to take up arms against the king in the Civil War. The concept of a strong ruler as head of a commonwealth was argued by Thomas Hobbes in his book *Leviathan* published in 1651. He based it on the idea of a social contract and seems to be referring to a literal contract drawn up according to seventeenth-century English formalities[7] by which the members of society in primeval times (perhaps corresponding in our terms to the Neolithic Age, although Hobbes was not concerned with actual prehistory so much as an

---

[6]   (1637) 3 St Tr 825.

[7]   *Leviathan*, Chapter 14.

idea) delegated the conduct of affairs to a sovereign head. The concept goes back to the Roman lawyers.[8]

The outcome of the mid-century struggles was that property, that is private ownership of land, became the most important value in political and national life. Hobbes' book was countered by John Locke in his *Second Treatise on Government* in 1689. Locke also accepted the idea of the social contract but considered that it could be varied by the parties. He had a more historical approach to the contract.[9] He was more emphatic about the importance of property and his ideas were influential.

The importance of property was not restricted to gentry and the owners of estates. Each landowner's home, however humble, was his own castle and he could do whatever he wanted with his land so long as it did not harm his neighbour. This complete control affected the way men saw the landscape and could alter it. Subject to the constraints in family settlements, which I consider later, and to the terms of any lease or copyhold customs, a landholder was free to put up or throw down a building. A great landowner could move villages, create or remodel parks, and plant or fell woods. Where several landholders together controlled all the interests in a piece of land, as was the case for some open fields or common wastes, they could get together to divide it up and reorder it without reference to any welfare of the wider community.

In 1660, Charles II was restored to his throne and apparently to power. Most men thought that Parliament, although it asserted itself, had nevertheless been relegated to something like its former subordinate position, but all was not as it seemed. On 22 April 1668, Samuel Pepys wrote in his diary:

> I by water from the Privy-stairs to Westminster Hall; and, taking water, the King and the Duke of York [his brother, later James II] were in the new buildings; and the Duke of York called to me whither I was going? And I answered aloud 'to wait on our maisters at Westminster,' at which he and all the company laughed; but I was sorry and troubled for it afterwards, for fear any Parliament-man should have been there; and will be a caution to me for the time to come.[10]

Twenty years later, James would not have thought it funny either as in 1688 the Glorious Revolution led to his expulsion by Parliament which, now supreme, offered the Crown to William of Orange and James's daughter Mary. The result was that if Parliament could unmake and make kings it could do anything. In particular, it could interfere with or at least redistribute rights of property so

---

8   Digest of Justinian, 1.4.1.1 (Ulpian).

9   Chapter 8.

10   Pepys, Samuel, *Diary*, 22 April 1688.

long as basic rights were protected. We will see how, over the centuries, it could authorise major changes in the landscape.

Parliament was seen as representing the realm. England was by no means a democracy: the very idea was abhorrent to most people both high and low. The people were represented by those with the greatest stake in the land, those who had property. There was a sense of unity from the greatest lord to the humblest cottager who knew his place in a settled society. This was not wholly new. From the time of the Hundred Years War, a feeling had developed that the people were one nation. Nationalism as we now understand it is a concept of the nineteenth century, but long before that men were proud of their country. After the Glorious Revolution, people came to feel that England was special. They expressed it as adherence to the three ideas: first, that England had a free constitution supported by a Protestant Church; secondly, that all Englishmen had a right to liberty; and, thirdly, that the prime duty of the law was to protect property.

People did not yet have the idea of the state as we understand it and therefore there was no state power to reorganise the landscape such as came to be exercised in the twentieth century. In Parliament, peers and commoners represented those with a stake in the country, but government was still the duty of the king. We saw how the idea of the law of the land had, in the thirteenth century, replaced the older idea of the law of people. At this time legal rules related to the kingdom or the realm or the commonwealth rather than to the state. The sixteenth-century political writer Niccolo Machiavelli used the word *stato* in the context of the North Italian cities in which he lived. His book, *The Prince*, was widely read in England. Even he more often used 'principality', 'territory' or 'kingdom'. He did not see the state as an entity distinct from the individual ruler or, in the case of a republic, from a collection of governors. People used the word to refer to a public state of affairs and in republics, such as Venice or the United Provinces of the Netherlands or, later, among the states of North America, they had to develop a collective concept, but it was not understood as a legal person in its own right distinct from the individuals who ordered affairs. At a time when people of status were educated in the classics, state was seen as much as anything as a translation of *civitas*, a legal community of leading men or a 'distinct political society'.[11] Although it could be used to refer to what we call state machinery, such as the armed forces or government agencies, it did not yet have the overriding power that emerged later.

After 1689, those with established power did not wish to alter either the constitution or the property laws which preserved the power of their family by determining the way their estates passed down the generations. But, as society

---

[11]   *Hepburn v Ellzey* (1805) 6 US 445.

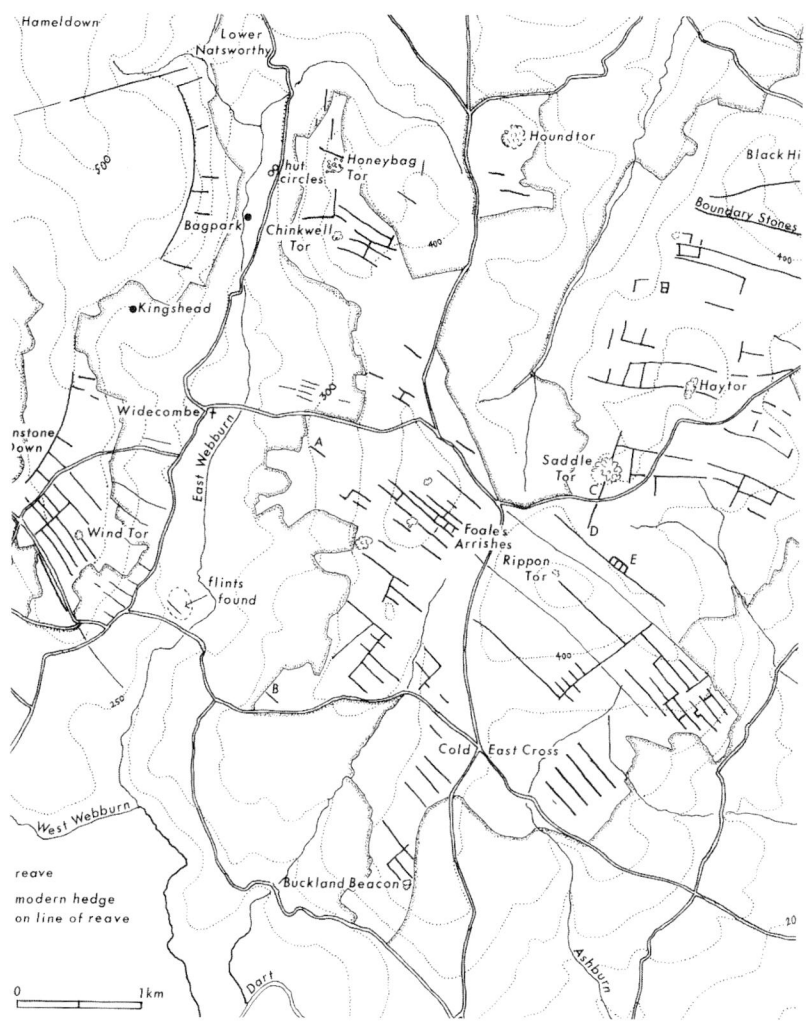

1. A map of part of the Dartmoor reaves (courtesy of Andrew Fleming from *The Dartmoor Reaves*)

2. Reconstruction of houses in Verulamium (courtesy of Guy de la Bédoyère from *Roman Towns in Britain*)

3. Offa's Dyke (courtesy of Clwyd-Powys Archaeological Trust)

4. Cottages in Church Street, Goldalming, Surrey (courtesy of Hugh Turrall-Clarke)

5. Tyntesfield House, near Bristol, once the property of William Gibbs now belonging to the National Trust (courtesy of Topfoto)

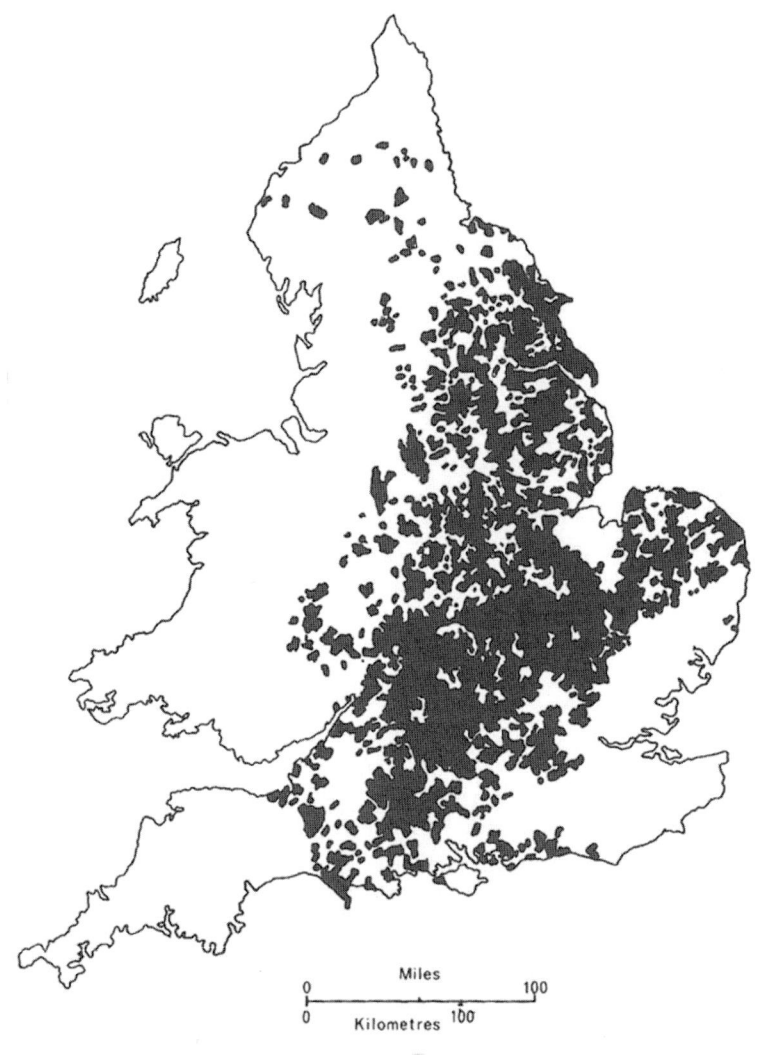

Miles
0   100
0   100
Kilometres

6. Map of Parliamentary Inclosure in England (courtesy of JA Yelling from *Common Field and Enclosure in England 1450-1850*)

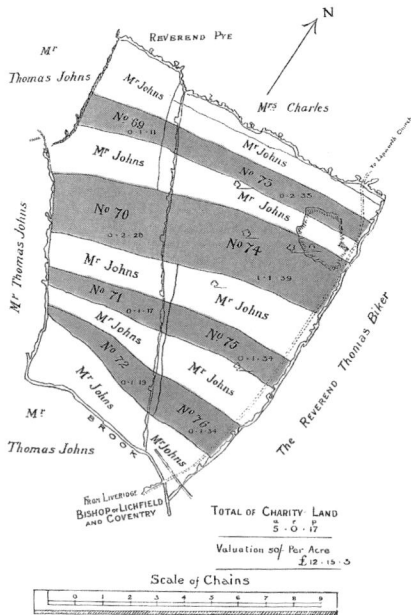

7. Strip fields in Lapworth, Warwickshire, from *Memorials of a Warwickshire Parish* by Robert Hudson

8. The Wey Navigation with railway bridge over it near Guildford, Surrey (photograph by the author)

9. Old road in the Surrey Hills (courtesy of Hugh Turrall-Clarke)

10. Stagecoach on Shepherd's Hill, Haslemere, Surrey
(courtesy of Haslemere Educational Museum)

11. The Mill at Saltaire circa 1880 (courtesy of Topfoto)

12. Birmingham Town Hall with the Alpha Tower behind (courtesy of Craig Holmes/Images of Birmingham)

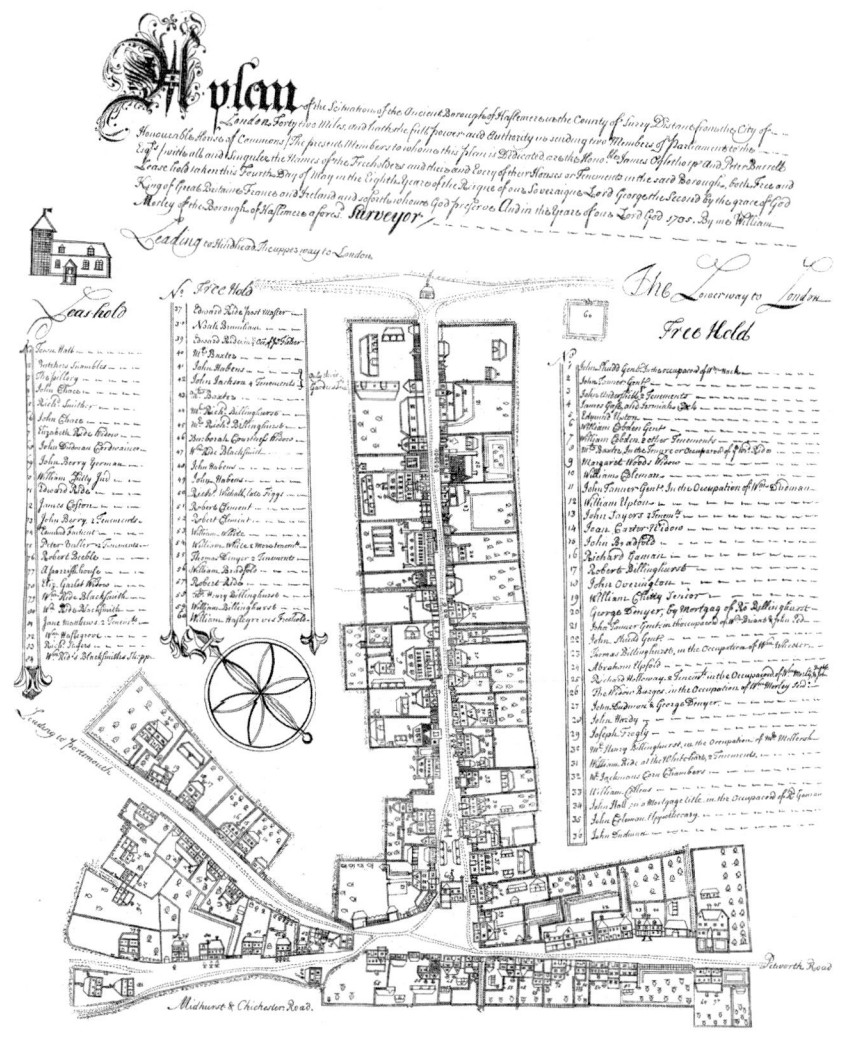

13. Map showing burgage tenements in Haslemere (courtesy of Haslemere Educational Museum)

and the economy changed, there had to be some way of reordering the landscape to meet the needs of industry and a growing population. I will look at the way that was done, but first I will consider the role of the settled landed estate, how it came to control land and how it was itself brought under control.

Chapter 11

Landed Estates – 1660 to 1900

Landed estates have given wealthy men and women power to control the landscape since Iron Age times, but in the eighteenth and early nineteenth centuries this control was exercised to a remarkable degree. In 1688, the aristocracy and gentry, working through Parliament, evicted King James II and over the next few years they took over the government. Their estates provided a source of wealth and the new ideas of what was implied in ownership of land allowed them to dominate the countryside, where most people still lived. This was accepted as a matter of course. Humbler people were expected to show deference to the squire and most of them believed that they should accept their station in life. There were of course independent farmers and small tradesmen working on their own freehold land, but over time many of them had to sell out to the wealthy, who then leased out the land and buildings on terms they decided. Such folk depended on the landowners for their livelihood either indirectly as labourers for the farmers who rented their farms or directly as domestics in the great house or working on the estate as gardeners or gamekeepers.

With power went responsibility and the squires protected the countryside on which they relied. Many loved and improved the landscape, as indicated by the care with which they laid out their parks, designed farmhouses and arranged coppices not just for hunting but also because they contributed to the view. But money spoke and, if there was a chance of profiting from development, then the landowner would take it. We will look at the developments brought by enclosure, undertakings and industry in the following chapters. Often, the great proprietors initiated those schemes. They wanted to rearrange the fields, build canals and railways and open mines in order to enhance the prosperity of their estates and therefore their own income.

However, this freedom conflicted with a different aim. In order to ensure that successive members of the family would uphold the ancestral status, it was essential to retain intact the estate on which wealth and power depended. This was done by using the judicial interpretation of the Statute of Uses to create future interests. These were combined with a tenancy for life in a settlement in such a way that in each generation there was a single head of the family who concentrated power but who could not do anything which prejudiced the inheritance rights of his successors. Therefore, because of a disposition made by his ancestor, he could not sell land to a canal or railway company or agree to exchange strips in the open fields farmed by his tenants. He could not even work minerals, fell timber or alter houses.

One of the major features of estates, therefore, is the way their identity continues down the generations. Some were inalienable by law, others by choice, and in this chapter I will look at the legal machinery for making them so. The result was that any given extent of countryside, from a few hundred acres to many thousands, retained a unity and coherence for centuries. This affected the design of buildings, the placing of villages and whether or not they could expand, the arrangement of farms, the layout of fields and even the colour scheme for painting doors and windows. I will focus on the affairs of the wealthy, but that wealth came from the work and intelligence of labourers, shepherds and farmers, and some was spent on the services of surveyors, architects and builders, all of whom contributed to the landscape.

THREE TYPES OF ESTATE

There were three types of estate, although they worked in similar ways. One was the estates of the Crown, which in the Middle Ages was the basis of royal income and therefore power. Once comprising up to a third of England, over the centuries much of it passed to private landowners. In the sixteenth and seventeenth centuries, the Crown sold off more of their lands. By 1700 this became a source of concern. Members of Parliament were worried by the generous gifts they thought William of Orange had made to his Dutch friends and they passed the Crown Lands Act 1702 to prevent the disposal of any Crown or government land. The Act is still in force but now affects little more than the inalienable royal parks and palaces. By the eighteenth century the Crown Estate, while extensive (which it still is in the twenty-first century) was not the dominant element it had been.

The second type of estate was institutional. This included Church bodies, such as cathedrals, as well as the glebe lands of a rector. There were others including schools, colleges and endowed charities. Like the royal estates they were run purely for income. They were also (with some exceptions) inalienable and so their bounds were fixed. As we have seen, by canon law Church lands could not be sold in the Middle Ages. At the Reformation, that law became subject to the general law of England, which allowed any land to be sold. If this was allowed to take its course the effects would be troublesome. A vicar could sell off his glebe or a bishop his estates and then there would be no income for his successor. So Elizabeth I's Parliament passed the Ecclesiastical Leases Acts in 1571 and 1575 which effectively prevented any sale. Colleges and most other charities were restrained by their own statutes or the terms of their original endowment from selling. Even where a town corporation had power to sell borough land there might be opposition from freemen who wished to exercise grazing rights over the town meadow or disport over a communal open space.

The third and in this period most evident type of estate were private family estates. Sometimes they were residential – that is the squire had his 'seat' on his estate, but estate and seat were distinct. In 1722, the journalist Daniel Defoe undertook a journey and he wrote about it in *A Tour through the Eastern Counties of England 1722*. In speaking of Suffolk he says:

> In this part, which we call High Suffolk, there are not so many families of gentry or nobility placed as in the other side of the country. But it is observed that though their seats are not so frequent here, their estates are; and the pleasure of West Suffolk is much of it supported by the wealth of High Suffolk, for the richness of the lands and application of the people to all kinds of improvement is scarce credible; also the farmers are so very considerable and their farms and dairies so large that it is very frequent for a farmer to have 1,000 pounds stock upon his farm in cows alone.

For his seat, the owner wanted an attractive landscape, perhaps with a view of hills or trees and waterfalls, with good communications to the local town and to London. It might be surrounded by an area called a park, often derived from a former deer park. Even if there were no deer left and the land lost its franchise status, most people still referred to the land as a park.[1] For his estate he wanted prosperous farmers with flat, well-drained land able to yield a steady rent. But being human, unlike the Crown and the institutional owners, he could develop an emotional attachment to the family estate. That explains attempts by many a twentieth-century owner to keep his estate intact even after it had lost its financial and political purpose.

THE STRICT SETTLEMENT

In order to concentrate their wealth in a line of male heirs, landowners used the settlement. The intention was to make the estate inalienable. It was only partially successful but it did work well enough to retain the structure of estates and the wealth and power of great families for 250 years.

---

[1]   *Howard's (Sir Charles) Case* (1626) Hutton 86, 123 ER 1119.

Because the Statute *Quia Emptores* permitted any holder of a fee simple to sell his land, private landowners could not simply prohibit any sales as such. There has always been a conflict between those who want to tie up land, to rule their heirs from the grave and arrange matters so that the family estates cannot be broken up, and those who have inherited those same estates but need to sell. There can be many reasons. One is to pay off debts. Another is to exploit part of the value, to work minerals or cut trees, because they are part of the land. Another reason is the disobedient heir. A son who knew that he was going to inherit the estates might not show proper respect, so his father needed to be able to use the threat to disinherit him.

This conflict appears in Anglo-Saxon times. I mentioned the law of King Alfred that where a land had been granted as bookland to a man on the terms that it remain with his family, then he could not leave it to someone else. We saw that the *Fonthill* case may have turned on this issue. By the thirteenth century there was an arrangement called the *maritagium* which, as the name suggests, could be made on a couple getting married. It provided that land given, say, by the bride's father to his son-in-law could not be sold if the couple were childless. However, the judges accepted that once a 'cry was heard within four walls' the restriction ceased to apply so that even if the child died after a few days, the land belonged to its father, who could sell it and keep the proceeds.

In 1285, Parliament passed the statute *De Donis*[2] which established the entail. Entails were known on the Continent and this brought them into English law. Because an entail was fee tail not fee simple, *Quia Emptores* did not apply to it. Initially, entailed land could never be given or sold away from the family as long as there were heirs. There were various types of entail. The most usual was tail male where land went from father to eldest son. If there was no son, then the right to it was traced up and then down the male line until a male heir could be found. For instance, Henry established an entail and had two sons. William the elder had one son, Walter, and Walter had one son, Wilfred. If Wilfred died without any son (it does not matter how many daughters there were), then on his death the lands would pass to the senior male descendant of Henry's second son, Edward. Another type was tail general, under which if there was a son, he inherited and if not all the daughters (or their husbands) inherited equally. There was also tail female but it was rare in practice.

No sooner were entails established than a generation grew up that wanted to break them. One reason was the new conditions after the Black Death when families died out or their circumstances changed and they wished to sell. More important in the eyes of many was the need to control heirs or, if the holder had no son, to prevent the land going to a nephew. So in the course of the fifteenth

---

[2]   13 El Stat Westm c 1.

century, landowners got their lawyers to find ways to break or bar entails. There were two main ways of doing it. One was by a warranty of title, sometimes reinforced by a collusive action of covenant known as levying a fine, but that only barred people descended from the person who arranged the action, so that if his own direct heirs died out but there were collateral heirs of the original holder to inherit, the barring was ineffective. That meant that even many years after the fine was levied and the land sold, the grandson of a cousin (who was now entitled) could claim it from the buyer's grandson. A more effective method which did bar collateral relatives was the Common Recovery, a collusive Writ of Right. Readers of novels were familiar with these issues and for instance the dramatic climax to *Sybil* by Benjamin Disraeli turns on the distinction. These collusive actions were recorded in formal documents many of which are beautiful examples of the art of the legal scribe. They involved applications to court with the parties represented by counsel and a host of formalities so that only rich families could afford them. A third even more expensive method was by obtaining a private Act of Parliament.

By the fifteenth century, it was established that any entail could be barred by a collusive action (except for the rare cases of entail by Act of Parliament). This suited the freer economic conditions of the time, but by the seventeenth century it was against the wishes of the squires who wished to settle their estates for the future. They wanted a secure system of inheritance. The solution was the Strict Settlement devised by Sir Orlando Bridgeman who was one of those who 'betook themselves to conveyancing in the time of the Civil Wars'.[3]

Bridgeman had to work against the rule that it was not possible to create an unbarrable entail or tie up land forever. His clients wanted at least to ensure that their immediate descendants would retain the estates, and not sell them to pay off debts or divide them among their own children. *The Duke of Norfolk's Case (Howard v Duke of Norfolk)*[4] in 1682 illustrates both the attempt and the limits. Until the Perpetuities and Accumulations Act 2009, this famous case was taught to law students but it has now lost much significance. It concerned the way life interests could shift from one person to another and the applicable time limits for contingent future interests to take effect.

It concerned the Howard family. At the time Bridgeman gave his advice, Henry Frederick Howard was Earl of Arundel but shortly afterwards became Duke of Norfolk. He had several estates and one of the smaller ones was the barony of Gostock and Burgh in Cumberland. The earl's eldest son, Thomas, was in poor health and unlikely to marry. By convention or possibly under an existing settlement Thomas had to inherit the main family estates. The earl expected his

---

[3]   Blackstone, Sir W, *Commentaries on the Laws of England*, Book 2, c 11.

[4]   (1682) 3 Ch Cas 1.

second son, Henry, to outlive his older brother. The earl wanted to provide for Henry during Thomas' life but also that if he did indeed succeed to the title and main estates, a third brother, Charles, would get something. He asked Sir Orlando to draw up a scheme to achieve this. Bridgeman complied and the documents were completed on 21 March 1647. The terms provided that Henry would have a right to Gostock and Burgh during his life but, if Thomas died without children in Henry's lifetime, then that estate should pass from Henry to Charles.

The earl (by then duke) died in 1652. Henry was well aware of the arrangements but wanted to keep Gostock and Burgh. He got his own lawyers to prepare some documents to make him entitled to it. Thomas died in 1677. Henry took the main estates and Charles claimed the Cumberland property. The case turned on whether the father's wishes and Sir Orlando Bridgeman's drafting would prevail or whether Henry's later devices had upset them. It was fought through the courts for several years. In the end the judge, Lord Nottingham, decided that Bridgeman's arrangement worked. He agreed that there was a rule that land could not be tied up forever with possible future contingencies for shifting interests, but that there was at the time no clear law as to how long it could be settled. It was not necessary to decide that in this case. At the very shortest it had to be for the lifetime of a living person, namely in this case Henry, and so the provision worked.

In fact, it appears that there must have been some form of family compromise because in 1684 Henry sold the Barony of Burgh to Sir John Lowther. Perhaps the legal costs had been so great as to exhaust the value of the estate. However, whatever the effect on the Howards, the case changed the law of the land and laid down a new rule that controlled the way in which family estates passed down the generations.

This is the Rule against Perpetuities. As it eventually developed, the maximum period during which contingent future interests could arise under a settlement was for the lifetime of someone living at the time the arrangement came into effect, plus 21 years, plus the period of pregnancy if an heir was then conceived but unborn. The strict settlement worked by combining the position of a tenant for life – the head of the family for the time being who enjoyed the revenues of the estate during his lifetime – with the entail. A tenant for life could only make arrangements to last during his life. He could not sell the land and could only grant short leases.

Suppose Sir John is tenant for life of the Dale Estate and on his death an entail will arise in favour of his eldest son. When that son James is 21, Sir John calls him into the library. They stand looking out over the gardens, over the park beyond, over the farms and woods of the estate beyond that:

One day, my boy, all this will be yours. But not yet. So far I have been paying for you and even given you an allowance. But now that might cease and you will be on your own. When I die you will come into the estate. It is entailed on you and you will then be able to make yourself owner and sell it if you want, but you can not do anything during my life and while I live you will have no right to any money. On the other hand I would like to provide for your mother and your brothers and sisters and safeguard the future. What I suggest is this.

We will get together and bar the entail on the estate. That will make the two of us acting together, I with my life estate and you with your reversion after my death, able to do whatever we want. So we will resettle the estate. I will retain my lifetime rights, and on my death you will also have a lifetime right so you will not be able to sell the land. We will make provision that when I am dead you will pay an annuity to your mother, and you will also have to make payments for your brothers and sisters. On your death there will be an entail to your eldest son, or, if you have no son, a life estate for your next brother and an entail on his sons. In return I will agree to pay you an income so long as I live.

So it happened. In due course, James married and had a son, Jonathan. Sir John died, James succeeded to the estates and, when Jonathan was 21, Sir James called him into the library. 'One day, my boy …'. That is how the great families of England preserved their estates, generation after century. It was a literary commonplace. The plot of Jane Austen's novel *Pride and Prejudice* turns on the fact that the heroine's father, Mr Bennet, was only tenant for life of the Longbourn estate. He had hoped for a son and if the son had arrived and become 21, the family could have made themselves full owners but he only had daughters. After his death, the estate was due to pass under tail male to a cousin, Mr Collins, so that Mr Bennet's daughters would have nothing to live on save a small annuity.

MANAGEMENT AND IMPROVEMENT

The whole purpose of the settlement was to tie up the estate so that no one ever had both the power and inclination to sell it or do anything which could diminish the value to the next holder. The restriction applied not just to sales but to other exploitation. A tenant for life had no power to authorise timber to be felled or mines to be worked. If the estate included manorial demesne strips in an open field, he could not exchange them for other land. He could not safely grant a long lease of a site for a factory because any arrangement he made would cease to apply on his death.

While a formal settlement with life interests and contingent remainders was expensive to set up, it was easy to create an entail. An owner could simply make a will leaving his land to 'my son Edward and the heirs of his body'. If he did so he locked it up as long as Edward had descendants unless the heirs were prepared to find the money for the legal procedure to free it. Even small farms might be tied up in this way. While a tenant in tail (unlike a tenant for life) could take timber or minerals, his other options were limited.

A family could bar the entail if they could agree and could afford it. As George Elliot's character, Mr Brooke, says in *Middlemarch*,[5] 'But I can cut off the entail, you know. It will cost money and be troublesome; but I can do it, you know'. That was accurate for the time the action was set in 1832, the year of the Great Reform Bill, but by the time the book was published in 1872 the cost issue had been largely overcome. Most readers knew that in 1833, Parliament passed the Fines and Recoveries Act which made it much simpler and cheaper to bar entails. This helped wealthy families but they could afford the costs of the old procedure. It was more important for more modest landholders.

During the nineteenth century, Parliament passed more general reforms to enable the development of settled estates. With the wider voting rights after 1832, the power that came from control of land began to be less important; indeed, the function of some estates had simply been to control the rotten boroughs which allowed the owner to nominate members of Parliament. A number of Acts[6] culminating in the Settled Land Act 1882 were passed to give tenants for life power to work mines, fell timber, sell land, grant leases and manage the estates.

Estates were communities. The focus might have been in farming, but they included all aspects of the landscape in the control of the proprietor. They tended to exist in closed manors where the lord owned all the farms and the village and there were no freeholders to be able to take an independent line. These were contrasted with open villages where either there was no dominant squire or, if there was, he might own some of the farmland and the woods but not all the dwellings or land whose owners could sell for housing, shops or factories. Closed estates tended to be in the west of England and open villages in the east, but there are many exceptions.

If the squire controlled the land, he could do what he wished. Subject to the terms of the settlement, he managed the estate by leases for fixed periods of time, such as twenty years, for uncertain periods, such as three lives (the lifetimes of the tenant, his wife and son), or by short-term tenancies. If he decided that he did not want to live next to the village, he could pull down the ancestral home and make a new mansion on what had been a farm or he could move the village, build a new one and transfer the occupiers. If his farm tenants needed cottages to house their labourers, he determined their siting and

---

5   *Middlemarch*, Chapter 84.

6   Principally, the Drainage Acts 1840 and 1845, the Improvement of Land Act 1864 and the Settled Estates Acts 1856 and 1877.

appearance. If he was a huntsman he could plant and protect coverts for foxes and decide where there should be fences and where gaps. If he shot then he could ensure proper game cover in managed woods. He could arrange the trees so as to provide an attractive prospect when seen from his seat. Until the Ballot Act 1872 brought in secret ballots, if those of his tenants who had the vote did not cast them as he wished, he could evict them.

Although many historians no longer consider that there was an agricultural revolution in the eighteenth century, it is clear that many owners tried (however unsuccessfully) to run their estates to produce food by more efficient methods. An enlightened landowner could let farms to progressive tenants ready to use the new farming techniques, and he could put them on the land either at will (on what later became a yearly tenancy) or on a long lease. There were advantages in both and landlords had different views on which was better. If a tenant held at will and did not prove to be a satisfactory farmer, the landlord could give six months' notice to quit at the end of the farm year. On the other hand, short-term tenants had no incentive to make permanent improvements, such as drainage or farm buildings, so a tenant on a longer lease may have taken better care of the farm. Similarly, the farmer may have wanted the security of a long term or preferred the flexibility of an annual arrangement. Rents under leases were fixed, while if the farm was at will they could be renegotiated every year. Both parties may have preferred not to be committed to fixed terms irrespective of whether or not the farm business flourished.

Improvements involved such changes to the landscape as building barns, walls and fences, putting two small fields together or dividing up a large one, making cottages for farm hands and sheds for cattle. The land could be fertilised by applying lime or guano: in the nineteenth century guano became an essential for any enterprising farmer and the money made by its importer, William Gibbs, paid for the building of Tyntesfield House, as shown in Plate 5. There were field drainage systems and farm roads. All of these were expensive and there was a problem in paying for them. Some landlords could afford them, but many had better things on which to spend their money, such as servants, a fine house, balls and dinners. Even if a landlord was ready to improve the land, in the hope of getting a better rent (because it was more productive and the farmer would make a better profit and could afford to pay more), he might not have had the spare money to do so. The system of settlement meant that although the land passed on the squire's death intact to the next male heir (who may have been a nephew or distant cousin), the testator's cash could have gone to his daughters. The tenant for life had many calls on his income from rents – to pay annuities to his widowed mother and sisters, and to provide portions for his younger brothers to fund the cost of a commission in the army or of a clergyman's benefice. He had little to spare to improve the farm.

There were two ways round this. Both involved borrowing: one indirectly through the tenant, the other directly from a banker or investor. The first was for the farm tenant himself to find or borrow the cash to build his barn, drain a field or get his own farm hands to do the work. He would take the land on a long lease at a rent fixed throughout the term (in an age without inflation) at the worth of the land in its unimproved state. At the end of the lease, if the tenant left he might have been entitled to compensation for the value he had added to the land. Parliament provided for this in a series of acts beginning within the Agricultural Holdings Act 1875. Initially, compliance with the Act was voluntary but it provided a model and tenants could use it as a basis for negotiation. The effect was to increase the value of the farm. If, when the tenant left, the landlord still had no cash to pay compensation, he could borrow it on mortgage.

The second was itself a loan secured on mortgage by the freeholder to fund the improvement, the interest being met out of an increased rent for a more profitable holding. We saw earlier that one function of the medieval lease was a form of mortgage, but it was not effective. The purpose of a mortgage is to give security to the lender. From ancient times there have been arrangements for one person who has money to provide it temporarily to another who needs it in return for a payment. The main problem of the lender is to be sure that he will be repaid. If the borrower has no money now, can the lender be sure he will have it later? The solution, for someone who has property, is to say that if the borrower does not repay, then the lender can sell the property and reimburse himself, but the lender can have no better power to sell than the borrower. If the borrower's land is tied up in settlement it does the lender no good, but in the Settled Land Acts, Parliament granted power for a tenant for life to mortgage land to fund improvements.

TRUSTEES

There was still a risk that a tenant for life might raise money ostensibly for an improvement but then misappropriate it. The solution came by adapting a device already developed in the settlement. One method, known as trustees to preserve contingent remainders, was sometimes used to anticipate and avoid the sort of spoiling technique tried by Henry Howard. Another developed out of the need to provide security for widows and younger children. Let us suppose in our account above that Sir James does not pay his mother her annuity. She may be unwilling to sue her son, but in his lifetime Sir John can ask some friends to be trustees for her after his death, so that if his son does not behave, they can move in and either collect the rents or even sell land to provide the widow's money. The trustees were often given a form of lease over the land which gave them power to take over the estate if they needed to. Many of these terms of years are referred to in documents and they can be confusing if the reader does not appreciate that they had nothing to do with any commercial or rent-paying arrangement. As we have seen, trusts could develop after 1660 once the Statute of Uses had lost its original purpose.

Once it was established that trustees could take income or hold capital money in the settlement for the benefit of widows and younger children of the testator, it was a small step to employ them where other money had to be raised for the good of the estate, for instance for building new farmhouses or cottages, reclaiming bogs or fencing heaths. The importance of trustees was precisely that they could be trusted where a family member might not be, and if the money was paid to them they would see that it was properly handled. So if the money for improvements was borrowed, when the loan needed to be repaid the settlement (or the Settled Land Acts) could authorise trustees to raise the money by selling some land.

The involvement of trustees was not just to transform the settlement. Trusts enabled other changes in the landscape because they allowed several people to pool their resources without going through the complications of incorporating by royal charter. Uses had long enabled charities to hold land. As I have already mentioned, an early function was to provide friaries. Other charitable uses survived the Reformation[7] and after 1660 they became trusts. More important in the long term was that trustees could hold land for a commercial purpose, allowing several businessmen to combine their resources to hold property. We will consider commercial trusts in relation to turnpikes and businesses in Chapters 13 and 14. Trustees could buy land or take a lease to operate a mine or build a mill or factory. Their beneficiaries, a number of companions investing together, could be referred to as a company. This was not a separate legal person like the medieval corporations or the modern limited company, but the trustees were still able to operate together as a legal group. Trusts also enabled a different form of keeping land in a family, sometimes called the trader's settlement. When a businessman acquired a town house or a country estate for his son, he could direct it to be held in the name of trustees rather than make the son tenant for life.

The invention of trusts, at just the time that rights of property had become paramount, led to another issue, namely who really owned the land. Was it the trustees who held it in their name? Was it the person who occupied the land or took its rents? Was it in some way the family for whose long-term benefit the trust was set up? The law came to distinguish two types of ownership of land. The nominal ownership, that is the name that appears on the deeds or in the land registry, is called legal title because it is of a type that used to be recognised by

---

[7]   Regulated by the Charitable Uses Act 1601.

the courts of common law. The beneficial ownership, which may be spread among many people, including generations yet unborn, is called equitable because the rule which governed it were developed in the equitable jurisdiction of the Court of Chancery. Much of the time these are the same. If a man or woman uses his or her own money to buy a house to live in there is no obvious problem. But where land is in the names of more than one individual, such as husband and wife or brother and sister, it has become simplest to regard them as trustees. They may hold the land for themselves but their rights may pass to others; for instance on the death of one a share may belong to children. If an owner dies, his executors may become trustees for his family.

END OF THE SETTLEMENT

After the repeal of the Corn Laws by the Importation Act 1846, the government of the United Kingdom was committed to free trade. This encouraged manufactured exports but in return the country freely admitted imports of food. After around 1860, cheap bulk grain came from North America and beef and lamb (in freezer ships) from South America and Australia. English farmers could not compete on price. Agriculture was less profitable, farmers could not pay high rents and the income, and therefore the power, of the great landowning families spiralled down. Owning an estate came to be seen as a sign of success in other fields, as with the Tyntesfield Estate (Plate 5), whose owner bought it and built the house from money made in trade.

At the same time, attitudes to inheritance changed. At one time the power and political influence of the great families came from ownership of land. For instance, if an estate included a rotten borough, as described in Chapter 15, the owner could nominate a Member of Parliament. When the Great Reform Act extended the vote to the middle classes this was no longer possible so those who subsequently came to power did not need to own land. Wealthy parents began to want to treat all their children equally. Other forms of wealth, in bonds and in the shares in joint stock companies, became more important so that land was less so. The Settled Land Acts of 1882 and 1890 conferred powers of sale of land on the tenant for life or tenant in tail in possession. These introduced the idea of a rotating fund which consisted not of specific pieces of property but a more abstract idea of family fortune. That might have taken many forms, as land was sold and reinvested in cash, shares or paintings while the underlying wealth remained intact.

A more significant threat was tax. In 1853, Parliament imposed a death duty known as succession duty but it was modest and easily borne. In 1894, the Finance Act replaced an old and inefficient system of collecting former taxes on death by a modern structure of estate duty on all possessions of the deceased which under various names (most recently inheritance tax) is still with us. In 1909, Lloyd George, the Chancellor of the Exchequer, introduced the People's Budget aimed at destroying the wealth and therefore the power of the landed classes by imposing heavy taxes. It was bitterly resisted, fought out through a general election and finally the opposition of the estate owners in the House of Lords was overcome in 1911 by the personal intervention of the king. Death duties became a major threat to landed estates. They could be avoided by giving away the land three (later seven) years before death. As they were cumulative, so that the richer the deceased the higher the rate of tax, they encouraged dividing wealth among children.

The last straw was the Great War and the death of many heirs in the trenches. All these causes led to many sales. It is reckoned that between 1915 and 1923 a quarter of the farmland of England changed hands.[8] Some of the buyers were wealthy investors (including those who had made their fortunes out of the war) who were able to afford whole estates. More often the estates were broken up. Farm tenants, seizing the opportunity and financed by loans, were able to buy the holdings they and their grandfathers had rented. New forms of mortgage, particularly through building societies, allowed householders to acquire the freehold of the homes they had formerly leased.

This spelt the end of the power of the great landowners, although it did not mean the end of estates as such. Although many private estates were broken up, some survived the agricultural depression from 1860 to 1939, the changes in society and the effect of controls on rents for cottages and farms mentioned in Chapter 16. During the twentieth century they tended to be strapped for cash so that there was little money to pay for new farmhouses let alone a new mansion house and there was neither the desire nor the money to lay out parks or create vistas. Many of those that lasted to our time now operate not as power centres but as businesses, able to pay their way as, in effect, large farms or by providing tourist facilities in cottages, horse riding and opening grand houses. Others are subsidised by royalties from gravel pits or from outside sources, such as dividends from investments or bonuses from financial dealings.

The Crown Estate and the Church Commissioners still retain some of their ancient holdings, although they are much diminished. They are run as, in effect, property companies, and many of their more valuable assets are not farms in the countryside but office blocks and shopping centres. Other former family estates

---

[8]   See Rothery, M, 'The wealth of the English Landed Gentry 1870–1935', (2007) 55(2) *Agricultural History Review* 251–68, Beckett, J and Turner, M, 'End of the Old Order', (2007) 55(2) *Agricultural History Review* 269–88, and Thompson, M, 'The Land Market 1880–1925', (2007) 55(2) *Agricultural History Review* 289–300.

have been passed to charities such as the National Trust or the RSPB and so become institutional. They are exempt from tax so long as they provide a public benefit such as nature conservation or public access. In that form they flourish and continue to have their effect on the countryside.

Chapter 12

Enclosure and Inclosure – 1660 to 1900

In a few places the open fields lasted for a thousand years until, as methods of farming changed in the eighteenth and nineteenth centuries, nearly all of those that remained were converted to closes. Much of the surviving common waste was also divided up. Just as the lords had acted with the farmers who cultivated the land to create the open system, so now their successors together brought it to an end.

This change is often called the enclosure movement. Enclosure, spelt with an e, is evident in the landscape of hedges, walls and fences around fields. The legal word is inclosure, spelt with an i, which means converting common land and common field to private (the legal word is 'several') ownership, free of the rights of others. Enclosure is a description of physical works on the ground; inclosure of a change in legal status. It is convenient to use enclosure to describe the process but here I will concentrate on the legal aspects particularly of statutory inclosure.

Enclosure took place across Europe as enlightened farmers and landowners wanted to change medieval ways of farming. In England, it mainly affected the midland champion districts where open fields had been the rule. In the woodland areas of northern and southern England, much common land became incorporated in farms but the process was more gradual and often did not need the full formalities of statutory inclosure. The clearest illustration of this is a map of England showing the areas affected by Inclosure Acts, such as Plate 6. They comprise a belt of country from Yorkshire and Norfolk on the north east coast to Somerset and Dorset in the south west, with only a few outlying parishes.

We saw that in the years up to 1348 in the crowded island before the Black Death, the processes of assarting and approvement began to encroach on the waste around villages. The enclosure movement started later and the motive was not subsistence farming but commercial agriculture. In that context I quoted the criticism of Sir Thomas More about sheep eating up the land. Sheep farming on a large scale was responsible for much early enclosure and landowners who adopted it could be ruthless in evicting small arable farmers. It was partly against that background that the law came to protect copyholders and leaseholders. Later, enclosure was also used for arable farming or for beef or dairy.

PRIVATE ENCLOSURE

While the lords and gentry were responsible for large scale reorganisation of the landscape they did it because working farmers found closes more profitable to manage and therefore could pay a higher rent. Many of them had to give up the struggle to run small uneconomic units. Others were able to expand through local deals, often of an acre or so at a time.

Suppose around 1530, Walter is farming four adjacent strips A, B, C and D in North Field in the village of Dale. Strip A is his own common law non-manorial freehold passed down his family for generations. Walter inherited it from his uncle and now holds it directly from the king. B is customary freehold and copyhold of the manor of Dale. The holder is free to sell it at will and Walter bought it two years ago. It is subject to suit of court and an annual quit rent of 2 pence to the lord of Dale. C is pure copyhold of the manor. It was formerly villein land and is subject to a heriot of his best beast payable on the death of the holder, a certain entry fee of 5 pounds when he took on the land and a quit rent of 1 shilling a year. It is held, as the manor rolls say, 'at the will of the lord'. Walter bought it last year by a procedure of surrender from the former copyholder and admission in the manor court. D is leasehold of the demesne of the manor. As an isolated strip it is not worth cultivating in hand as part of the Home Farm. The lord's bailiff has therefore decided to let it for a modest rent on its own. Walter negotiates to take it for a term of three lives (himself, his wife and his son) paying an entry fee of 10 pounds and a rent of 6 pence per year.

Walter wants to put all the strips into one close to cultivate the land with a horse plough and put a hedge against the headland at the ends of the former strips. He can only do this if the open field is not a common field but a commonable one. In a common field the strip holders (or some of them) have legal rights of common, which they can enforce in the common law courts in Westminster Hall, to graze over the whole extent of the open field. That is unusual. More often the field is commonable, that is there is a practice, not amounting to a legal right, that cattle can stray from one strip to another without hindrance. If in such a field Walter wishes to enclose his strip he can do so. He can keep out other people's cattle but in return he must cease putting his own stock out in the open field. A field was also called commonable if the rights of grazing were all copyhold and so could only be enforced in the manor court, but in that case they could be released in that court without needing the more formal procedures of the common law.

Assuming he can clear out any grazing rights, Walter is free to do what he wishes with strips A and B. In relation to C, changing the boundaries is in law regarded as waste. This is in the sense of wasting the lord's property, even if by improving it as any change was so regarded by the law. Such action renders the copyhold subject to forfeiture. However, when he took the lease of D he negotiated for the right to put the fields together.

The result is that he will have a (more or less) rectangular field and he pays the lord a total of 1 shilling and 8 pence per year. When he dies his widow or son will have to pay a heriot and a further sum of 15 pounds. If he wants to sell there will be a series of transactions. If he dies before 1540, his common freehold land will pass to his heir, although he could before 1535 during his lifetime convey the land to feoffees to the use of his will. After 1540, the Statute of Wills allows him to leave it by will. His leasehold can be left by will in any case but as it is by reference to three lives it is most likely that it will pass in the family. Both his copyholds will pass according to the custom of the manor, although he may be able to surrender it to the use of his will (copyholds could not be directly left by will until 1815[1]). In the meantime, he regards himself as effective owner of the whole of what is now one piece of land and refers to 'My close at Dale'. In practice as time passes and records are lost, the different tenures of separate parts of the close may be forgotten. As we saw in relation to land taken from the waste, so with former open fields it could be a matter of chance if it comes to be regarded as common freehold, copyhold or leasehold and in a generation there might be a lawsuit about the status of the land. Plate 7 shows parts of some strips at Lapworth in Warwickshire assembled in a close.

Another method of enclosure was exchange. If two or three farmers held strips scattered across the common field they could agree to swap them so that each of them had his pieces of land consolidated together and he could then fence them round. They may have been subject to restrictions if they were copyhold or leasehold so sometimes the farmers would simply let one another into occupation without any formal document. That could give rise to later disputes.

A third method was a collusive court action. If all the people with interests in the land agreed on a redistribution of their holdings they could ask a judge to issue an order declaring that their respective rights were to be rearranged. This was only practicable where there were a few landowners, but where it applied it

---

[1] Preston's Act 1815 (55 G3 192).

was a straightforward means of adjusting ownership without all the complications of normal conveyancing. It could be done through the Court of Exchequer, which was a common law court, but it was more usual to seek the wider jurisdiction of the Chancery to make a decree governing the rights of the applicants.

RIGHTS OVER THE LAND

Sales, exchanges and collusive actions only worked if all the people with rights in the land being reshaped agreed to the arrangements. Often that was not the case. There were three principal sources of difficulty. The first was the ancient rights belonging to others in the locality, derived from the manor and similar institutions. By the eighteenth century these were seen as private rights, not in any sense communal, but they were enjoyed by many folk, often humble in status, proud of their independence and not to be overborne even by a rich landowner. Secondly, there were the rights of the landowner's own family, protected under settlements and other rights related to the estates of the institutions. Thirdly, there were commercial rights.

There were a great many ancient rights. There were rights of common not only over the waste but sometime over the open fields. Such rights included Lammas lands often found near ancient towns where the burgesses had the right to put their beasts out to graze the stubble after harvest on Lammas Day, 1 August. More important were the rights of tenants of the manor, some humble, others more independent, in the waste. The most obvious was grazing but there were also turbary, the right to take turfs as fuel, botes, to take wood for fuel or to repair a house, and so on. They included pannage, the right to put out pigs in the woods, but unlike the great herds of pigs of the early Middle Ages, by the eighteenth century these benefited cottagers with one or two animals.

There were others, such as right of way across the open fields to reach strips. There were many tracks winding across the common. Some were public footpaths and roads across the country which anyone could use. Others were customary ways for local inhabitants to lead their beasts to pasture. Others were private easements of way leading to specific closes or houses. All of these needed to be diverted in the interests of efficient agriculture.

There were rights in the soil, some of which allowed tenants of the manor to take sand or loam to fertilise their fields while others could be exploited for valuable minerals. There were various sporting rights to game or wild birds as well as hunting. The ancient payments of Church tithes still existed. Originally, they were one tenth of a farmer's income, but by this time the law on tithes had become convoluted with detailed rules about different products and holdings. The parson was still entitled to tithe in some parishes. Elsewhere, many tithes had passed to monasteries in the Middle Ages and on the Dissolution they often passed to a layman, typically the buyer of the monastic estate but sometimes to a different person. The tithe owner was entitled to a proportion of the income from cultivated land not waste, but it was an important issue on inclosure of the open fields.

The second source of difficulty involved restrictions on dealing with land. The most important were the family settlements which, as we have seen, were designed to ensure that no part of a family estate, not even a strip or a piece of the common, could ever be disposed of. If the estate was subject to annuities or rentcharges to another member of the family, then the security attached to each piece of land in the settlement when it was created. If the tenant for life tried to give it to someone else, even if land was received in exchange, the rentcharge or entail still attached to the original piece so the person who took it needed to be sure that the rights were released.

Even if there was no formal settlement there could be complications. For instance, if a man died without a will and had no sons, his land passed equally to his daughters. If a daughter was married, her husband owned it while they were both alive and, if he survived his wife, he might have a right to one third of her lands by the right of curtsey during his life. If she died as a widow, her rights passed under her will or to her own children or to the family. So land could easily come to be owned in small shares by many people. For other estates, there were different restrictions. As we have seen, institutions such as the Church or a university college could not part with land, even in exchange for other land of equal or greater value; nor could the Crown. A charity could also have a rentcharge over a piece of land; for instance, in the seventeenth century, a landowner could leave an annual sum of money to provide a marriage portion for poor spinsters of the parish charged on his property.

The third source of difficulty was the commercial rights of occupiers and others. Even if the freehold belonged to someone who farmed it himself, it might be subject to mortgage. If it was let to a tenant, the leaseholder had rights to the land and could not be evicted against his will, even to be given a replacement, so he had to agree to any reorganisation of the fields. There could be a whole range of tenants, with a head tenant having a lease for 99 years, a sub-tenant for 20, and the cultivator in occupation from year to year. If the land was copyhold, both lord and tenant had to agree as well as anyone holding a lease from the tenant. If there were valuable mineral deposits, then someone could have rights to them either under a lease or sale or under ancient custom.

Finally, the difficulties of title were such that it was sometimes impossible even for experienced lawyers to know who did actually own all rights to the land. Someone could be in occupation, farming the land under a lease granted 200 years before for a single payment and no rent. Or the farmer could be paying rent but only to someone with a right to take it for his lifetime, and after that the person entitled could be unknown. It might not have been possible to know who would be the heir until the current landlord died or he could be a child, insane, live overseas, or be a married woman living apart from her husband. The land could be copyhold of a manor where the lord could not be traced.

INCLOSURE ACTS

For these reasons it could be unsafe to proceed to inclose either by agreement or under a court order. In the eighteenth century Age of Enlightenment, many advanced thinkers wanted to sweep away medieval survivals, which in their view prevented the proper running of society. Others were more interested in private profit and the need to put what was seen as idle land to productive use. Nevertheless, the law protected existing property rights, whether of local people, members of the squire's family or commercial occupiers. The way forward, to adjust these rights, was an Inclosure Act.

As we have seen, an Act or statute is a law passed by Parliament which sits at Westminster. Because we are so used to it we do not notice just what a remarkable thing it is that a handful of middle-aged or elderly men sitting in committee in London can decide the layout and ownership of fields in parishes in distant parts of the land. How and why could this happen? The answer is that Parliament could, by changing the law, change people's rights and property. It could do this either on a grand scale, across the whole kingdom, or for individuals or for particular areas. There was no clear distinction between the various matters Parliament had to deal with.

After the Glorious Revolution, Parliament exercised the legal sovereignty that formerly had belonged to the king and could do anything. The landowning lords who sat in the Upper House and the gentlemen who controlled the election of the members of the Commons did not like to upset the existing condition of affairs. They believed that the lesson to be learnt from Oliver Cromwell's abuse of power in the Interregnum was that any change bought disorder and a challenge to property rights. They wanted to run their estates in peace. But Parliament had a power to intervene if needed. It is that power which we will see used to authorise the making of new roads and canals. It could also be applied to the rearrangement of country estates. If the major landowners wanted to do it, then Parliament would help them.

We should not overstate this bias towards the powerful. As much as helping the petty squires of distant localities to inclose their commons, most members of Parliament saw themselves as protectors of rights of property, however humble the owner. While there were exceptions, especially at the height of the two inclosure booms, the first between around 1760 and 1780 and the second between 1800 and 1815, as a rule an Inclosure Bill would not proceed over strong local opposition. The parliamentary procedure did allow the majority to overrule a recalcitrant minority, and this was determined not by the number of individuals but by the value of the land, but Parliament would always listen to an objector who had the money or the time to come to Westminster to address the committee. Many Bills either did not get passed or were not even introduced because those who might have planned them knew there would be trouble.

There came to be an established procedure. First, the promoters, who included the principal landowners affected, took informal local soundings. Although the idea was most often put forward by great landowners, many farmers, both small freeholders and tenants, may have supported a more rational distribution of land and favoured the idea of converting what was seen as useless common waste to productive farmland. In open parishes there may have been no dominant squire. There could be opposition particularly from those who had no legal rights over the land but who, nevertheless, supplemented their living by gleaning in the fields or gathering rushes from the marsh, but they would have little influence.

If the initial explorations were favourable the promoters called a local meeting to put forward their ideas for discussion. If that was also in favour, the next step was to instruct lawyers to prepare the Bill. That could take a long time. The drafting of most of the Bill was not a problem as it would largely be made up of standard clauses. It was the negotiations on local detail which could be difficult and hard fought. The Bill appointed commissioners who were named in it and were responsible for implementing it. Who were they to be? Usually they were the main landowners who in practice appointed deputies to represent them. Which land was to be included? Sometimes only part of a parish was inclosed, even part of a common. It was possible, if the parties agreed, to include ancient inclosures, that is land which had been converted to closes many years, perhaps centuries, before but which would have rough or inconvenient boundaries. There may have been a proposal to allot land for local purposes, as a quarry for sand or road-making materials, as a public ground for recreation or as a paddock to be let out at a rent to be paid for the benefit of the parish poor. Anyone could have an idea for special terms.

Most Inclosure Acts look alike. Much of the wording is identical from one to another. The Bill, after appointing the commissioners and setting out their duties and what happened if any of them died or retired, went on to state what matters they had to consider and to govern evidence before them. There was often a long definition of persons interested, that is those to be regarded as having rights in the process. These could include freeholders, people having rights under settlements, copyholders, leaseholders, those entitled to rights of common or tithes, and so on. There had to be provision if there were any married women involved (who acted through their husbands), any children, persons of unsound mind or any corporations, such as a town council or an Oxford college. There may have been special rules where someone had several properties with different titles. There were lengthy procedural provisions to cover the way the act was to be implemented, including where a jury could decide issues, and for appeals against decisions.

Once the Bill was in shape, the promoters had to find an MP or lord to present it to Parliament and steer it through one or other House. The Bill was read like any other and then sent to committee. If there was opposition, this is where the battle was fought. Many Bills were not opposed and could pass on the nod but some were contested. The committee had to decide, first, if the Bill should go ahead at all, or, secondly, if it could (and perhaps no one objected to the idea as such) how the rights of different parties should be adjusted. The parties appeared, as in a court of law, by their counsel who addressed the committee and the members could then amend the Bill. It was, after all, for Parliament to say what the law (even local law) should be.

Once it had been through the first House it had to undergo a similar procedure in the second House. Again, there was a committee although often if matters had been fought out in the first there was no need for a repeat. Finally, it was passed and became an Act.

INCLOSURE AWARDS

That was just the beginning. The commissioners appointed a valuer to allot lands. He obtained full particulars of all the land and all rights over it recognised by the law. There were of course many practices which had grown up over time and did not produce legal rights. For instance, local people may have gathered berries from the common or a cottager might have grazed her goose on the green. The valuer disregarded those (as a judge would have if the issue had gone to court). In reckoning legal rights he computed the value of the tithes, he found out what was freehold, leasehold or copyhold. He determined rights of way, rights of grazing, turbary, and so forth. He then valued all these rights and how much value belonged to every proprietor involved whether great or small.

Then he prepared a map. Often an inclosure map was the first ever made of a parish, so the valuer had to start by surveying the landmarks, houses, woods and roads. Then he proceeded to redesign the locality, clearing away ancient strips and common lands diverting highways obliterating paths and hedges. Early inclosures might have included village greens, although that was prohibited by section 15 of the general Inclosure Act 1845. He then allotted the lands in proportion to the values. Someone who had rights which were worth eighty-five parts in a thousand of the total value of everything before inclosure would get land valued at eighty-five parts in a thousand of the total value of the land as inclosed. Not all pieces of land were worth the same – some were on good soil or on south-facing slopes, others were boggy or far from the village. So everything was done by value. He then redrew the map, laying out straight lines to distinguish one allotment from the next. He wrote a detailed account of the work, describing each new holding, determining who had rights of way over new roads, who contributed to their upkeep and who was responsible for making the new hedges between the newly designed farmlands.

He allotted new leasehold land for old, to be held by the same tenant from the same landlord, so the boundaries had to suit both. He could allot new copyhold land for old, although in practice tenants often agreed with the lord that the new land should be freehold with a bit of extra land being allotted to the lord in return for releasing his rights.

Most valuers tried to be fair, allotting suitable land to each person affected. In particular, a good valuer awarded to smallholders land which was not too far from their homes. He could not please everyone and some valuers had more regard to the interests of their powerful patrons than was strictly fair. But a professional valuer made his living from this work and if he got a reputation for being too partial he would not get the next job because someone would object to him. He then published a draft award. People could examine it to see whether there were any mistakes or to raise points of valuation. Once the award was either beyond challenge or any legal proceedings were over, the award took effect.

Inclosure then had to be carried out. This was expensive. The new owner had to plant a hedge at least around his boundaries and perhaps also to divide up his fields. He may have had to drain former waste, fell trees, root out gorse and brambles and fertilise the land. Also, the parties each had to find their share of the costs of the process. If a tenant for life under a settlement had no money of his own, he may have had to raise it by selling part of his allotment, so the Act could include power to do that. It is said that these costs were too much for some smallholders who had to sell their allotments, but many managed to clear and fence their land by using their own labour. Sometimes the commissioners allotted land to be sold to meet the expenses of the Act and in such cases one of the main promoters may have bought that land.

From 1756 onwards, Parliament passed a number of general Inclosure Acts which governed various aspects, including one in 1773 which dealt with fencing and boundaries.[2] Broad provisions were included in a series of major general Acts between 1845 and 1859, parts of which are still on the statute book. These set out in standard form many of the provisions which otherwise had to be repeated in each individual Act, but by then the great age of inclosure was over. The Inclosure Act 1836 permitted inclosure without needing to obtain a specific Act if enough of these interested agreed. That freedom was restricted by section 12 of the Inclosure Act 1845 and reversed by section 1 of the Inclosure Act 1852, which required parliamentary authority for any inclosure, although this may have been by order without a full Act. People were becoming aware of the beauty and interest of common land and its value for recreation. Besides, by the middle of the century most of the suitable land had already been inclosed. In 1876, the Commons Act provided that thereafter land could only be inclosed if the Inclosure Commissioners, a statutory body which by then oversaw inclosures, had taken into account whether the proposal was for 'the benefit of the neighbourhood'.[3] After 1876 there were only 29 applications for inclosure, the last being in 1914,[4] and section 194 of the Law of Property Act 1925 in effect prevented any more.

One effect of enclosure was to strengthen the control which the owners of estates, both great and small, had over the countryside and the people who lived there. It defined rights, many of which belonged to the landowners and their more prosperous tenants. By extinguishing common rights and dividing up the open fields, it reduced the scope for landless cottagers to benefit from unenclosed land. Even where a smallholder was allotted land in exchange for his former strips and common rights, he may not have been able to gain the same livelihood from the new arrangement. There is some evidence that this encouraged such people to sell up and move to take jobs in an industrial town and the most likely buyer was the squire.

The enclosure movement not only changed the countryside, it changed attitudes to change as such. In remote villages across the land, people became aware of the power of Parliament to reorganise their lives. Furthermore, the techniques pioneered to enclose the land could be adapted to other purposes. Parliament was asked to pass Works Acts which authorised the construction of what we would call the infrastructure of Victorian England, and it is that we consider next.

---

[2] The Inclosure Act 1756 (29 G2 c 36) and the Inclosure Act 1773 (13 G3 c 81).

[3] Commons Act 1876, s 7.

[4] See *Hampshire County Council v Milburn* [1991] 1 AC 325, at 339.

Chapter 13

Roads, Canals and Railways – 1660 to 1900

WORKS ACTS

The enclosure of open land for more profitable farming was only part of a wider transformation of society and the economy in the eighteenth and nineteenth centuries. There were new sources of wealth in trade and industry and those who established them needed better means of travel and transport than the ancient ways of the kingdom could provide. New roads, canals and railways transformed the countryside. We would call them infrastructure. People at the time called them undertakings and particular projects were known as works. Methods were developed to confer the legal right to carry them out. Those methods could also be used for projects such as a reservoir to supply Manchester, a new cemetery, gas lighting for a market town or a new quay for a harbour, but it was the great transport corridors by land and water which caught the eyes and imagination of the age. The methods involved two legal institutions. I will look at the private works Acts in this chapter and the company in Chapter 14.

Works Acts were necessary because works interfered with rights of property. If people wanted to improve a road, dig a canal or build a railway, they could not just go and do it. That would be a trespass against the landowner, his tenants and anyone else with property rights in the land which could not be overridden even for public benefit without statutory authority.

Private Acts could authorise enclosure but Works Acts involved wider issues. Enclosure involved a limited number of landowners and farmers in a single parish or manor. In principle they could (and often did) arrange matters between themselves and they only asked Parliament for a Bill where that was not possible, in order to displace rights, either public, such as footpaths, or private, such as entails or rights of common, which could not be removed in any other way. Private Bills must include a statement (which has to be proved to the parliamentary officials) that the purposes of the Bill cannot be achieved except by the authority of Parliament.

The nature of works was precisely that they extended over long stretches of country and affected many people, not just in one locality. In particular, they often had to be built in populous towns or needed a lot of land to operate, which might involve taking property from many owners along the route. They were also seen to be more for the public benefit than simply enabling a handful of rural landowners to rearrange some fields. So the promoters needed an Act.

There are a few early instances of statutory powers for works, sometimes financed by the Crown. An Act of 1512[1] concerned bulwarks (sea defences) on the coast. Another of 1523[2] concerned diversion of highways in the Weald of Kent. The reclamation of Plumstead Marshes involved Acts of 1530, 1562 and 1566[3] to authorise the drainage of the marsh land. This was a form of enclosure but, like the subsequent works in the fens of East Anglia under Charles I, it had to be carried out by undertakers albeit under royal authority.

After 1660, lawyers developed the technique of using the power of Parliament. Acts came to be classed in one of two types. One was public and dealt with matters such as taxation, crime, trade or a change in the general law. The other was variously called local, municipal, personal or private. The distinction between the two types was never (and still is not) altogether clear. In principle, public Acts deal with matters affecting everyone in the country while the other sort affects specific localities or people or undertakings, but the boundaries of the two were uncertain and promoters sometimes used a public Act where we might have expected them to use a private one. In particular, promoters of early Acts affecting highways or navigation often used public Acts because they affected the rights of all members of the public.

The modern classification of Acts was introduced in 1797. In the following full year, 1798, there were thirty-nine public Acts, of which nineteen concerned roads. There were seventy-two Acts now classed as local, of which thirty-seven also concerned roads, seven canals (including the Kennet and Avon and the Grand Junction), one a bridge, one a harbour and two drainage. There were also eighty-eight Acts classed as private or personal, of which fifty concerned inclosures. A quarter of a century later in 1825 there were 212 local Acts. Most were roads Acts but there were also canal Acts, navigation Acts, harbour Acts, dock Acts as well as the new railway Acts. Each dealt with specific localities, often very small. In addition, there were improvement Acts, for example one for

---

[1]   4 H8 c 1.

[2]   14 & 15 H8 c 6.

[3]   22 H c 3, 5 El c 7, 8 El c 4.

the city of York and another to lay out Tothill Fields in London. Also in 1825 among the public Acts were those for Pembroke Dock[4] and Regent Street.[5] The landscape kept Parliament busy.

ROAD ACTS

Suppose that around the year 1700 the merchants and landowners in a country town, fed up with the twisting, muddy, potholed tracks which passed for many of the highways of the country, wanted to straighten out a road, embank it and resurface it for public use. Public highways were classified into three types, namely footpaths (travel on foot only), bridleways or driftways (travel with horses or other animals) and carriageways (travel with wheeled vehicles).[6] Roads were already in principle a public responsibility. The Highways Act 1555[7] provided (spelling modernised):

> that the constables and churchwardens of every parish within this realm, shall yearly upon the *Tuesday* or *Wednesday* in *Easter* week call together a number of the parishioners, and shall then elect and choose two honest persons of the parish to be surveyors and orderers for one year, for the works for amendment of the highways in their parish leading to any market-town

Every landholder in the parish was to contribute:

> and every person and carriage above said shall have and bring with them such shovels, spades, picks, mattocks, and other tools and instruments, as they do make their own ditches and fences withal, and such as be necessary for their said work.

During the Interregnum, Oliver Cromwell sought to reform highways law in an Ordinance of 31 March 1654, 'for the better amending and keeping in repair the Common Highways within the Nation'. Although all legislation of the Interregnum became void on the Restoration, Parliament in 1662 passed a new Act partly based on the Ordinance.[8]

But the legal responsibility was to maintain what was already there, however inconvenient it might be. Although some ancient roads had been made by the Romans, most were either inherited from Saxon times or had come into existence more recently. Some had been laid out as a result of a deliberate dedication by the

---

[4]   6 G4 c 36.

[5]   6 G4 c 38.

[6]   Coke on Littleton 56a.

[7]   2 & 3 P & M c 8.

[8]   14 C2 c 6.

authority of a king or abbot. Many more had simply emerged from long use by people regularly passing using the same route to pass from house to house, village to village. They wound across country in no obvious pattern, diverting to the site of a long abandoned farm or avoiding a wood which had been felled centuries before. In some places, they were narrow lanes where travellers had eroded the ground surface until it tunnelled between high banks. An example of such a road in Surrey now long abandoned to traffic, is shown in Plate 9. In others, especially where they crossed waste or open country, roads could be broad expanses of mud or pitted with potholes, some large enough to swallow a cart. Few were suitable for the growing commerce of the age after 1660 and the new designs of carriages, such as the stagecoach shown in Plate 10.

So the promoters wanted to straighten the road. They may have intended to cut off a corner by making a new route across a field and then to close the bend of the former road which became obsolete. Both presented problems. The owner of the field to be taken may not have wanted to hand over part of his property. It was, and still is, easy for a landowner voluntarily to dedicate a piece of land for public use as a highway but he has to agree to the dedication. Sometimes the law presumes he has agreed even if he has not in fact done so but only if he has tolerated public use for a long time. In the age which followed the Civil War which had been to a great extent about property and the liberty which went with it, how could he be made to give it up against his will? The only way was through Parliament, which has power to make any legal change, including depriving an owner of his land. He would of course be compensated but members of Parliament were ready to accept that sometimes the common good could even override rights of property.

The other problem concerned the land cut off and no longer needed for a road. Perhaps the landowner was prepared to give up his land for a new road if in return he could take the old road into his farm. There was and is a rule: 'once a highway always a highway'.[9] There was an ancient procedure under a writ of *ad quod damnum* to divert a highway but it was of uncertain use especially after an Act of 1697 regulated appeals and therefore challenges.[10] A surer means to compel the public to give up the ancient rights that they had to pass over a piece of land, even if it had become superfluous and no one used it, was by Parliament authorising it. In 1773, Parliament authorised a simpler procedure under which the justices of the peace could authorise it.[11]

Bridges need to be maintained and, over the centuries, governments tried to get this done by local landowners. We saw that one of the basic public

---

[9]   *Dawes v Hawkins* (1860) 8 CB 848.

[10]   8–9 WIII, c 16, s 6.

[11]   13 G3 c 78, ss 19–22.

commitments in Saxon times was the *trinoda necessitas* which included bridge repair. Over the centuries this responsibility became attached to the property of great landowners. The procedure was for the jury of a Hundred to make a presentment in the royal court that a bridge was out of repair. If the person named did not agree that he was responsible, he could then appear and defend the case. Thus in *R v Countess of Pembroke* in 1351[12] a claim was made against Mary Countess of Pembroke that she was responsible for repair of a bridge at Braxted Park in Essex and another called Briddynghobrigge at Rivenhall. She claimed that the Rivenhall bridge was a private one set up for her servants to get to a private mill and she had no public duty. She also said that the bridge at Braxted, for which she was responsible, was in good repair. Similarly in *R v Abbot of Abingdon* in 1387[13] the jurors of the Hundred of Ock supported a case against the Abbot of Abingdon that he had failed to repair a bridge and causeway at Marcham then in Berkshire (now in Oxfordshire). His attorney appeared and said that the causeway was not part of the king's Highway and it was maintained by a local arrangement among commoners called Bryggewryghtters by collecting subscriptions. This defence was not accepted.

By 1700 this system was badly disrupted. Two cases, *R v Sir John Bucknall*[14] in 1702 and *R v Duchess of Buccleugh*[15] in 1704 involved an attempt to pin responsibility for maintenance of a bridge at Delamore in Hertfordshire on the local landowners by reason, it was said, that the liability attached to the lordship of the manor. The court accepted that might be the case in principle but the attempt failed because there was insufficient evidence that the lord was liable. Thereafter, the attempt to uphold medieval responsibilities was largely abandoned although it may still exist in a few cases.[16] Most highway bridges now are maintained under statutory powers.

Some bridges were maintained out of charitable endowments. Charitable purposes are described in the Charitable Uses Act 1601 and they include the repair of bridges. As well as a great variety of public benefits including schools, hospitals and almshouses, charities included funds for such public benefits as repair of highways and bridges. The most famous is the City Bridge Trust of the City of London which maintained London Bridge and others from medieval times, although it is now a general charity. The trustees were and are the Mayor and Corporation of London.

---

[12] (1351) (1915) 32 Selden Society 60.

[13] (1387) (1915) 32 Selden Society 13.

[14] (1702) 2 Ld Raym 792 and 804, 92 ER 29 and 37.

[15] (1704) 6 Mod 150, 87 ER 909, 1 Salk 358.

[16] See Highways Act 1980, s 49.

Bridges, although important, are small local features. They pass over rivers and even with their approaches do not take up much room, however prominent in the landscape, and do not involve many landowners. Roads were different. If the local investors wished to improve an existing road and even more if they wanted to make a new one across open country, they needed powers to do so and then the ability to maintain the road once built. The solution, allowing for parliamentary powers, was the turnpike trust.

TURNPIKE TRUSTS

Although the old highways law catered to a limited extent for the repair of existing roads it did not deal with the provision of new ones suited to the commercial needs of the eighteenth century. The natural response at the time was not to invoke either local or central government but to use private enterprise. A group of businessmen could combine to set up a turnpike trust. These were not charities but investments designed to make money. The promoters needed to cover the cost of building and repairing the new road, and make a profit from their investment. They did this by getting authority from Parliament to build new roads or improve ancient ones and to charge tolls to travellers who used them.

Tolls are an ancient form of exaction and go back to prehistoric times. Wherever a powerful man controlled a river crossing or a valley entrance, he could seek to charge travellers. All across Europe the independent nobles of the Middle Ages charged tolls on roads, fords and mountain passes. The English kings were better able to restrict them and most English tolls were (at least in theory) granted by royal favour for public benefit. A few ancient rights, known as toll thorough, survived in some places. This allowed a local landowner who was responsible for the repair of a stretch of road to charge travellers for the cost of maintenance. In most places the public have the right to use the king's highway without payment. Therefore, Parliament had to authorise the road builders to collect from local people the tolls to provide money to do the work.

The earliest turnpike is said to have been established in 1663[17] on Ermine Street (originally a Roman road) but the main development of trusts date from the reign of Queen Anne when initially they were set up by public Acts[18] although later they were created by private Acts. As with inclosure and indeed any other works, the Act (which itself followed negotiations) was only the start of a long process as the road had to be designed, workmen hired and the road built. Once

---

[17] 15 C2 c1.

[18] Eg Hockliffe and Woburn, 1706 6 A c 13, and Devizes, 1706 6 A c 26.

built, it had to be operated and tolls collected. A few toll houses still survive beside roads made at this time. Turnpikes were not a long-term solution as they depended on the ability of private investors to manage the road and there was a temptation to charge high tolls. By a series of changes during the nineteenth century, Parliament wound up the system and replaced it with local authority responsibility.[19]

CANALS AND RAILWAYS

The works procedures developed further with the canals and even more with the railways. The immediate precedents were a series of Acts to improve navigation on existing rivers, by removing obstacles, such as weirs, dredging and raising bridges. Early Acts were concerned with the improvement of existing rivers, for instance in 1651 Sir Richard Weston obtained an Act from the republican Commonwealth Parliament for the improvement of the navigation of the River Wey at Guildford.[20] After the Interregnum, the Act needed to be amended and confirmed and this was done by an Act of 1671.[21] Part of the waterway is shown in Plate 8 where it is crossed by a railway bridge for the North Downs Line constructed by the Reading, Guildford and Reigate Railway Company.[22] In 1698, there were public Acts for navigation of the Aire and Calder Rivers[23] and on the Trent.[24] The first formal canal is said to derive from 1755 when the Common Council of Liverpool (an existing borough which had held a charter since 1207) obtained an Act[25] for 'making navigable the River or Brook called Sankey Brook'. In practice, there was no prospect of improving this little stream except by using to the full the power to make new cuts and the result was a canal nearly 12 miles long which used the Brook for a water supply and, for a short length, as part of the waterway. There followed innumerable canals, improved rivers, locks, tunnels and aqueducts across all parts of the country where they could profitably be constructed, as well as a few ambitious designs which went beyond the limits of prudence, over 5,000 miles in all.

Most of the canals were not trusts but were operated by companies. These are corporations with legal personality separate from their members. Until the introduction of modern companies, it was necessary for them to be formed

---

[19] See Law Commission Report, *Repeal of Turnpike Laws*, February 2010.

[20] CJ, vi, 593.

[21] 22 & 23 C2 c 52.

[22] 9 & 10 V c clxxi (1846) as amended.

[23] 11 W3 c 25.

[24] 11 W3 c 26.

[25] 28 G2 c 8.

either by royal charter or by special Act of Parliament but if the promoters already needed an Act in order to take powers to build and operate the canal, this was no problem. The companies were organised and run by small committees, rather like a modern board of directors. They had a larger class of investor shareholders and if the enterprise was profitable (and most were) they paid a dividend, often a good return on the original investment. The shares could be bought and sold and were in themselves a form of property.

The actual work of digging the canals was done by navigators or 'navvies'. Some were hired by gangs run by a hag-master; others were hired directly by the engineer responsible for the canal. Often the early terms of employment were restrictive so that if a man was hired and then wanted to go to another canal which paid higher wages, he could be brought back. This return to serfdom did not last but the gang system did. Navvies were not common labourers but were skilled in the techniques of tunnelling and excavating. They worked hard as they were paid by piecework according to what they achieved. They were also hard-drinking men who, when they came in great numbers to a country area, could terrify the residents while the canal was going through.

When railways became a practical proposition they were modelled on the canal companies but the investment involved was much greater. The men who dug the railway cuttings and piled up the embankments also came to be called navvies. Once a canal was built, it needed some maintenance and supervision but the major cost was over. Not so with the railways. There were always new expenses: the rails, engines and carriages had to be replaced, stations had to be staffed and repaired and a much bigger workforce was needed.

The promoters of both canals and railways needed parliamentary authority first to acquire the land and secondly to run the undertaking. The route ran across country and while it was often designed to go through the land of a major investor – the Duke of Bridgewater was a supporter of early canals and was able to site a substantial length on his own estates – the promoters had to acquire pieces of land from many owners, large and small. Some were willing sellers; many were not. In practice, the promoter had to reach agreement with each major landowner along the route as the landowner was in a position to prevent its passage though Parliament (especially if he was a member of the House of Lords), but the compulsory powers could be used to overcome the opposition of smaller landholders. As with inclosure, there were many owners, such as colleges or family settlements, who had no power to part with land even if they wished, but an Act of Parliament could override any restrictions on the title. If a railway went across common land (and it might be designed to do so in order to minimise the value of the land to be paid for), then the rights of commoners had to be bought out.

The procedure was based on Inclosure Acts but with a difference. The promoters did not have to represent a majority of the community but they did have to demonstrate a need for the project and of course they had to have the funds to carry it out (or at least they had to appear to do so even if, as events turned out, the money was not enough). They deposited the Bill in Parliament with a map of the lands to be taken, or over which they wanted to have rights, such as rights of access. The maps included limits of deviation so that if there was some obstacle, such as particularly hard rock or unexpectedly soft ground, they could change course slightly without having to return to Parliament for a fresh authority. The landowners sought to restrict this deviation as far as they could so a preliminary survey was important. The Bill included provisions for building canal locks or railway stations and marshalling land. A particular source of debate was accommodation works. A farmer whose land was split in two or users of the public highway which was cut by the work might want a bridge or tunnel to cross the canal or railway. It was expensive to provide these so the promoters tried to keep them to a minimum. Sometimes this had to be fought out in committee. There may have been restrictions on the amount of fares and other details could get into the Bill but their outlines became standard. Many provisions were included in the Railways Clauses Consolidation Act 1845 and the Lands Clauses Consolidation Act 1845 (still in force) from which they could be incorporated into each individual enabling Act.

There were other works, including new and enlarged harbours, sluices in watercourses and marshes, and rivers, as well as reservoirs to supply towns. For instance, in 1816, a number of individuals who had organised themselves as the Company of Proprietors of the Keighley Water Works obtained an Act of Parliament[26] to buy land compulsorily (and incidentally to authorise lords of manors and landowners to sell) in order to create a reservoir to supply the town. The company continued to operate until the Keighley Water Works Act 1867 provided for it to be passed onto Keighley Corporation.

These works were a necessary part of the Industrial Revolution and created an environment which had not been seen before. The new means of communication opened up the countryside in a way not possible with the former rough-surfaced roads. The roads, canals, railways, docks and reservoirs were built not for their own sake, but to link mines and industry with the towns. It is to those we now turn.

---

[26] 56 GIII c 43.

Chapter 14

Industry and Business – 1660 to 1900

During the eighteenth and nineteenth centuries, England became a nation of industry and commerce, and the country had to accommodate mines, factories, offices and shops. Those who constructed them did so in the hope, often realised, of generating profits but they were expensive to make. Their builders needed to have security in their right to occupy the land and put up the buildings and to be able to recover their investment either by sale or out of the revenue generated by the structures. If the works were made by an entrepreneur who intended to occupy them for his own business, he needed to be sure that he would be able to stay in them unmolested and at a known cost so long as he wished, and perhaps have the ability to sell the business along with the right to occupy when he retired.

MINES

There has been mining in England since prehistoric times and its traces are still visible. There were Neolithic flint mines at Grimes Graves in Norfolk. It is likely that they were organised by practices which we would regard as mingling law with religion and social and moral control. In the Bronze Age, the tin of the south west was mined and made its way into tools and weapons on the Continent. This was by exchange or a system of mutual gifts since there was no coined money. The Romans worked the mineral resources of Britain under imperial authority although there could have been some private mines. There were lead mines in the Mendips and iron works in the Weald. The Domesday Book[1] indicates that a system of mining and trading customs had developed in Saxon times around the salt works at Middlewich in Cheshire.

Our first detailed accounts of English mining law come from medieval customs in the lead mines of Derbyshire, particularly in the High and Low Peak and also

---

[1]   The Domesday Book, Cheshire, 268, Middlewich.

in the tin mining Stannaries of Cornwall and Devon. These were important for the economy of the whole country. The miners obtained special privileges and some came to be confirmed by royal grants. Cornwall had the most developed and elaborate system which had two special features. One, which was invoked up to the nineteenth century and which still exists in theory, was the custom of tin bounding in certain manors in the eastern part of the county. A miner who wished to prospect or work in a defined area could lay out his bounds on any land without permission (save that in some places he needed the consent of the Duke of Cornwall). He could dig out the tin and keep it but he had to observe the customs, including paying a defined dish or royalty to the landowner. Originally, as the tin was raised out of the workings in baskets and laid out on the ground, the steward of the landowner could come and select any one basket in fifteen. Later, this became a royalty of one-fifteenth of the value. The other feature was a special Stannary Parliament which was elected by and represented professional tin miners in the county and which could make regulations to govern the tin industry.

Miners have worked coal from the Middle Ages largely from surface pits either under local customary rights or under licence from the landowner. As the accessible deposits were worked out, they had to go deeper with shafts and tunnels, which involved surveys of the deposits, a large work force, and the expense of pit props and equipment to extract the coal. One of the main incentives to develop the steam engine was as a resource to extract water from mines liable to flood. Coal became ever more important as time passed, not just to heat homes but to power industry and eventually the great steamships that crossed the oceans.

All of this required a lot of money. The returns were great. Tin, lead and ironstone all produced good returns and the greatest fortunes were made from King Coal. But before the royalties could be paid there had to be investment and that needed both security and finance. The enterprise first needed security in access to and working the subsoil deposits. The mine operators did not need to own the surface land itself but did need to be sure of access to the mineral levels for long enough to recover the cost of the initial investment. One aspect of mineral working was the area immediately around the pit head where the mine machinery, spoil dumps, offices and other facilities were located. The other was the workings, deep out of sight where the mine tunnels could run far under the adjoining land. Above the seams of coal, farmers could continue to raise crops or graze their cattle. Sometimes the surface subsided and then there could be disputes and claims for damages by a farmer who had lost his land.

In most land the minerals belonged to the surface owner, although he was free to sever the ownership and sell or lease the surface separately from the minerals.

One exception was copyhold land where the lord of the manor had the property in the minerals – that is he owned them – but the possession – the right to get at the minerals and work them – belonged to the copyholder. The reason was that in medieval times minerals could only be obtained by digging from the surface and since the copyholder (like the villein who preceded him) had a duty to cultivate the land, the law gave him a corresponding right to prevent anyone (including his lord) disturbing him. This principle extended even to deep minerals which were far below the surface. This created a stalemate since neither lord nor copyholder could work the minerals without the agreement of the other. Copyholders could therefore demand a share of mineral payments and as many of the best coal deposits were in champion country where copyholds were widespread, this became a general practice.

The second requirement for the mining enterprise was a source of finance to operate the mine. Usually, the mineral operator did not want to own the freehold in the minerals, both because he preferred not to tie up his capital and because once the mine was worked out he did not want to be left holding abandoned workings in and under the ground. Equally, landowners did not want to sell or could not because the rights were in a settlement or the owner was an institution. Many great families improved their fortunes from the lucky accident that there were mineral deposits under their hereditary lands. Once again, the settlement had a part to play since under normal rules the tenant for life was impeachable for waste, so that his heir could prevent him working the mines as that was seen by the law as damage to the land. One way round was to obtain an Estate Act allowing the landowner to grant a lease to an operator to work the minerals and set aside part of the royalties for his heirs, often by paying them to trustees who could invest them. This of course was expensive and only the wealthy (or those who could do a deal with a substantial mining enterprise) could afford it.

The operators raised the cash to work the mine partly from their own funds but more often from investors and lenders. A mining lease would be made for a long period. Ideally, it was drawn as an asset which could be sold or mortgaged so that if the particular enterprise failed, the operator or his lender could sell the lease to someone prepared to try the venture. Investors may have contributed their money as partners in the business. Partnership could be risky since, if the business failed, each partner was liable for the debts of the enterprise and a creditor could seize all his assets.

The mining lease set up an elaborate structure under which the owner of the minerals granted to the operator the right to extract them and to make shafts, install roads and machinery and deposit spoil on the surface. The parties gave little thought to the longer term, to what would happen after the mining finished. As a result, the area became covered with abandoned spoil tips, derelict machinery and mine buildings. Some have since become conservation habitats for unusual plants or valued monuments to industrial history lovingly protected by archaeologists. Others are dangerous and unsightly heaps of mine waste or rubble disfiguring the locality even where they are not a danger to nearby villages or walkers.

COMPANIES AND COMMERCIAL LEASES

A modern company is a form of corporation, created for a business. We have seen how, before 1189, abbeys, cathedrals and some ancient towns were recognised as corporations which gave them the right to be regarded as if they were legal people. After that date any group, such as townsmen or traders who wanted to be formed into a borough or a livery company, or any other group who wanted corporate status, needed to obtain a royal charter.[2] This allowed them to accumulate funds and carry on enterprises for longer than a natural lifetime. The Crown even authorised some commercial companies, such as the Merchant Adventurers chartered in 1390. In the seventeenth century, a number of trading companies obtained royal charters to operate as businesses. The best known are the Hudson's Bay Company and the East India Company but there were others most of which operated overseas.

The Bank of England was established under the Bank of England Act 1694.[3] It took deposits and provided finance by discounting bills of exchange. More importantly, it was the head of (and ultimate lender to) a system of banks. Many of them were in London but part of their business was to act as agents for numerous local banks around the country. This system made possible the provision of capital for many projects which changed the landscape. The emergence of companies in the modern sense as corporations was long delayed because of a national scandal known as the South Sea Bubble. A company invited inflated expectations, many people invested in it and in other similar enterprises and then the bubble burst in 1720. The investments lost their value and the investors lost a lot of money. Even before the burst, Parliament imposed tight restrictions on the formation of new companies.

Businesses had to be financed and run as true partnerships with their property held under a trust. Some partnership shares could be bought and sold. Many were successful and much of the prosperity of the eighteenth and nineteenth centuries came from such enterprises. Others continued to be family businesses and many wool and cotton mills were run in that way. These were the basis of

---

[2]   Statute of Quo Warranto 1290 (18 E1).

[3]   5 & 6 W & M c 20.

middle class prosperity, son following father and grandfather in the same trade, buying comfortable houses and fine furniture, hiring domestic servants in addition to those at the business and educating their children. But these little enterprises were at risk from an improvident speculation or a downturn in the trade, or just misfortune. If things went wrong, all the wealth built up, perhaps over generations, may have been lost in a moment as the proprietor could not keep his personal wealth separate from the misfortunes of his business. If he was successful he might buy and settle land on his son to keep it out of the reach of creditors, but if so it was not available for the business either. Also, it was not a simple matter to sell a business since all the assets, property and debts had to be transferred separately and the servants rehired.

Furthermore, as businesses expanded, the cost of buildings and machinery grew and they needed more finance. Proprietors and investors needed a better form of organisation. The Joint Stock Companies Act 1844 allowed investors to form companies which had their own personality but this did not solve the problem of unlimited liability. If the business failed, often owing a lot of money, all the investors were liable for the debts. As a result it was difficult to get funds from the public because of the risk. So, in 1855, Parliament passed the Limited Liability Act which enabled limited liability companies to operate under strict supervision. The way was then open to accumulate ever greater funds not just from a few wealthy men, but from anyone in the land who was prepared to risk their money in equities.

A typical industrial plant was the cotton mill. Some were vast buildings employing great numbers of workers. A few of the early entrepreneurs, such as Richard Arkwright, are famous but there were many smaller operators. In order to have a good power supply the mill needed to be on a flowing watercourse, and therefore often had to be built in the country. Such a building dominated the landscape. Mills were expensive to build and run and the mill owner therefore needed security in order to be able to work the mill and recover his outlay. Plate 11 shows a mill at Saltaire near Bradford.

In particular, a mill owner needed to be able to control the land for the mill and its surrounds. The most suitable land was likely to be on an estate. He may have been able to buy the freehold but often neither he nor the landowner would wish to do this since putting money into owning land and buildings tied up capital which could otherwise be used in the business, to buy machinery and materials such as wool, which then generated profit. Although sometimes it was worth having the freehold of his works, often the mill owner preferred instead to take a lease at an annual rent paid out of his turnover. Equally, if the site was in a settlement the landowner may not have had power to sell and, even if it was not, he may not have wished to lose control of an area in the middle of his lands. He, too, may have preferred a lease structure with a rent coming in every year.

The result was that lawyers developed commercial leases alongside the existing forms for farms, houses and mines. Most often these had fixed rents although sometimes the parties used turnover rents. An instance is the famous case of *Walsh v Lonsdale.*[4] It concerned a weaving shed where the parties agreed terms for a lease for seven years but the lease was never actually granted. The landowner agreed to put the shed into good condition and provide steam power by means of an engine house and boiler house. The tenant agreed to pay a rent for each loom, the amount of the rent depending not only on the number of looms but also on whether the landlord or the tenant provided the steam. In fact, the tenant was able to provide his own steam power. There was a dispute about the amount of rent due and the court came up with a solution which reflected the bargain the parties had intended. The case illustrates the sort of deal industrialists were making. It is taught to law students for the way the courts were ready to uphold commercial agreements by using the equitable principles developed in Chancery rather than the stricter rules of the common law. The Chancery also developed legal techniques which enabled businessmen to obtain damages calculated by reference to the profit and loss accounts of a firm which gave a more realistic remedy than common law damages for breach of contract. Such methods made commercial ideas enforceable through the courts and thereby supported the growth of business and industry.

POLLUTION

There might be other disputes. An instance is one of the most important cases in English property law, *Rylands v Fletcher,*[5] decided by the House of Lords in 1868. In 1850, Thomas Fletcher took a lease from the Earl of Wilton of some coal mines at Ainsworth between Bury and Bolton, north of Manchester. Over the years, he extended his underground workings north westward under the land of adjoining owners towards some other land of Lord Wilton near Old Wood Lane. As his workmen did so they came across the traces of some much older mine workings, including some abandoned mine shafts upwards from their level. They had been filled up with marl and rubbish but they did not interfere with Mr Fletcher's workings and so they were left alone.

Nearby at Ainsworth there was a mill belonging to John Rylands and Jehu Horrocks. Rylands, who was born in 1801, was the owner of a substantial business which manufactured ginghams, calicoes and linens. After his death in

---

[4]   (1882) 21 Ch D 9.

[5]   (1868) 1 LR 3 HL 330.

1888, his widow wanted to erect a permanent memorial of her husband which led to the building of the John Rylands Library in Manchester opened in 1899. In 1860, Rylands and Horrocks needed to expand their water supply. There was a suitable site on the Wilton Estate and so with the consent of the earl they began to construct a new reservoir near Old Wood Lane to the north of their mill. Their workmen also came across some abandoned vertical shafts downwards from the construction level which appeared to be filled up and so they were left as they were. In December 1860, the reservoir was sufficiently advanced for water to be let in.

On the morning of 11 December the old shafts gave way and water poured from above into Mr Fletcher's workings. He sued for his losses from being unable to work the mine for a long time, for the cost of pumping and for other costs caused because workmen were afraid to work in such a dangerous mine. Presumably, he had difficulty in getting men and had to pay them more. The judge awarded the substantial sum of £5,000 in damages. The House of Lords upheld the decision. The rule that developed from the case is that if someone brings onto his land and keeps there something which, if it escapes, might cause damage, then he is liable for any losses irrespective of any fault on his part. It has implications in our own times for pollution from past enterprises and so is the basis of much environmental law.

The growth of industry did indeed lead to a good deal of pollution of the landscape. This was long before there was any idea of government intervention to protect the environment so any claims had to be brought by the people affected. There were cases over rivers, over drainage and many other issues between landowners. An instance is *Crossley & Sons Ltd v Lightowler*[6] in 1867. Crossleys had a large carpet factory at Dean Clough on the banks of the River Hebble near Halifax. They needed a supply of pure water which they could take from the river. Unfortunately, it was polluted. There were several dye works, one of which was Mr Lightowler's. That was built on the site of a former smaller dye works run by Messrs Irving up until around 1840 when it was abandoned. Lightowler had now made a new works, much larger than Irvings', which contributed much (though not all) to the pollution of the river. Crossleys applied to court for an injunction to prevent further pollution. Lightowler had two arguments. One was that the use was established by the Irvings twenty years before, but the court held that that use had stopped and Lightowler could not rely on it. He also argued that there were other polluters, such as a worsted mill, but the court did not think that relevant. Crossleys got their injunction.

In the absence of any planning or zoning laws, men of commerce could build factories wherever they wished and in many towns these were mixed among the

---

[6]   (1867) 2 Ch App 478.

houses. Until the workers could travel to work by train, they had to live within walking distance of their work. In much the same way, offices and shops mixed in with residential areas. As we will see in Chapter 15, the developers of towns tried to use covenants to control the occupations in residential areas and to exclude unwanted uses. They had some success, especially in the suburbs of the growing towns, so that much industry began to be restricted to business areas. But landowner power was hardly enough in the long run and in the twentieth century the state had to intervene.

WORKERS' ACCOMMODATION

Industry needed workers and they had to be housed. Often, mills had to be built in isolated sites, perhaps where there was enough water power. Workers had to live within walking distance of their work and the obvious course was for the mill owner to put up the houses for the workforce. In addition to his factory, he could take a lease of the land for dwellings for his mill hands. Some employers cared for their workers and built good dwellings but others wished only to build them cheaply in quantity. The mill hands were obliged to live in them as tied accommodation only so long as they worked there. If they had a dispute or became ill they would be dismissed and lose their home as well as their job. Sometimes the mill operator may have paid slightly more in a wage and sublet at a modest profit rent. As landowners realised this, they too came to take a more direct hand in housing, and, especially in a district with expanding towns and many employers of working men, it suited employers for someone else to build and let out dwellings. Often, this was done by investors who could acquire land for dwellings, either freehold or on long lease, put up houses and let them to the workers. Houses could be rented by the week, the month or the year. In such cases, the housing was not tied although a worker who lost his job would not be able to pay rent and the result would be the same. Often, the housing was of poor quality in monotonous terraces or around small courtyards and liable to degenerate into slums.

Whether they rented or had tied accommodation, the law took the view that free men and women could accept any conditions by contract. While this would not compel someone to work for a specific master, if the alternative was to starve, the worker had little choice but to accept the terms offered. There were scandals. Novels such as Disraeli's *Sybil* and Dickens' *Hard Times* described in gripping detail the conditions in which many were made to work and live. Some politicians also made much of the issues and there is no doubt that bad employers did exploit their workers. But there were also many good and fair masters who did not go to the publicised extremes.

Other towns developed for miners. These tended to be rougher than industrial towns but many of the same principles applied. Although tin, iron or copper mines operated on a small scale, the coal mines which provided fuel for the great smokestack industries were on a different order and so were the mining towns. At their peak, the mines employed thousands of workers all of whom needed houses. This was not just the rough miners themselves who worked deep underground and surface workers who collected, graded and removed the coal – they could be given tiny cottages. But there were also engineers to maintain the equipment and foremen and bookkeepers to run the business, and such people wanted more substantial and respectable dwellings.

Any housing, whether for mining or industrial towns, involved a good deal of administration. A substantial landowner could employ staff to look after the farmers and cottagers of a rural estate, but it was another thing in a large expanding busy town with thousands of people living closely together in cramped dwellings. Great landowners came to let the housing estates on long leases to head lessees who managed the estate by subletting to occupiers at weekly or monthly rents.

Farming used a different approach but attitudes were influenced by those in industry. Farm workers could be employed casually when needed but often they were hired by the year. Particularly in the north of England, this might be at hiring fairs held once a year. If a farm worker depended on seasonal employment life could be hard, but if a farmer knew he was going to need labour for the spring sowing and even more for the harvest, he needed to be sure that conditions were not so harsh during the winter that he would lose his labour and therefore often employed farmhands throughout the year. On many farms, rows of small cottages were built to house workers and their families, usually constructed by the landowner but occasionally by the farm tenant as an improvement to the land. Most farm workers lived in tied cottages.

To some extent, the hard conditions were alleviated by the system of relief for the needy, paid for out of the local rates, which in turn were levied by justices of the peace, who were also the landlords of the farmers who needed the labour so that the system was made to work. After the 1830s, this was replaced by a statutory system of workhouses, solid buildings paid for out of the rates, and many survive, sometimes converted to small industrial units.[7]

Workers' cottages, whether in industrial towns or on farms, could be situated anywhere, but over time ever more people of all stations in life came to live in towns, which I look at next.

---

[7]   The Poor Law Amendment Act 1834.

Chapter 15

Towns – 1660 to 1900

The growth of towns has been one of the biggest changes in the landscape. They have spread over the countryside and are where most people live and work. They contain the hospital where people are born, the funeral parlour which prepares their bodies for burial and every need in between.

This shift to urban living involved a shake-up in the former social and legal structure which had evolved over the millennia. Until the mid-nineteenth century, most people lived in villages or on isolated farms. As towns grew, the factories and offices which provided employment and the houses and flats where the people who worked there lived could not just appear; they were built on someone's property. Nearly all towns were enlargements of an existing borough or village but they could only expand over land which belonged to someone and under conditions laid down either by the landowner or in laws made by Parliament or often both.

EARLY TOWNS

We have seen how the principal Roman towns were plantations, introduced to civilise Britain and provide a congenial environment for settlers from the more developed parts of the empire. Many Anglo-Saxon towns began as defences and later became centres for traders. Medieval towns developed because they provided work. The boroughs were market towns and ports. Merchants collected the produce of the countryside and arranged for its distribution here and overseas. Towns became centres for tradesmen and those who provided services, such as doctors and lawyers.

Like much else, the development of towns paused with the Black Death. After the fourteenth century, most boroughs settled down to a steady regime where little changed over the generations. Some towns became rotten boroughs, where the franchise was limited to particular properties and the lord of the manor controlled either them or the employment and income of the occupiers. For example, in many towns there had since the Middle Ages been a special form of landholding known as burgage tenure. It came to be seen as a form of socage but it had some unusual features, for instance the land could be left by will. That was because in towns, a shop or even a house was part of a business along with the goods sold or the money earned and, as the proprietor could leave his trading assets to any of his children or to a business associate, it would have made little sense for his land to be bound to go to his eldest son. By the eighteenth century, the franchise in some boroughs was restricted to burgage tenants. If a rich man could buy them up or bribe the owners, he controlled the votes, and as a result after 1660, many boroughs fell under the control of the local gentry. In others the voters retained the independence to make their own choices. Plate 13 is a copy of a map of the town of Haslemere in Surrey in 1735 showing burgage tenements with voting rights.

Many important towns in the midlands and the north developed as industrial centres. For instance, as the wool trade expanded, weavers came to live and work together. At first they lived in villages where each weaver owned or rented his own home and had a frame set up in it where all the family worked. Where weavers could command good incomes there was a demand for house sites. This tended to happen in open villages where there was no dominant squire. The new occupier could buy or rent a piece of land from a farmer to put up a house. This was simplest if the farmer was a freeholder. Copyholders and leaseholders were accountable to the lord or landlord for waste which included changing the nature of the land including erecting a house and in many manors there was a custom that copyholds could not be divided up. If the lease was long enough, the leaseholder could either assign part of the land or, more often, sublet for the rest of this term. But all these were liable to objection from the owner of the freehold, so new dwellings were often made in areas where there were numerous small proprietors.

In some open villages anyone might be able to put up a house on the waste. If the main employment was weaving, or even if it was arable farming where the plough was drawn by horses not oxen, owners of animals no longer needed the waste for grazing. It could become covered with scrub. If a homeless family decided to put up a dwelling perhaps no one would stop them and, as with the assarting of fields in the Middle Ages, if the owner of the waste did become aware of it he might permit it for a small rent. There was said to be a custom in parts of Wales that if a house was put up within one night (*ty un nos*) the squatter could remain. This was never the law in England, but in practice many small dwellings could appear and often were allowed to remain. Over the years, such encroachments grew into suburbs, much as shanty towns do in some countries now. But this piecemeal expansion was not satisfactory. It did not provide for roads and drains; as the occupier had no title, his position was precarious and no one wanted to spend a lot of money on building a good house without security. However, the law came to recognise squatters' rights after occupation for a time and many modern freehold titles derive from such arrangements.

HOUSING THE MIDDLE CLASSES

The middle classes also needed housing. Commerce, not just in London but throughout the country, needed clerks and other literate employees to deal with the vast quantity of paperwork needed to run an empire and its business. Such men were paid much better than industrial workers. Others were in their own professions or ran their own businesses. They wanted good solid houses which their wives could manage and where their children grew up. Some of them could afford the wages of at least one maid, and the more prosperous might have several staff and a house of a size to accommodate them. After the railways began to spread across the countryside, middle class employees could afford to commute, and housing estates for office workers followed the railways in suburbs around the great towns. Where they were built on agricultural land, the boundaries of building estates often reflected the former field shapes.

Some landowners were able to put up housing estates for the middle classes at their own expense and then lease them out at a substantial rent, but only a few could afford to, had or could employ the expertise to do that. In addition, many middle class occupiers wanted to have the benefit of long-term security and of being the owners of their houses, whether or not they owned the freehold, and sometimes they wanted to design and build a house to their own liking. In any such case, they had to have good titles which had to derive from an acknowledged landowner.

Landowners used three methods to profit from these disposals: the outright sale (perhaps leaving part of the price outstanding on mortgage), the rentcharge and the ground rent lease. All depended on the economics of building. The key to housing finance in the nineteenth century was the availability of a steady dependable income in an age where there was virtually no inflation. In 1900, £10 bought much the same as £10 in 1800. Someone who had spare cash might invest in government stocks, notably Consolidated Stock (Consols) which went on forever paying £3 for every £100 invested (until 1888 when it was reduced to 2¾%), backed by the government and administered by the Bank of England. But many landowners did not really understand stocks and bonds and preferred the security of land. Control of land could bring other benefits, such as regulating the buildings erected on it.

Professional building firms developed to meet the demand for housing. Suppose a builder knew that a completed house was worth £400. He was in business to construct the house and sell on. He did not want to be a landlord. His return came from turnover in bricks and mortar. He knew it would cost £250 to build that house. Adding in the expense of running the business, of interest on his borrowings and to make a profit for himself he needed another £50. So the total cost was £300 and that meant there could be £100 for the landowner for each plot of land for a single house. In practice, the builder might take on a dozen or so house plots at any one time.

From the landowner's point of view he might not want the £100 in cash. He might prefer the security of a steady income return from land and be unwilling to invest in stocks. If he was tenant for life he might not be able to sell. Suppose in Jane Austen's *Pride and Prejudice*, Mr Bennett had wanted to develop a field next to Meriden for housing; he could not do so without the consent of Mr Collins and even if they had agreed on this, they would have to go through the expense of a common recovery in order to make title to the buyer.

Assuming that the landowner had or could obtain the necessary powers, there were two principal ways of disposing of land while retaining an income from it – by rentcharge or by long lease. In practice, they worked in a similar way and both have now been effectively prevented by modern legislation.[1] The choice of method varied in different parts of the country for no obvious reason beyond fashion. The house owner had the advantage that he did not have to find the £100 for the landowner as a lump sum but could pay an annual sum instead.

In some areas, notably Bristol and parts of the Midlands, the landowner would part with the freehold in return for an annual rentcharge. If the landowner could have invested the £100 in Consols and produced a return of £3 per year, he would instead sell the plot for a rentcharge of £3. The house buyer paid the builder £300 and if he did not pay his annual rentcharge then the rent owner (former landowner) could take back the house and sell it, compensating himself out of the proceeds and paying the house owner the balance.

But the landowner may not have wanted to part with the freehold or may have been prevented by his settlement. Instead, he could grant the builder a long lease of the undeveloped plot, for 99 years or 999 years at a ground rent of £3 per year. Many settlements included power to grant building leases for up to 99 years and if not the Settled Land Act 1882 conferred it. The builder put up the house and sold the lease for £300 to the occupier who went on owing the ground rent to the landlord. The landlord expected his heirs would get the land back, with a house on it, after a century. As it turned out it was the expected expiry of

---

[1]   The Leasehold Reform Act 1967 and the Rentcharges Act 1977.

such leases, many granted in Wales in the 1860s, which led to the dismantling of the ground rent system in the Leasehold Reform Act 1967. Longer leases of up to 999 years (more common in the north and west) were more like freehold sales with a rentcharge. In such cases, the landlord never expected his heirs to get the house itself; he was interested only in a secure fixed income. A lease could also include provisions to control nuisances, such as pollution or rubbish, and to regulate the appearance of the buildings. It provided a long-term investment which was as safe as houses.

In practice, as the house owner might have himself needed to borrow there would also be a mortgagee to pay – and many of the suburbs of England were built out of money advanced on mortgage. Although some banks lent on mortgage, many loans were from trustees, often on behalf of the original landowner, so that an alternative to the foregoing arrangements was to sell for £100 but give a mortgage for that amount at 3% or 4%. Mortgages were considered proper investments for a trustee to make (as Bernard Shaw satirised in his play *Widowers' Houses*) and this was confirmed by section 32 of the Law of Property Amendment Act 1859. Generally, prudent lenders limited their mortgages to two thirds of the value of the property and that remained the law for some trustees until the Trustee Act 2000. Another early source of finance was a building society. They began as mutual arrangements for groups of people to pool their savings, so that individual members could borrow on mortgage from the pool to build or buy a house. However, in the nineteenth century, these tended to be for less affluent householders, especially in the Midlands and the North.

Mortgages of long leases were often made by sublease. Mortgages of freeholds were created by a conveyance of the freehold to the lender with a provision that when it was paid off the lender would transfer the property back. Any mortgage document of the time looks confusing and, because it takes a legal form which does not reflect its true nature, it constitutes a legal fiction. One judge famously said 'no one, I am sure, by the light of nature ever understood an English mortgage of real estate'.[2]

CONTROLLING THE TOWNSCAPE

The owner of a building estate often wanted to have his cake and eat it too. He liked to have the proceeds from selling or the income from letting the land for building but he also wanted to control the appearance of the house to be put up and often to control undesirable activities. This may have been for his personal

---

[2] *Samuel v Jarrah Timber & Wood Paving Corp Ltd* [1904] AC 323, per Lord Macnaughten.

benefit if he lived in the vicinity. More often, it may have been to protect the amenities of the building estate in the interests of all the house owners, so that values would be maintained and future buyers would pay a good price to come to a high class residential area where standards were also maintained. Before the development of town planning, the quality of a housing estate could only be controlled by private means and the law developed to permit this. A benefit of a leasehold estate was that the landlord could include covenants to keep the house in repair and to maintain gardens and walls so that the estate remained of high quality.

Even where a landlord was ready to sell his freehold for a single purchase price, he still expected control of the urban setting. This became possible after the case of *Tulk v Moxhay*[3] in 1848, which concerned the preservation of an open space in London. In 1808, Mr Tulk, who then owned Leicester Square and many of the houses around it, sold to Mr Elms the garden or pleasure ground in the middle with an equestrian statue in the centre and iron railings around it. The terms of the conveyance required Mr Elms and any future owner to keep up the garden 'in neat and ornamental order'. The garden area was sold and resold and, by 1848, Mr Moxhay had become the owner. He announced his intention to build on it. A later member of the Tulk family still owned some of the houses in the Square and claimed an injunction to stop him, which was granted by the court.

The case established that the seller of freehold land could impose restrictions on building. They had to be negative in nature but ingenuity might allow them to be used to positive effect. Thus a covenant may have laid down a building line between the house and the street and prohibited any structure in front of it, so that each house had a front garden, or say that any house must not cost less to build than a minimum amount (so ensuring only a prosperous family could afford it). The terms may have, in effect, provided that it could only be used as a dwelling. Covenants may have prohibited a use the landowner did not like, such as sales of tripe (because of the smell) or indeed any non-domestic use (other, perhaps, than a professional man such as a doctor or lawyer), or be more specific so as to prevent use as a public house or as a dissenters' meeting house. They could restrict the design or require an architect's plans to be approved by the original seller.

Most of these were drafted so as to be enforceable only by the landowner or anyone who bought land from him. Others were set up as building schemes with a common set of covenant on a building estate laid out in plots where all the owners could enforce the covenants against any of their neighbours. The leading case concerned such a scheme at Felixtowe in Essex set up in 1861 where the

---

3   (1848) 2 Ph 774.

court granted an injunction against a buyer of land subject to a restriction that it could not be used as a hotel.[4]

EQUIPPING THE TOWN

The towns of course needed more than just houses. There were shops, offices, factories and warehouses. There were public amenities such as theatres, parks, and municipal offices. More than this were the basic infrastructure of undertakings such as sewage works. A mixture of private and public money provided these.

Private money would produce anything which could make a profit, and the places of entertainment, the pubs and music halls and galleries, could pay for themselves. Most often, the premises were held on lease at a rent. Other buildings had a less tangible but still strongly felt benefit. A good landlord may have provided land for public recreation, or if he did not, the leading citizens may have clubbed together to buy land for either a genteel promenade for the respectable inhabitants or a grassy area for the working classes to see a bit of greenery. Some municipalities, often under the influence of benevolent landowners, acquired open spaces called parks after the amenity land which surrounded a mansion.

Churches were prominent features in medieval towns which were well supplied with enough churches for all the population. At the Reformation, these all belonged to the Church of England and everyone was expected to worship there. After the Civil War, Parliament acknowledged that independent churches or dissenters could exist but in order to avoid their clergymen competing with the Established Church, the Nonconformists Act 1665 ('the Five Mile Act') forbade them from living within five miles of their former parish which was often a market town. Some therefore settled just outside that limit, so that their congregations could reach them easily on Sundays and there still survive some splendid chapels which are, and always have been, far too large for the small villages where they are found.

The church was the biggest and most solid building in a medieval village. If in the nineteenth century the village expanded to become a town, the church would still be in the centre but it would now be too small for the population. It might be enlarged but more often a landowner provided land, either out of piety or because he thought a church was good for public morals and order. An outright owner was free to do as he wished but Parliament also conferred a power on

---

[4]   *Elliston v Reacher* [1908] 2 Ch 374, at 665.

tenants for life.[5] Then the townsfolk would raise the money to build a new church by local collection or through one of the national religious societies. Parliament also provided funds under the Church Building Act 1818 and its successors. The churches with their towers and spires were sited to draw attention and stood out in the townscape but they were also social centres. They were not just a gathering place for the respectable middle classes on Sundays – many of the clergy were active in charitable work for the relief of suffering – and they were regarded by the middle classes as places where the working classes might learn temperance, decency and morality. They were of course also places for spiritual release and for teaching.

Schools were associated with the Church which saw education as part of its responsibility. The School Sites Act 1840 authorised tenants for life to give up to one acre for schools or for housing schoolmasters but only so long as the land was used for that purpose. In a similar way to churches, the school building was paid for by local subscription or by the National Society for Promoting Religious Education. This and other societies were set up to collect subscriptions in a common account and once enough was given the work could begin. The money and the land were in the name of trustees, often the vicar and churchwardens, holding for charitable purposes. As local education was reorganised in the twentieth century, many such schools closed and the person who had become entitled to the assets of the settlement claimed the land back.[6]

The judges, by interpreting and enlarging the effect of the Charitable Uses Act 1601, gave charitable trusts special privileges. Unlike private trusts, which under the rule against perpetuities could exist only for a limited time, charitable trusts could exist forever and carry on their work down the centuries. Many are still operating under nineteenth-century trust deeds often still in their original offices. They built working men's institutes where mechanics who wished to better themselves could go to a reading room. They provided hostels for fallen women. They established hospitals and almshouses. The solid buildings, often with their name and purpose proudly displayed in moulded brickwork, are still to be found in many towns.

More important for the future were municipal building and works. The old town corporations had been set up as an arrangement for a number of burgesses to manage their own affairs. They were not accountable to the people at large and by the eighteenth century many of them had become little more than clubs. They existed for the benefit of the freemen of a town and any money they had was, quite legally, divided among those freemen. Meanwhile, most parts of the country and particularly the new towns had little in the way of local

---

5   Now in Settled Land Act 1925, s 55.

6   Such claims are now regulated by the Reverter of Sites Act 1987.

government. In some parishes, the churchwardens were able to administer the public interest. In others, the burden fell on the manor court. In a few, the court leet survived as the last relic of Saxon local administration. In practice, most local government depended on the justices of the peace, who were substantial landowners with an interest in maintaining the peace of their own estates, and who met four times a year in the county town at Quarter Sessions to administer justice and to decide on major works such as the repair of roads.

None of this suited the new towns. There was a half-hearted reform of local government under the Municipal Corporations Act 1835. Birmingham Corporation was established under that Act, its Town Hall (illustrated in Plate 12) having already been built the year before. Manchester was incorporated in 1837 and in 1847 obtained a private Act[7] to construct the Longdendale Reservoirs in the Pennines. However, the major reforms had to wait until the Local Government Act 1888. By the end of the nineteenth century, many people had come to the conclusion that private arrangements, whether governed by personal profit or by piety and charity, were not sufficient to deal with social problems of housing, public heath and infrastructure. Since the sixteenth century some local government, notably poor relief, had been financed by local rates. Under the reforms, local government was run by councillors accountable at elections to ratepayers. It was not up to the task of providing for the mass of working class people. National democracy, on the other hand, gave a voice to ordinary people who far outnumbered the propertied middle classes, and in a world of one man one vote (women were not given the vote until after the Great War) numbers counted. So government had to intervene. It did so in the twentieth century on a large scale to control housing, industry, local government and much more.

---

[7]   10 V C cciii.

Chapter 16

The Twentieth Century – 1900 to 2000

The landscape changed more in the twentieth century than in all previous times put together. Some changes were made by individuals around their homes and farms, others by companies operating for profit or by government acting in the public interest. They have, as always, involved the law, but in new ways. In response, those who tried to prevent or control change, either to protect their homes and surroundings or, increasingly as the century progressed, to conserve the countryside and the townscape, also invoked the law. The law of landscape has therefore become particularly complex in our time.

Some dwellings were built by government under housing legislation; others by private developers who spread them over the land and raised blocks of flats high above the city streets. Office blocks came to dominate city centres as once churches and town halls had done. Plate 12 shows behind Birmingham Town Hall the Alpha Tower built between 1969 and 1973 as the headquarters of a television company. Transport authorities built motorways and airports on land taken by compulsory purchase. In this chapter, I will look mainly at the built environment and the changes affecting towns and villages as well as controls on leases of homes, businesses and farms. In Chapter 17, I look at the effect of European agricultural policy, environmental controls and leisure access which have longer-term implications for the countryside and will lead to future changes.

The most evident control of building has been by the planning laws. These restrict, though they do not initiate, the position and design of houses and workplaces. Planning regulates in two ways. New structures need planning permission while in contrast others, often, reckoned as part of the heritage, cannot be demolished or altered without consent. These two controls have weakened the idea of ownership and the rights of property established in the seventeenth century. Although there were already a few, mainly local, controls in 1900, people saw them as special exceptions to the rule that an owner of land had the right to do whatever he wanted with his own land. By 2000, that was far from the case. This revolution came about through two linked causes: first, state sovereignty and, secondly, democracy influenced by socialism. The detailed story is beyond the scope of this book but we need to understand some of the ideas to see how and why the law developed as it did.

DEMOCRACY AND SOVEREIGNTY

Although their origins are older, the ideas of democracy and sovereignty both emerged in their modern form in the nineteenth century from the same underlying cause. We saw that, ever since prehistoric times, wealth in an agricultural society came from control of productive land. Since there was only a little surplus, that led to a society dominated by a few powerful landowners. That meant that at the summit both of society and government were a small group of men who knew one another. The law relating to land reflected that during the centuries of our history. With the Industrial Revolution this ancient balance was upset. Industry and commerce brought massive wealth which, while it needed land to operate, did not itself derive from land. While at first it was still concentrated in a few hands, once the underlying logic of control of land had gone, so society changed and the law changed with it. No longer did landowners need to settle their estates down a succession of eldest sons, and the landowners themselves lost influence and power. That power passed to the men who had the new wealth.

It did not stop there. The new ways of making a living involved large numbers of educated middle classes as professionals, managers and clerks. Just as important were the workers. They lived clustered in towns. There they met and agreed to combine their strength in trade unions. The right to vote, extended in 1832 to the new commercial middle classes, was in 1867 also given to manual workers. Politicians had to take note of the needs of their new electorate and satisfy their demands.

They did this through what we must regard as a new institution, the state seen as something distinct from its governors or members. Although we may talk by analogy about the Roman state or the Plantagenet or even Tudor state, the state in the modern sense was an invention of the nineteenth century. Although they recognised that there was a public state of affairs, Roman and medieval people had no concept of the state as such. Government was by the emperor or king or in his name. As we have seen, the idea of state power developed in Italy in the sixteenth century and influenced the government of Charles I, but he saw government very much in personal terms. The result of the Civil War was to emphasise the rights of private property and to reduce the scope of government.

The German philosopher GWF Hegel, who wrote at the beginning of the nineteenth century, developed the idea in its modern form. He had predecessors including Thomas Hobbes but Hegel saw the state, *Staat*, as a separate entity not only comprised of its members but as more important than them. His ideas were popularised in simplified forms and adapted to the power hunger of politicians. He cannot be blamed for the abuses in the totalitarian societies of the twentieth century by those who misread his writings. Hegel's concept of the state was then combined with the legal idea of the corporation, particularly as the company came into use in the nineteenth century and was widely understood. People began to think of the state as a super corporate legal person. It acted through ministers and civil servants, just as a company acts though its directors and agents, but it was distinct from them, powerful and not restrained by any morality beyond its own survival. The remark of Hobbes is often quoted in the context of 'kings and persons of sovereign authority' that 'The notions of right and wrong, justice and injustice, have there no place. Where there is no common power, there is no law; where no law, no injustice'.[1] In the Middle Ages, Bracton had said that the king, although he made law, ought himself to be under God and the law. The modern idea of the state was that although it made law, it was not itself subject to law. In Britain, the state did not become a legal term as such and government is still in the name of the Queen, but the reality even here is that the state, often called the Crown, operates as a corporate person. In the end, the concept of an unfettered state not even bound by morality was seen to lead to totalitarianism and world war and came to be rejected across the globe, but we are still seeking to work out the implications for international law.

As it became accepted that the state was sovereign and not subject to any law, it came to have ultimate power over its citizens and, indeed, anyone for the time being within its geographical borders. This is quite different from the idea that a sovereign Parliament, made up of individuals who are representatives, can make laws binding everyone. We saw how around the year 1200 the idea developed of the law of a place rather than of a people. Within the boundaries of each independent territory the sovereign (at first an individual king or emperor, later in association with an assembly) was supreme legal authority, much as within the traditional landed estate the squire was owner. Just as squires might have other dependent estates around the country, so sovereigns might have other territories comprised in an empire. After the First World War and under the influence of President Wilson of the United States, the growing international community began to adopt the idea of a nation state. Each nation (broadly a group of people with a common language and culture) was to have its own territory within which it was sovereign. States were not necessarily either nations or democratic but that became the ideal. Under the new ideas, the state

---

[1] Hobbes, Thomas, *Leviathan*, Chapter 13.

represented the nation and it knew what was best and could decide what the people should have, even if that involved taking their property.

This idea of the nation state became mixed with socialist ideas. Karl Marx studied Hegel although he adapted what he read. In particular, he taught that rather than exist as a super being the state would wither away. He believed that all people were naturally good, kind and generous and were only corrupted by the economic system in which they lived. If they were allowed to develop their full potential, society could subsist in which each gave according to his ability and each received according to his need. The way Marxism worked out in practice was rather different but socialist ideals influenced many people for most of the twentieth century and affected many of the laws which control land. Marx himself wrote '... the theory of the Communists may be summed up in the single sentence: Abolition of private property'.[2] In this context property meant land.

THE 1925 LEGISLATION

In 1926 there was, for lawyers, an English revolution. It was not a Bolshevik one (and had nothing to do with the struggles which led to the General Strike of May that year). It occurred on 1 January at the instant after midnight and most people slept through it. The Property Legislation of 1922 to 1925[3] came into force on the first day of the new year. It did away with many of the ancient laws we have considered.

The process had started 100 years earlier, with the efforts of the Whig administration after the Great Reform Bill. More or less timid reforms were passed through the 1830s and thereafter during the century but 1926 saw a new system. It was no longer based on family ownership or rights derived from tenure or seisin. Instead, it developed the existing idea of distinguishing the beneficial rights to enjoy the use of land or receive its revenues, known as equitable interests, from the nominal ownership of land, known as the legal estate (which confusingly has little to do with landed estates) seen as a commercial asset. Legal title is held by between one and four persons (either individuals or companies) who have power to deal with it. They can buy, sell, lease, grant rights and behave as if they are full owners. That title may, and in the case of a single landholder in most cases will, correspond to equitable ownership but instead the proprietors may be trustees holding for other people. So far as anyone else who does business with them is concerned it does not

---

[2] Communist Manifesto.

[3] Notably, the Law of Property Acts 1922 and 1925, the Settled Land Act 1925 and the Land Registration Act 1925.

matter. A buyer or tenant can safely deal with the apparent owners without being concerned with trusts or family rights, or the rights of investors in a farm or factory.

Parliament swept away a lot of ancient rights and procedures with provision for some compensation to those who lost by the changes. Copyholders now acquired the freehold of their land from the lord of the manor in return for a usually modest sum to buy out the manorial rights so that manors became historic titles instead of sources of revenue for the lord. Tenants for life acquired the fee simple, although they had to exercise their rights in the interests of the settlement (which was preserved, although new ones cannot be created after 1996[4]). The Statute of Uses was repealed. Feoffment with livery of seisin was abolished, as was the status of heir and a mass of rules connected with it. Leases for lives were converted to 90 years. Mortgages of freeholds were no longer made by conveyance.

The promoters intended the changes to make it easier to deal with land. In that they only partly succeeded. Current methods of conveyancing are a world away from the cumbersome, slow and expensive system before 1926. As the formalities of transfer of title to land have been simplified, that has supported a strong market in land which in turn allows it to pass into the hands of new owners who want to make changes so that they can make better or more profitable use of it.

But there were also, increasingly as the century went on, more state controls and laws affecting land which lawyers advising buyers had to take into account. Although the formalities of making title are not often a problem now, land transfer did not become as simple as the reformers of 1925 had hoped. Any lawyer acting for the buyer of land has to make many searches in various public registers and ask many questions of the seller before advising the buyer that it is safe to proceed with the purchase. Even if the buyer does not personally want that information, most buyers of houses and flats, and many of agricultural or commercial property, need a mortgage and the lending bank will insist on the procedures being followed.

THE CONTROL OF LEASEHOLDS

Parliament also intervened to redress what was seen as the power of landlords to exploit leaseholders. For much of the twentieth century, laws were in force to modify the terms agreed between landlords and tenants of farms, businesses and

---

[4]   The Trusts of Land and Appointment of Trustees Act 1996.

homes. This was straight intervention on political grounds by a powerful state which overrode private rights. It came as a reaction to the unfettered freedom and abuses in the nineteenth century. We saw how a few freeholders held most of the land in England. They granted that land out to tenants. In some cases the tenants were, in effect, the owners of the land. If you hold a lease for 99 years at a fixed rent of £10 a year, you have a far greater right to the land than someone who is the nominal landlord. But most leases were shorter and at fuller rents and even long leases run out some time. Landlords still had much power. They not only took their profits but also exercised control by restricting alterations to the building, prescribing special methods of cultivation or refusing consent if the tenant wished to sell his lease.

Ordinary people, whose votes now far outnumbered those of the rich, saw no need to defer to their betters. Following Lloyd George's attack on the great estates, other politicians sought to remedy what they saw as an unfair use of rights of property. Tenants wanted security so they could not be evicted when the term ran out. The result, in a fast-changing world, was to allow some people to stay where they were and thereby to keep their holdings unchanged.

Farm tenure was a particular problem. We saw how after 1860 cheap foreign imports of food undermined the profits of agriculture and therefore the rents and income of owners of estates. In the First World War under threat from U-Boats, the country needed food. In response the government granted farmers rights to run their holdings free of interference by the landlord and free of the risk of being evicted. But after the war and despite promises that farmers would be looked after, those controls were removed in 1921 in what became known as the Great Betrayal. This did not last. In 1939 war broke out again. Once again, England was at risk of starvation and, once again, the farmers were needed.

This time the protection was permanent. Farm tenants gained lifetime security to remain on their farms.[5] In 1976, that was enlarged to three generations.[6] That was overkill since, as a result, landlords could not expect to get possession of the land for perhaps a century. The old system of accepting that generations could follow in tenanted farms was now long gone and so landlords stopped letting land. The government slowly responded and, partly in 1984 and more fully in 1995, relaxed the controls.[7] While the system continued, the physical condition of the protected farms tended to remain unaltered as neither the landlord nor the tenant had any incentive to improve them, and nether could change the boundaries to a more efficient unit without the agreement of the

---

[5]   The Agriculture Act 1947, now in the Agricultural Holdings Act 1986.

[6]   The Agriculture (Miscellaneous Provisions) Act 1976.

[7]   The Agricultural Holdings Act 1984 and the Agricultural Tenancies Act 1995.

other. But where there was more freedom, those who, in the new jargon, were said to manage land were free to experiment with new systems of farming.

Much the same happened with other commercial leases. In 1954, the Landlord and Tenant Act granted business tenants security to stay in their premises and that still continues. It means offices, shops and factories often remained in use long after the owner might otherwise have redeveloped the site because although, in theory, a landlord could get the building back to demolish, in practice it often involved a fight with a tenant who was trying to save his business. Again, these rules caused problems and in 1969 they were partly relaxed.[8]

More important for most people was security in their homes. The Increase of Rent and Mortgage Interest (War Restrictions) Act 1915 granted residential tenants the right to remain. These controls again were relaxed after the war, and controls were on and off until the Rent Act 1965[9] gave a strong degree of protection to most residential occupiers; they had security for their lives and often two generations afterwards.

By itself this would not have affected the landscape, since landlords might have been content to keep their tenants provided they were paying a full rent. Instead, government fixed rents at a level intended to be fair. In practice, this turned out to be uneconomic for the landlord who, under the Housing Act 1961,[10] also had responsibilities for repair of the house and if the rent was fixed he could not pass on the cost of maintenance. So landlords did the minimum. Houses with sitting tenants were not repaired or modernised and tended to decay. Landlords used every effort to evict tenants and then sell the house. The government encouraged people to own the freehold of their homes (or long leases for flats) and new forms of mortgage enabled many people to borrow to buy. The planning system restricted the number of new houses being built, which meant that prices tended to spiral higher.

In the end, these together destroyed the private rented sector. These rules in turn had to be changed and most new private tenancies granted after the passing of the Housing Act 1988 were no longer protected, again allowing flexibility and experiment, and encouraging private investors once again to provide housing.

Public sector council housing only partly filled the gap, and often did so in an ugly way. Instead of small groups of individually let dwellings whose occupants paid rent to a private landowner, there were vast stretches of identical rows of council housing. The local authority took the land to build them under

---

[8]   The Law of Property Act 1969.

[9]   Now the Rent Act 1977.

[10] Now the Landlord and Tenant Act 1985.

compulsory purchase, often for slum clearance. The new homes were certainly better than the slums they replaced. However, the cost of building them and then keeping them in repair had to be paid for either out of the rates (and councillors were under pressure to keep them down) or out of government grants (which were never enough). As a result, the dwellings were often cheaply built and had no character. Councils imposed a strong policy of uniform management and tenants could not even paint their front doors in the colours they wished.

In 1980, the Conservative government introduced a Right to Buy.[11] This fitted in with the policy of home ownership. As a result, instead of the blocks owned by private estates in the nineteenth century or local government in the twentieth century, these houses passed into the hands of individuals. In time, they planted their own trees, made their own extensions and adaptations, changed widows and doors and began to make a more varied townscape.

STATE CONTROL OF LAND

But it was in the provision of national equipment and infrastructure, the successor to the nineteenth-century works, that the power of the state was most evident. Some were provided under statutory powers, either under regulation or under direct state ownership. Water and sewerage came to be the responsibility of local government. Both electricity and telephone were nineteenth-century inventions. Telegraphs and subsequently telephones were regulated by the Telegraph Acts from 1863 onwards and electricity was regulated by the Electric Lighting Act 1882 and its successors, and poles, pylons wires and cables spread across the countryside.

The great change occurred in the Second World War, although most of the procedures had been pioneered before. In the emergency of national survival, there was no time to pass individual acts for separate works. The Victorians had anticipated this with general provisions (as on inclosure or railway construction) which could be incorporated in special Acts, although most of them included protections for private rights. But now government could rule in effect by decree in order to equip the nation to fight a total war. The War Ministry took land for training, coast defences and airfields. To maximise food production, a County War Agricultural Executive Committee could evict an inefficient farmer. Although the power was rarely exercised, the threat was there and affected the attitudes of farmers. A great mansion might be requisitioned as a hospital or for housing troops. Land could be taken for an airfield or for the construction of defences. Such works might directly affect the landscape but the implications

---

[11]   The Housing Act 1980.

were more important for the long term, and the legal techniques developed under the pressure of war could be applied to peacetime reorganisation.

In 1945, the people elected a Labour government. State ownership of land had been in the party manifesto since 1900 and clause 4 of its constitution aimed at the nationalisation of the means of production. In practice, it was not politically or financially realistic to try to nationalise all land. The UK government did, however, try to take over, by taxation, all or part of the development value of land, so that a landowner who had land ripe for building could retain the value for its current use, perhaps as farm land, but would have to forfeit to the state any additional value due to its suitability for development. The first attempt at this had been in Lloyd George's budget which imposed an undeveloped land duty.[12] That was repealed in 1920 without coming into force. More determined efforts were made repeatedly after the Second World War in 1947, 1967 and 1976 but none got very far.[13]

There had been some planning legislation since the Town Planning Act 1909, notably in the Restriction of Ribbon Development Act 1935. The post-war proposals were made possible by the Town and Country Planning Act 1947. It was administered by local authorities, initially county councils and after 1974 district councils. This had perhaps more of an effect on the landscapes than anything which had gone before.

Planning has existed for thousands of years. We saw how in the Bronze Age vast areas of the countryside were laid out in reaves. The Romans built towns on well-prepared patterns with streets on grid plans and laid out fields in standard sizes by centuriation. The lords of late Anglo-Saxon England established their villages with dwellings set out along a street or around a green. The kings, earls and abbots of the high Middle Ages designed new towns round market places and churches. But after the Black Death there was little incentive to plan and, with the triumph of property, the rights of individuals to do what they wished became more important.

In the eighteenth and nineteenth centuries, some parts of towns were laid out and built by private initiatives. For instance, the parades and squares of London and many important provincial towns were the expression of the aesthetic ideas of the great landowners who profited from urban expansion and, as we have seen, restrictive covenants could be used to protect the designed layout. However, with the invention of the motor car, swathes of new suburbs and building estates spread in ungainly fashion across the countryside, and those

---

[12] Finance (1909–10) Act 1910, s 16.

[13] The Town and Country Planning Act 1947, the Land Commission Act 1967 and the Development Land Tax Act 1976.

who valued it argued that unrestricted rights to build wherever there might be a profit were no longer acceptable. Steps were taken to deal with this even before the Second World War.[14] After 1947, virtually all building across the country was controlled although, because farmers were still favoured as producers of food, this affected the towns more than the rural areas. Rights of property were too entrenched to be dismissed, but the law provided that anyone who built a structure which needed planning consent and did not get it could be made to pull it down. By use of this weapon, all new development came under control. The authorities zoned land for housing, industry or as green belt.

But the state did not just react to what landowners were doing. It initiated much of the major changes and did so by legislation. The motor car required a new type of communication system. Instead of a few canals and railway lines crossing the country, cars needed an intricate network of surfaced roads and government rapidly provided them. In a democracy it could do no less and although cars were expensive at first, after around 1960 they were relatively cheap and became a necessity for everyone. Highway authorities – usually the county council – improved existing roads and exercised compulsory powers to straighten out bends. The sheer number of purchases ruled out any similar procedures to those used by the turnpike trusts. Road improvements for motor cars began with an Act of 1909[15] and the construction of national routes, such as motorways, was authorised by the Special Roads Act 1949.[16] Road improvements affected every corner of the land. It was not necessary to pass a new Act for each new road work: there was a standard procedure involving a public enquiry at which those affected could object, but there was little point in doing so and landowners tended to settle for arguing for the best compensation.

It worked like this. The ancient roads of the kingdom twisted about the country. As motor cars became common, councils resurfaced the former roadways to make them suitable but they did so on exactly the same lines. A curve that would not trouble a horse drawn wagon might be dangerous for a car or impassable for a lorry. If there was a fatal accident, the police investigated and perhaps the coroner at the inquest commented on the unsafe road. A member of the Highways Department drew up a report saying it would be best to straighten the road. The matter went to a committee of the council which agreed to ask for an order. Council officials drew it up and presented it to officials in the Ministry of Transport. If they approved it, it was advertised in the local press. If the landowner whose land was to be taken objected, there had to be a public enquiry. The inspector reported in favour of the change and the Minister approved the order. The council sent a copy to the landowner and issued a

---

14   The Restriction of Ribbon Development Act 1935.

15   The Development and Road Improvement Funds Act 1909.

16   Now the Highways Act 1980.

Notice of Entry, requiring him to permit the council workmen to go onto his land to construct the new road, and a Notice to Treat saying that the council needed to acquire either the freehold in the land or highway rights over it. The council paid its value as farm land and may also have compensated the farmer for incidental losses, for instance if the new road cut off grazing land from his farm buildings so that he had to replace them.

Toward the end of the century the pace of compulsory acquisition slackened. People saw the public sector as inefficient. Private housebuilders could make good profits out of development and they were able to buy up fields and back gardens in order to erect houses which they could sell to owner-occupiers. The motor car (encouraged by state roads) allowed people to live far from their work. More houses spread across the country, restrained only by the planning system.

But the bonanza had to end. The pace of change, not just in Britain but across the world, was such that it began to threaten what came to be called the environment. In 1990, the first Environmental Protection Act was passed and we will see in Chapter 17 how the law is beginning to control the landscape even further.

Chapter 17

The Law of the Landscape Today

In this final chapter, I will consider the way the law of the landscape is evolving in our own time. We have seen how it has worked over the centuries to define rights to control land and that, by the seventeenth century, this led to a clear idea of property. Individual rights of property are still fundamental but they must now be seen in a wider context. Since the eighteenth century, Parliament has intervened to override them in the public interest. This is especially important in the context of public access and in the control of land in the interests of conservation. In the nineteenth and twentieth centuries, the focus of much of the law had been on the built environment of houses and towns, of railways and roads. In the twenty-first century, the emphasis has shifted. The cities are as important as ever but the law relating to them has matured and the basic principles are established. Now there is much new law about the countryside. It cannot be called a natural environment. As we have seen, it has been organised by humans for over 6,000 years and there cannot be any square inch of England that has not been rearranged many times but, as it now changes faster than ever, more law is needed. Some of this law is domestic but much of it comes from overseas. Although the law of England has never been wholly isolated from ideas developed in other legal systems it has, since the thirteenth century, tended to develop on its own. Now it is affected by laws originating not just in Europe but also across the globe.

There are three linked themes. The first is the way people see the countryside, with a public interest in leisure and conservation which can conflict with the wish of landowners to preserve their privacy either in their residence or for commercial purposes. The second is the way English law is becoming integrated with international regulation. The third is the extent to which state power impinges on private rights.

PUBLIC ACCESS AND CONSERVATION

Many people, especially those who live in towns, now see the countryside as a facility for leisure to enjoy a green landscape away from the crowded streets. In the past, the law recognised few such rights of the public. In some communities, local people could take exercise on the village green. Apart from that, the principal public right was over highways, such as roads and footpaths. There were a few statutory public rights, for instance access to monuments under the guardianship of the Secretary of State under the Ancient Monuments Protection Act 1900[1] but protection was limited, guardianship was voluntary and such rights were very much the exception.

This was emphasised in *Attorney-General v Antrobus*[2] in 1905. Sir Edmund Antrobus was the owner of Stonehenge and was concerned at the damage done by visitors. He did not accept guardianship but instead put up a fence and charged for admission. The archaeologist Sir Flinders Petrie and others brought a case under the relator procedure which allowed them to use the name of the attorney-general claiming the public had a right to visit the remains. The judge decided that such a right was unknown in English law and although there had been a path for many years it was not a public right of way. In any case it was settled law that even if there was a highway, it could only be used to get from one place to another, not for leisure or antiquarian purposes.[3] This aspect has recently changed. In 1995, Margaret Jones and others took part in a public demonstration on the roadside verge of the A344 also at Stonehenge.[4] They were charged with being an unlawful assembly and the issue was whether, being on a highway for the purpose of a demonstration rather than just to go from one place to another, they were trespassing. The House of Lords in 1999 decided they were not. In contemporary conditions a highway is not just for passage – in a democratic society it could be used for a political demonstration or for any other purpose, such as taking a photograph or even having a picnic so long as it did not cause an obstruction.

Ever since the railways gave urban workers a chance to leave their towns, they have appreciated access to open rural areas. This could lead to conflict as landowners sought to protect open areas from trespass. Sometimes this was to protect grouse moors; at other times it was simply to assert their property right free from what they saw as invasion by agitators. On 24 April 1932, there was a mass trespass on Kinder Scout in the Peak District opposed by the gamekeepers

---

[1]   Now the Ancient Monuments and Archaeological Areas Act 1979.

[2]   [1905] 2 Ch 188.

[3]   *Harrison v Duke of Rutland* [1893] 1 QB 142.

[4]   *DPP v Jones (Margaret)* [1999] 2 AC 240.

of the landowners. There were prosecutions which provoked a national outcry which, in turn, led to the ineffective Access to Mountains Act 1938. In 1949, Parliament passed the National Parks and Access to the Countryside Act which was intended to open up the country by providing for access agreements or, if the landowner refused to agree, compulsory access orders. These also were largely a dead letter. In 2000, the Countryside and Rights of Way Act introduced a right to roam on common land and waste of the manor as well as mountain, moor, heath and downland. In 2009, the Marine and Coastal Access Act began the process of extending this around the coast.

Similarly, the Commons Registration Act 1965 and the Commons Act 2006 have changed the rules for town and village greens. Formerly, these could arise only by local custom, in theory dating to before 1189, or under an Inclosure Act. Now they can be created if local inhabitants have carried on sports or pastimes for 20 years. As many open spaces on land intended for development have been left unoccupied and so available for people to walk on, there have been several disputes, fought up to the highest court, between development companies and local amenity groups, which have established that such sites cannot now be built on.

Apart from access rights, Parliament has imposed many controls for conservation purposes. Some relate to buildings. As mentioned, heritage bodies have long protected from demolition or change ancient monuments and listed buildings, structures which as we have seen were once new and functional, from Neolithic burial mounds and Norman castles to the Palladian mansions of the squires.[5] Conservation areas protect the character and appearance of village streets as areas of special historic or architectural importance.[6]

Other provisions concern growing things or their biological setting. The Town and Country Planning Act covers tree preservation orders which protect specified trees mainly in towns. Other legislation plays a more positive part in the landscape. The National Parks and Access to the Countryside Act 1949 provided for protections of the countryside by creating National Parks, Areas of Outstanding Natural Beauty as well as Nature Reserves (now called Sites of Special Scientific Interest and governed by the Wildlife and Countryside Act 1981). Opponents of change have used the procedures of the planning legislation to seek to frustrate landowners wishing to build on their land.

So a landowner may have to tolerate public access and may be restricted in making changes not just to buildings but even methods of ploughing or grazing.

---

[5]   The Ancient Monuments Protection Act 1882, now the Ancient Monuments and Archaeological Areas Act 1979.

[6]   Planning (Listed Buildings and Conservation Areas) Act 1990, s 69.

He will be subject to inspections and directions by numerous authorities, ranging from health and safety to conservation of habitats, buildings and ancient monuments. He may need permission to drain boggy land or to flood dry land. He may need consent to fell existing trees[7] or to grub out a hedge to combine two fields.[8] If the land belongs to institutions, such as government, local authorities, public companies or charities, any changes may be subject to public debate and even private landowners may be exposed to less formal but nevertheless intrusive comments in the media.

EUROPEAN AND WORLD LAW

Some of these legal influences on the landscape come from the European Union, notably through the Common Agricultural Policy. The Policy has two pillars. One pillar is designed to protect and preserve rural communities, particularly important in countries such as France which has suffered from rural depopulation since the First World War. The other is intended to ensure a secure supply of food for the peoples of Europe. That was a lesson learnt in both world wars when every country endured either a threat to their food supplies or actual famine. The second pillar has been outstandingly successful – so much so that it produced meat and butter mountains and milk and wine lakes but at great cost to the payers of value added tax and, by intensive farming, great damage to the countryside. Starting with one reform in 1983[9] and with another bigger reform in 2003,[10] the European Union has tried to control surpluses. Now farmers are encouraged to protect the environment by a system of cross-compliance They are entitled to payments from European funds but only so long as they observe some limited environmental standards. Failure to keep to these standards leads to a loss of payment. European rules also require environmental assessments before certain major developments, not just buildings such as power stations or motorways but even afforestation or large-scale pig units.[11] In addition, European law protects the purity of watercourses and the conservation of breeding grounds of birds, including the Habitats Directive[12] and the Birds Directive.[13] An important source of income for farmers is the Environmental Stewardship Scheme administered in England by Natural England on behalf of

---

[7] The Forestry Act 1967.

[8] The Environment Act 1995.

[9] Council Regulation (EEC) 3950/92 on Milk Quotas.

[10] Council Regulation 1698/2005 on the Single Payment Scheme.

[11] Council Directive 85/337 on Environmental Impact Assessment.

[12] Council Directive 92/43/EEC.

[13] Council Directive 79/409/EEC.

the Department for Environment, Food and Rural Affairs but governed by European law.[14]

The United Kingdom is a party to the Landscape Convention of the Council of Europe which came into force in 2007. Although this is a statement of intention between governments and does not directly create rights or duties which affect citizens, it is a legal document. It sets out the common aspiration of the countries of Europe to conserve and protect their landscapes as an important part of their common heritage. Natural England, a government body, is responsible for its implementation here.

This is linked to globalisation. The effects of acid rain and oil pollution do not stop at national borders. If an endangered species or habitat is lost, it affects not just those who live nearby but the ecosystem of the whole world. Likewise, buildings important for historical or architectural reasons are seen as part of the inheritance not just of one country but of all human beings. Therefore, many of our laws now come not only from the European Union but from international conventions on the environment and wildlife. Many of our important monuments, such as Stonehenge and Hadrian's Wall, and natural features, such as the Dorset Coast, have been designated as World Heritage Sites.[15]

THE STATE AND THE LANDOWNER

Environmental controls operate in two ways: the 'stick' of prohibiting certain acts and the 'carrot' of encouraging other acts by means of payments. The use of subsidies and grants is only possible because of the wealth generated by industry and commerce. Since the nineteenth century, the state has been able to take a share of the profits of industry and world trade, in a way impossible in an agricultural community. The expectation that everyone will be taxed has given governments vast funds to administer. They are used to pay civil servants, inspectors and bureaucrats, many of whom are engaged in supervising and controlling the activities of their fellow citizens. Thus the state has the resources and means to control town and country. As we have seen, it does so not only for its own needs, such as defence, prisons and efficient transport by road, rail and air, but it imposes planning in the wider interest.

The former unfettered power of Parliament to override private ownership is to some extent limited. The European Convention on Human Rights, produced in 1950, was accepted into English law in 1998.[16] Its first protocol, signed in 1952,

---

[14]   Council Regulation 1698/2005 and Commission Regulations 1974/2006 and 1975/2006.

[15]   UNESCO World Heritage Convention 1972.

[16]   By the Human Rights Act 1998.

says 'Every natural or legal person is entitled to the peaceful enjoyment of his possessions. No one shall be deprived of his possessions except in the public interest and subject to the conditions provided for by law and by the general principles of international law'. It goes on, however, to say 'The preceding provisions shall not, however, in any way impair the right of a state to enforce such laws as it deems necessary to control the use of property in accordance with the general interest or to secure the payment of taxes or other contributions or penalties'.

Rights of property are therefore still very much alive. More people than ever before own the freehold in their land. This is partly as a result of government policy as well as the ready availability of mortgages. Many just have their homes and gardens but the ownership of all types of land is more widely spread. Therefore, all sorts of people are ready to resist state interference with their property. There are still, in any case, wealthy men and women, some the descendants of the squires who have been able to keep their family wealth, others who have made their fortunes, such as bankers, industrialists and pop stars, and have purchased country properties to give themselves privacy and solitude. Such people are able to afford the cost of law suits against the government and have influence. Although their wealth does not now derive from the control of land, they still want a home in the middle of their own land, to enjoy playing on a golf course, to keep horses, to use private airfields, to run a hobby farm or simply for the pleasure of being the owner of all the eye can see. Many of these people care as much for a beautiful environment as any eighteenth-century aristocrat, although they have to be content with only a few hundred acres instead of a few thousand. They, too, wish to control the landscape.

Much land is once again owned by institutions. Some are public bodies which have buildings and use their grounds for functional purposes, such as schools, hospitals and local government offices. There are also wider extents of land ranging from a town square to a country park of hundreds of hectares. There are state bodies, such as the Forestry Commission which manages woodland or British Waterways, which owns the canals. They are set up with their own aims which they are expected to defend even against other organs of government.

But there are also independent conservation charities, such as the National Trust and the Royal Society for the Protection of Birds, and innumerable others down to a local trust set up to preserve a piece of woodland. Many owners of traditional family estates have also been able to put the mansion house with its farms and cottages into a charitable trust to preserve them as entities free from a break up which would destroy their character. That is because charities benefit from many tax reliefs, including freedom from death duties. The mortmain laws were repealed in 1960[17] but Parliament has imposed other controls in their place.[18] Charities have to be for the public benefit and therefore encourage public access, either to educate people about the countryside or its buildings or simply to make land available for recreation.

CONCLUSION

Like every other aspect of our lives, the law of the landscape is changing fast and it is hard to keep up. Even so, there are some wider themes we can see to help understand how it may develop in the future.

We should expect change to build on what has gone before. We have seen that there are good reasons for property law to respect established rights and to be cautious about unexpected consequences. A freeholder is still legally a tenant in fee simple in free and common socage, a concept going back to Norman times. Other rights derive from procedures introduced under Henry II and still show signs of their origins. Although the thinking of the nineteenth century improvers is already looking quaint and the state-centred concepts of the twentieth century will soon become old fashioned, they are still on the statute book and they will stay there for some time to come.

Likewise, the landscape always has been, and continues to be, used. Farmers need to be able to produce crops and raise animals with the maximum economic sufficiency, in a world in which they have to compete with others in distant continents and where, in the future, increased competition for food may mean we have to grow more of our own. While there are some large farms where companies run thousands of hectares with a handful of skilled farm employees, the family farm still survives as the successor of the *tributarii*, *ceorls*, socmen and 40 shilling freeholders. We need to work mines and quarries, to employ people in factories and offices, and everyone needs housing. These can only be done in the landscape.

It follows that the law will have to reflect the needs and aspirations of owners and occupiers. In a crowded country, people may be less tolerant of interference by others and some have the money to try to do something about it. That has led to many court cases between neighbours over boundary disputes and a growth in claims in the law of nuisance to prevent un-neighbourly uses of land. It has also led to tighter private control. When an owner sells part of his land but still owns property nearby, he may impose covenants restricting what the buyer can do

---

[17] Charities Act 1960, s 38.

[18] Charities Act 1993, s 36 (likely to be replaced by Charities Bill (before Parliament at the time of writing), cl 117).

with the land. Landlords impose ever more restrictions in tenancy agreements and arrangements for occupation get ever more complex, with head leases, underleases, sub-tenancies, occupation licences and the like, until the sheer complexity of different rights in any piece of land is hard to follow. Each of these is documented in ever more detail with longer provisions in elaborately drawn documents now made possible by word processing and other computer techniques.

At the same time, public interest will involve more intervention into what was formerly regarded as private land. This includes access to open country, conservation of landscapes and buildings, planning, new roads and other public works, prevention of pollution and attempts to enhance wildlife and the beauty of the countryside.

This will be reinforced by the increasing public availability of information about rights in land. Although rulers such as William I in the Domesday Book and Henry VIII in his Statute of Enrolments[19] did from time to time seek to secure knowledge about tenure of land, in general the conveyancing methods of previous generations were designed to keep ownership confidential. That has now changed. Title to most freeholds and to leases over seven years is now shown on a government guaranteed register of title which anyone in the world with access to the internet can inspect. Physical title deeds are becoming obsolete since, under the Land Registration Act 2002 which came into force in October 2003, title to all registered land was dematerialised and now consists of entries in the Land Registry database. Apart from that, there is now more information available about the landscape, its use and who occupies it than ever before.[20] Much is available on the internet, including satellite photos, maps of land liable to flood, land contaminated by past uses, land accessible to the public and land designated as listed buildings.

Some of this is relevant to what many people think is the most important issue for the future, namely climate change. It could bring rising sea levels and fierce storms which will flood or destroy land both coastal and inland, rough winds and rising temperatures which affect woods, crops and the future design of buildings. If so, these can only be controlled on a world scale. Although there are some institutions, such as the European Union and the United Nations, which transcend state borders, they are not designed for this. There is a need to gather the relevant information and develop and implement a policy. There may have to be coordinated control of methods of farming, the planting of forests, industrial emissions, mining, the use of roads and many other activities, all of

---

[19]　27 H8 c 16.

[20]　The Freedom of Information Act 2000 and Council Directive 2003/4/EC on Public Access to Environmental Information.

which will affect the rights of owners as well as powers of state control. If that is to be done by the law, there will need to be new ways of making and enforcing it.

All of these factors will develop the law of the landscape. While respecting the needs and wishes of those who live on or derive livelihood from the land, it will take into account wider issues of public benefit. As a tool that helps us live together, the law will reflect, as it always has reflected, however imperfectly, the needs and relationships of people.

Note on legal sources

For the Prehistoric period, virtually all evidence for England comes from archaeology. Excavation reports and general accounts deal with issues such as Neolithic fields and Bronze Age systems of landscape management. Much is known of contemporary legal systems in Europe and the Middle East but, although it is possible that people here were influenced by such ideas, they are unlikely to have been suitable for societies in England. For the end of the Iron Age, Julius Caesar uses some technical legal terms but, as he wrote political propaganda to support his ambitions in Rome, they should be treated with caution. Other Roman writers provide some information but it is not always reliable. There are a number of modern books on 'primitive law'. The best known by Sir Henry Maine was published in 1861. It focuses on the law of the Greeks, Romans, Hebrews and Hindus and is influential but dated. More recent works are *Primitive Law* by AS Diamond (Longmans Green & Co, 1935, revised 1970) and *The Law of Primitive Man* by EA Hoebel (Harvard University Press, 1954), which also discuss ethnographic parallels. There is a mass of ethnographic literature, although much of it is written by anthropologists who naturally write from the standpoint of their own discipline.

There are extensive sources for Roman law. The most comprehensive is the Code of Justinian issued in 533. This includes much imperial legislation in the *Codex* and the *Novels* but the most important part comprises an anthology of opinions of lawyers, mostly from the second and third centuries, known as the *Digest*. Foremost among the writers included was Gnaeus Domitius Annius Ulpianus, known as Ulpian. There are also some earlier legal texts, such as the *Institutes* of Gaius. The Edict/Rescript to Pacatianus is preserved in the *Codex Theodosianus* and the rescript of Honorius is mentioned in Zosimus *Historia Nova*. Much law is referred to in general writings as most educated Romans had some knowledge of the legal system.

In Saxon times, there are the laws of several kings, although as mentioned they shed little light on land law. More important for land law are the surviving *boks* or charters or copies. There are some genuine texts and a great many forgeries, but many of them are based on original documents which have been adapted and therefore have some value.

The most important Norman source is the Domesday Book and its associated volumes, with other contemporary surveys. A number of original writs and charters have survived and there are copies of others. By the high Middle Ages, materials become abundant. Two early outstanding works are the *Tractatus de legibus et consuetudinibus regni Angliae* of Ranulf de Glanvill, who was Chief Justice under Henry II and the *de Legibus et Consuetudinis Angliae* edited by Henry of Bracton but probably based on an earlier manuscript perhaps by William Raleigh. There are numerous administrative records, notably the Pipe Rolls starting in the twelfth century and continuing until the nineteenth century. There are also the Year Books, starting in 1268, which report on legal arguments in the royal courts. There is a mass of manorial rolls and records. Statutes are recorded on the Parliament Roll. Many of the sources have been edited and published in annual volumes issued by the Selden Society. The writings of FW Maitland, especially *Domesday Book and Beyond* (Cambridge University Press, 1897) and his *History of English Law before the time of Edward I* (2nd edn, Cambridge University Press, 1898) (known as 'Pollock and Maitland' but Sir Frederick Pollock contributed only his name and an introduction), are important and still highly regarded.

In all subsequent periods, the primary sources are overwhelming. Statutes and law reports continued to be produced. There are textbooks on every possible subject. The two most important were (first) a commentary by Sir Edward Coke on the *Tenures* of Sir Thomas Littleton, which also became the first volume of his *Institutes of the Lawes of England* and therefore known as Co Litt or Co Inst 1 and (second) Sir William Blackstone's *Commentaries on the Laws of England*.

There are a number of legal histories. The most thorough is WS Holdsworth's *History of English Law* in 12 volumes (1903–38), now gradually being replaced by the *Oxford History of the Laws of England*. The most accessible on land law is AWB Simpson's *An Introduction to the History of the Land Law*, and my debt to that will be evident throughout this book. Other legal history textbooks include accounts of aspects of land law.

Many strictly legal sources, such as decided cases in the High Court, county council enquiries into footpaths and the series of Commons Commissioners hearings under the Commons Registration Act 1965 (www.acraew.org.uk), include a good deal of historical material, as do records of disputes in earlier centuries, but I would sound a note of caution. It may be necessary for either or both parties to a lawsuit to produce historical materials sometimes going back many centuries in support of their case. In theory, the limit of 'legal memory' is 1189 but in practice they may wish to refer to earlier materials. Judges and other decision makers have to consider such evidence and, because the law of

England is regarded as continuous since 1066, those trained in modern law schools have to express authoritative views on ancient materials. Some are better at this than others, and all are dependent on the materials produced by one party or the other in evidence to suit that party's case.

The principal sources of English law are law reports and statutory materials. From the thirteenth century to the sixteenth century, we have the year books which record argument in court on difficult issues. From the sixteenth century, we have reports of judgments which themselves create precedents. An early set was edited (and mostly written) by Sir Edward Coke who was Chief Justice under James I. These are known as Coke's Reports, abbreviated as Co Rep. Thus *Semayne's Case* decided in 1604 is in volume 5 at page 91a and the reference is 5 Co Rep 91a. In subsequent years, other people produced sets of so-called nominate reports under their own names but these were of varying reliability and had no official standing. These reports have been included in a set known as the English Reports, so the reference to *Semayne's Case* is also 77 ER 194.

The Incorporated Council of Law Reporting was established in 1865 to produce good quality reports. The initial reports were in sequential volumes so that, for instance, *Walsh v Lonsdale* in 1882 is in volume 21 of the reports of cases in the Chancery Division at page 9, giving the reference 21 ChD 9. In such cases, the year is often included in the reference but in round brackets to indicate that it is not an essential part. Later, the Council changed the reference to annual volumes where the year is part of the reference and shown in square brackets. Thus *DPP v Margaret Jones*, which was appealed to the judicial committee of the House of Lords, appears in the second volume of appeal reports for 1999 at page 240, so the reference is *DPP v Jones (Margaret)* [1999] 2 AC 240. Since 2001, there has also been an official neutral designation, so that *Hall v Moore* is reported in the cases for the English and Welsh Court of Appeal Civil Division number 201 and the reference is [2009] EWCA Civ 201.

Many reports are on the internet, often the full text. Some law reports, particularly more recent ones still in copyright, are only available on subscription through legal publishers. Very recent cases are on the British and Irish Legal Information Institute website at www.bailii.org, which is free to use. Other material is in legal or public libraries. Many old series of law reports now out of copyright are reproduced through Google Books.

Statutes are published in annual volumes. The most accessible source for statutes is on the internet at www.legislation.gov.uk, which includes the text of all statutes currently in force. Often, a later Act will amend an earlier one, so the website sets out the text as amended, but in most cases the text as originally enacted is included, as are a few repealed statutes. Otherwise, it can be difficult to locate the text of old Acts of Parliament. Most law libraries and many public libraries contain sets of Acts.

Acts were initially cited by reference to the regnal year of a king in which they were passed. In each session there was originally a single statute divided into numbered chapters. Later, each enactment was itself called a statute but the reference was still to a chapter. Thus the Statute of Uses was the tenth enactment passed in the legal year 1535 which was the twenty-seventh year of the reign of Henry VIII. Its reference is, therefore, 27th Henry VIII chapter 10 or, more briefly, 27 H8 c 10. Since 1962, the citation has changed to the calendar year, so that the Land Registration Act 2002, the ninth enactment in the year 2002, is 2002 c 9.

Books and Articles Referred To

Books

Anglo-Saxon Chronicle
Austen, Jane, *Pride and Prejudice*

Bede, The Ven, *Historia Ecclesiastica Gentis Anglorum*
Bentham, Jeremy, *Works*
Blackstone, Sir W, *Commentaries on the Laws of England*
Bracton, Henry of, *de Legibus et Consuetudinis Angliae* (SE Thorne (ed))
    (Harvard University Press, 1975 and later)

Caesar, Gaius Julius, *de Bello Gallico*
Coke, Sir Edward, *Commentary on Littleton's Tenures* (*Institutes*, Vol 1)
Collingwood RG and Wright RP, *The Roman Inscriptions of Britain* (Oxford
    University Press, 1965 and later)

Defoe, Daniel, *A Tour through the Eastern Counties of England 1722*
de la Bedoyere, Guy, *Roman Towns in Britain* (Tempus, 2003)
Dickens, Charles, *Hard Times*
Disraeli, Benjamin, *Sybil*

Elliot, George, *Middlemarch*

Fitzherbert, Anthony, *Natura Brevium*
Fleming, Andrew, *The Dartmoor Reaves* (Batsford, 1988)

Gaius, *Institutiones*
Gerontius, *Sanctae Melaniae junioris Acta*
Gildas, *De Excidio Britanniae*
Gray, CM, *Copyhold, Equity and the Common Law* (Harvard University Press,
    1963)

Hart, HLA, *The Concept of Law* (Oxford University Press, 1961)
Hobbes, Thomas, *Leviathan*

Hoskins, WG, *The Making of the English Landscape* (Hodder & Stoughton, 1955)
Hudson, Sir Robert, *Memorials of a Warwickshire Parish* (Methuen, 1904)

Law Commission Report, *Repeal of Turnpike Laws*, February 2010
Locke, John, *Second Treatise on Government*

Machiavelli, Niccolo, *Il Principe*
Maitland, FW, *Domesday Book and Beyond*
Maitland, FW, *Collected Papers*
Marx, Karl, *Communist Manifesto*
More, Sir Thomas, *Utopia* (Ralph Robinson (trans), 1551)

Pepys, Samuel, *Diary*
Plinius, Gaius Secundus, *Epistolae*

Shaw, Bernard, *Widowers' Houses*
Sherwin-White, AN, *The Roman Citizenship* (Oxford University Press, 1973)
Simpson, AWB, *An Introduction to the History of the Land Law* (Oxford University Press, 1961)

Tacitus, Cornelius, *Agricola*
Tacitus, Cornelius, *Annali*

White, Lynn, *Medieval Technology & Social Change*
Wormald, Patrick, *The Making of English Law – King Alfred to the Twelfth Century – Vol 1*
Wulfstan of York, Archbishop (attr), *Rectitudines singularum personarum*

Yelling, JA, *Common Field and Enclosure in England 1450–1850* (Macmillan, 1977)

Articles

Beckett, J and Turner, M, 'End of the Old Order', (2007) 55(2) *Agricultural History Review* 269–88

Rothery, M, 'The wealth of the English Landed Gentry 1870–1935', (2007) 55(2) *Agricultural History Review* 251–68

Stevens, CE, 'A Possible conflict of laws in Roman Britain', (1947) 37 *Journal of Roman Studies* 132–4

Thompson, M, 'The Land Market 1880–1925', (2007) 55(2) *Agricultural History Review* 289–300

Tomlin, RSO, 'A five acre wood in Roman Kent', in *Interpreting Roman London*, Oxbow Monograph 58 (Oxbow Books, 1996), pp 209–16

Turner, EG, 'A Roman writing tablet from Somerset', (1956) xlvi *Journal of Roman Studies* 115

Williamson, T, 'Early co-axial field systems on the East Anglian boulder clays', (1987) 53 *Proceedings of the Prehistoric Society* 419–31

Index

References are to page numbers